BATTLEGROUND
NEW YORK CITY

Related Potomac Titles

*Bullets, Bombs, and Fast Talk: Twenty-five Years of
FBI War Stories*, James Botting

Endless Enemies: Inside FBI Counterterrorism,
Raymond W. Holcomb, with Lillian S. Weiss

*One Marshal's Badge: A Memoir of Fugitive Hunting,
Witness Protection, and the U.S. Marshals Service*,
Louie McKinney, with Pat Russo

BATTLEGROUND NEW YORK CITY

COUNTERING SPIES, SABOTEURS, AND TERRORISTS SINCE 1861

THOMAS A. REPPETTO

Potomac Books
Washington, D.C.

Library of Congress Cataloging-in-Publication Data
Reppetto, Thomas A.
  Battleground New York City : countering spies, saboteurs, and terrorists since 1861 / Thomas A. Reppetto. — 1st ed.
    p. cm.
  Includes bibliographical references and index.
  ISBN 978-1-59797-677-0 (hardcover)
  ISBN 978-1-59797-880-4 (electronic edition)
  1. Subversive activities—New York (State)—New York—History. 2. Crime—New York (State)—New York—History. 3. Espionage—New York (State)—New York—History. 4. Terrorism—New York (State)—New York—History. 5. Police—New York (State)—New York—History. 6. Secret service—New York (State)—New York—History. 7. Intelligence service—New York (State)—New York—History. I. Title.
  HV6795.N5R47 2011
  363.25'931097471—dc23
                                    2011028461

Printed in the United States of America on acid-free paper that meets the American National Standards Institute Z39-48 Standard.

Potomac Books
22841 Quicksilver Drive
Dulles, Virginia 20166

First Edition

10 9 8 7 6 5 4 3 2 1

To the memory of Insp. Thomas J. Tunney,
commanding officer of the NYPD bomb and
neutrality squads, 1914–1917, and, as a U.S. Army
captain, commander of the first American military
counterintelligence unit, 1917–1918

CONTENTS

INTRODUCTION

"Here begins the great game."
—RUDYARD KIPLING[1]

On a bitter cold night in February 1993, New York City police commissioner Ray Kelly allowed me to witness a secret drill by the NYPD. Hundreds of officers from all over the city were mobilized to deal with two thousand unruly demonstrators who had illegally assembled at the Vietnam Veterans Plaza, in Manhattan's financial district. As the scenario called for, when the demonstrators (actually fifty cops dressed in old clothes) refused to disperse, they were arrested.

Thirty-six hours later, many of us who had been at the exercise returned to the same area. This time it was not a scripted sit-in but a real act of war. Terrorists had detonated an explosive device inside a truck parked in a garage below the World Trade Center. The blast ripped through several floors, cut off power, and sent thousands of people fleeing for their lives. Six people were killed; another thousand required treatment for injuries, smoke inhalation, or shock. Within a few days, FBI agents, assisted by NYPD detectives, arrested a group of Islamic militants for the crime. Over the next two years, all the defendants were convicted and given long prison sentences. Terrorist groups had previously blown up American embassies, Marine barracks, and airplanes in various parts of the world, but they had not struck on U.S. soil. Now, America's principal city was the target.

After the first World Trade Center bombing, foreign intelligence services such as Israel's Mossad warned U.S. authorities that terrorists would try again to attack some high-profile objective, most likely in New York City. NYPD detectives, carrying out follow-up investigations, discovered lists of possible targets, such as the United Nations complex, the Statue of Liberty, and Rockefeller Center. In addition to the possibility of bombing buildings, police and federal agents uncovered plots to attack the subways or to send commando teams to shoot up corporate headquarters and posh hotels. The one form of attack the NYPD did not canvass was an air raid. However, on September 11, 2001, Islamic hijackers flew airliners into the twin towers of the World Trade Center, killing nearly twenty-eight hundred people and achieving a level of destruction that most Americans never imagined possible.

Viewed from a historical perspective, the Trade Center attacks should not have been unexpected. New York City has always been the principal arena in which America's domestic security conflicts have been fought. In the nineteenth century, bloody riots were a common occurrence. The greatest urban insurrection in American history took place in 1863, at the height of the Civil War, when mobs comprising mainly Irishmen swarmed through the streets burning, looting, and killing (mostly African Americans) to protest a newly enacted draft law. During the fighting, U.S. troops fired artillery at the rioters. Even today it is not certain whether the number killed was as low as a hundred or more than a thousand. In the last third of the century, protests over ethnic, political, or economic grievances were frequently put down by police or soldiers.

Significant as they were, the events of the nineteenth century have little relevance to security problems of our own time. In contrast, those of the early and mid-twentieth century have a great deal. The modern era of U.S. domestic security began in 1914, when a relatively young country, with limited experience and understanding of security policing or intelligence work, became involved in the struggles of European powers that were much more skilled at playing what was called the "great game." The term originally referred to spying, counterintelligence, and political warfare carried on between the British and the Russian empires in Asia during the nineteenth century. In 1901, it was popularized in Rudyard Kipling's novel *Kim*. Peter Hopkirk, author of books on the great game, wrote that in World War I, "A new and more sinister version of the old great game [was] fought out between the intelligence services of King, Kaiser, Sultan and Czar."[2] Eventually, it extended to the United States.

The chapters that follow will describe security operations in the World War I and World War II eras, concentrating on New York City. It was natural that terrorists, spies, and saboteurs made New York their number-one target. It was, and still is, the country's most important city—the center of its economy, culture, and communications. A major attack on the city strikes at the de facto capital of the United States and the Western World. During World War I, the Hudson River piers were the place where munitions for the Allied armies were loaded onto ships. Starting in 1915, German agents used Irish dockworkers to plant bombs in the vessels' cargo holds. In 1916 they blew up an ammunition dump in New York harbor known as Black Tom Island. So powerful was the explosion that the noise was heard as far south as Philadelphia. In Manhattan thousands of windows were broken, and the Brooklyn Bridge swayed. One postwar history described New York as "the heart of the great and intricate system of German espionage. . . . It was imperative that the vast protective agencies of the national government focus here . . . [so] every force was rushed to the danger line in New York."[3]

In the 1930s, Hitler's spies smuggled U.S. secrets out of the country on German liners that departed from the Hudson piers. In 1935, and again in 1938, Nazi spy rings were unmasked when federal law enforcement officers seized German nationals on the dockside. During the late '30s and early '40s, in liberal New York City local "führers" addressed their followers in public places as large as Madison Square Garden, while native storm troopers roamed the streets beating up Jews. In 1940 a bomb planted in the British Pavilion at the New York World's Fair killed two NYPD detectives. German, Soviet, and British intelligence always deployed their strongest contingents in New York.

━━━━━━

It could be argued that a focus on New York is too narrow because it does not deal with major security problems in the western states, such as bombings and shootings by the Industrial Workers of the World (IWW) or Japanese espionage. In this respect it is like a history of World Wars I and II that concentrates on France, to the exclusion of the Eastern European, Mediterranean, and Pacific areas. However, critical events of both world wars occurred on French soil.

While key decisions about U.S. security were usually made in Washington, they were often based on conditions in New York City. Many New Yorkers played leading roles in formulating policy and directing security operations in both world wars. Among them were the scions of America's most distinguished families, such as the Roosevelts, Biddles, Polks, and Astors. To better understand the New York story, we will occasionally jump across the Atlantic to examine the British model of security. In both world wars it was the Brits who tutored the Yanks in how to carry out domestic security operations.

This account will reveal much of the hidden history of espionage, sabotage, terrorism, and subversion directed against America. It will assess the operations of agencies such as the U.S. Secret Service, military and naval intelligence, the FBI, and the NYPD—organizations that we characterize as "the security forces." Many readers will be surprised to learn that the New York police have always been a major bulwark for U.S. domestic security. The final chapters will describe U.S. security from the end of World War II to 9/11. Then, drawing on knowledge of the past, we will analyze the present situation and the possible course of future events.

———

Though there is a vast literature on intelligence, the subject is not well understood by the public, which often compares apples, oranges, and tomatoes. So a few explanations are in order. Intelligence is usually classified as either foreign or domestic. The foreign variety (sometimes known as positive intelligence) seeks to determine the political, military, and economic capabilities and intentions of another nation or entity. While this is often taken to mean spying, the bulk of such information is obtained from open sources. Because intelligence agencies operate secretly, governments sometimes use them to carry out tasks with which it does not wish to be publicly identified, such as assassination, sabotage, and fomenting disorder. But these are special operations, not primarily intelligence gathering. The oft-cited example of the difference between the two is that an intelligence officer counts the number of enemy tanks crossing a bridge; a special operations officer tries to blow it up. Domestic intelligence or counterintelligence (aka "negative intelligence") involves combating threats to a nation's internal security. Its most glamorous component is spy catching or counterespionage; its most controversial role is spying on its own citizens.*

In the United States, the organization of intelligence duties has been muddled. Agencies gathering foreign intelligence, such as the CIA and its predecessor, the OSS (Office of Strategic Services), frequently engaged in domestic spying. Countering threats to internal security has never been the responsibility of a single organization. Instead, it has been carried out by military and naval intelligence, by some private groups, and, most commonly, as an adjunct to the primary duties of federal, state, and local law enforcement agencies. There has never been an American organization comparable to Britain's state security service known as MI5.

During the world wars and other crisis periods, the operations of U.S. domestic security agencies have followed a regular cycle. In the opening phase, agencies are slow to recognize and respond to threats. As Black Tom demonstrated, two years into World War I, U.S. security forces could be caught off guard. Then comes a period when security organizations move front and center, beefing up staff and battling rivals for primacy. In both world wars, some security agencies spent nearly as much energy fighting each other as they did countering the enemy. During World War II, in addition to the FBI, military and naval intelligence, and the NYPD, President Roosevelt formed three secret organizations in New York City—all of which reported directly to him, with their chiefs frequently running to the White House to complain about rival groups.

In the next phase, it is damn the torpedoes and full speed ahead, with agencies disregarding constitutional and legal "technicalities," which they believe might interfere with winning the war. In World War I, the Bureau of Investigation (it did not acquire the prefix Federal until 1935) supplemented

---

* Counterespionage is concerned with apprehending spies. Counterintelligence collects information of general relevance to security. U.S. agencies that gather foreign intelligence, like the CIA, also have counterintelligence sections to protect their own security and keep an eye on enemy spy services. But theoretically they are not supposed to engage in domestic operations.

its three hundred agents with thousands of untrained citizen volunteers, who were furnished with "Secret Service" credentials and sent out to hunt spies and antiwar dissidents. Finally, after the crisis period ends, the security services come under heavy criticism for their activities, and the government (federal or state) promises that never again will its agents exceed their authority. To ensure that they don't, restrictions (both reasonable and unreasonable) are placed on them. Then, when the next crisis arises, the restrictions are lifted, security forces are given the green light, and the cycle begins again.

Our narrative will trace the continuing tension between efforts to safeguard national security and to uphold the rule of law. There has never been a consistent institutional position in this area. An agency that operated with regard to the law in one era might function unlawfully in another, and vice versa. In World War I, the U.S. Department of Justice strove, with varying degrees of success, to keep security operations within relatively restrained guidelines, while military intelligence believed that in a national emergency legal restrictions should be ignored. After the Armistice, under a new attorney general, it was the Department of Justice that led security forces into the excesses of the "Red Raids" while the Army took a back seat.

We will analyze the question of why America has not developed a well-defined, comprehensive domestic security system. One reason for the division among security forces is that the U.S. maintains two systems of government, federal and state. This fosters competition between them even in conventional crime fighting. Often G-men and municipal detectives working on the same crime will conduct separate investigations and strive to obtain exclusive credit for solving the case. The United States has yet to build a real partnership between local police and federal agencies, especially in matters of national security. As recently as November 2008, a front-page article in the *New York Times* reported on the rivalry between the NYPD and the Department of Justice in New York, observing: "Even in the best of times, the police and the FBI's New York office can be quarrelsome partners, and current and former officials say the dispute between the two—which share overlapping responsibilities for security in New York—has brought the relationship to a new low."[4]

In domestic security, the feds have the national jurisdiction and international connections. But big-city police can call on their vast resources and community contacts to obtain information about local terrorist cells. They are also the ones who, as first responders, must deal with the consequences of terrorist acts. In present-day New York, the NYPD has assumed an international role. Early in the twentieth century, American security forces learned that federal, state civilian, and military agencies must work together. The problem has always been how to achieve this in practice.

Organizational arrangements are one aspect of a security system. Individuals are probably the most important component. Any discussion of U.S. security operations in the twentieth century must look closely at J. Edgar Hoover. Although he was a man of many accomplishments, his narrow views and insatiable desire for power sometimes harmed U.S. security. At age twenty-four he was the brains behind the Department of Justice's 1919–1920 crackdown on alleged subversives, which became known as the Red Raids. In World War II, as director of the FBI, he strove to obtain absolute power—an attempt that was thwarted by other powerful players.

Despite the views of Hoover's admirers and critics (and today the latter greatly outnumber the former), he was not the be all and end all of domestic security. To understand the entire picture, it is necessary to examine the careers of other security chiefs from a variety of agencies. These include men such as Col. Ralph Van Deman of Military Intelligence; Capt. Ellis Zacharias of the Office of Naval Intelligence; William Flynn, head of the U.S. Secret Service; William Burns, who became the country's leading private detective chief and later director of the Bureau of Investigation; and William Donovan of the OSS. There were also Brits such as Col. Claude Dansey and Churchill's World War II spymaster in America, the Canadian Bill Stephenson.

The most important figure of all was Franklin Roosevelt, probably a more active player in the game of intelligence and counterintelligence than any other American president then or since.* During World War I, as assistant secretary of the navy, he oversaw the Office of Naval Intelligence. In the 1920s he maintained a close relationship with a group of multimillionaire New

---

* Although he was not the only one to play at it. Unlikely as it would seem, President Herbert Hoover initiated a mini Watergate-type operation in New York City.

York security buffs known as the Room. As president, he made the ultimate decisions that produced the U.S. intelligence establishment that has existed to this day.

═══════

One advantage of focusing the present study on the first half of the twentieth century is that it makes it easier to arrive at informed judgments about the perennial problems of U.S. domestic security and the agencies that sought to deal with them. The facts about the two world war eras are mostly known. No powerful interests from that time remain to try to hide or distort the truth.

An additional benefit of studying past eras is that it may cause some people to rethink their views about domestic security. Many Americans who have lived through the McCarthy era, the Vietnam War, or the current counter-terrorism drives have come to regard virtually any kind of security policing as wrong; such views are especially popular among the most educated segment of the population.

In the chapters that follow, I have striven not to become a partisan of any particular ideology or bureaucratic faction.* It is my hope that the analysis will shed light on two important periods in American history, help us understand the present situation as regards domestic security, and weigh current policy proposals against the experience of the past.

---

* Because I frequently write about the past, I am sometimes referred to as a historian. However, my training and experience is in the area of government, public administration, and criminal justice. Thus, I approach my subject from a different perspective than a professional historian. My focus is on organizational analysis and the exercise of power.

GUARDING AMERICA'S GREATEST CITY

Security Policing Before 1914

In 1863, with the North and South locked in a bitter civil war, the most powerful man in America's greatest city was John A. Kennedy, superintendent of the New York Metropolitan Police. At 7 a.m. on Monday, July 13, he was notified that the Irish workers who maintained the streets in the city's Nineteenth Ward had not reported to work. Measured alongside the news that Gen. Robert E. Lee's army was retreating after being repulsed at Gettysburg, the actions of a few New York City laborers seemed of little consequence. However, Kennedy recognized it for the ominous sign it was—a warning that New York might be plunged into a battle as important as Gettysburg. The previous Saturday, military officers had begun selecting lottery numbers to determine which New Yorkers would be inducted into the Union Army under the recently enacted draft law. For weeks there had been reports that attempts to enforce the law would meet with violent resistance from the city's Irish Catholics. Under the watchful eyes of a detachment of police, the Saturday drawing had been conducted without incident. On Monday the lottery would resume, and one of the locations where it would be held was Forty-Sixth Street and Third Avenue in the Nineteenth Ward.

Blacks and Irish were frequently pitted against each other in the competition for low-paying jobs. In 1853, when Irish laborers had struck against the Erie Railroad, seeking a salary of a $1.25 per day and a limit of ten hours' work, management hired blacks as replacements and equipped them with revolvers. The Irish did not relish the prospect of fighting for a Union victory that might send masses of freed slaves into the labor market. The law also provided that an individual selected in the lottery could be exempted if he paid $300 or hired someone to go in his place. Either option was beyond what Irish workingmen could afford. On Sunday, July 12, the papers carried the names of the men selected in Saturday's draft. Many were Irish, including some who had been promised exemption because they were in occupations essential to the war effort, or they served as volunteer firemen. In the saloons that were the center of social life in poor neighborhoods, there was much grumbling about the unfairness of it all. As the drinks flowed, violent talk filled the air and conspiracies were hatched.

New York had always been a turbulent city. Its strengths were also its weaknesses. From colonial days its great harbor—the finest in North America—had made it the principal port of call for ships arriving from Europe. With the opening of the Erie Canal in 1825, New York became the link between the Old World and the American heartland. The city's merchants grew prosperous as middlemen, handling both imports and exports. Given its location and flourishing economy, New York attracted vast numbers of immigrants from Europe and the hinterlands of America. With land scarce on the narrow island of Manhattan, the immigrants were packed into areas of shabby, overcrowded tenement buildings. It was these slums that produced the violent gangs of New York. Still, people poured in. Between 1825 and 1860 the population rose from one hundred thousand to eight hundred thousand; counting those residing across the river in the separate city of Brooklyn, the number was over a million.

From the outbreak of hostilities in 1861, the city had been a hotbed of antiwar sentiment. When the Southern states seceded, Democratic mayor Fernando Wood suggested that the city do likewise and become a free port. President Lincoln commented that that would be like the front doorstep setting up housekeeping on its own. The leader of the city council, Tammany boss William Magear Tweed, was also a strong opponent of the war. In contrast, the police were a bulwark for the Union cause. Unlike the situation in most cities, the mayor and council in New York did not control the cops. In 1857 the state legislature had abolished the municipal police department and replaced it with a metropolitan force that covered not only New York City proper (then mostly the island of Manhattan) but also Brooklyn and areas of Queens and the Bronx. The Democratic governor of New York, Horatio Seymour, opposed the war and was an outspoken critic of the draft law. Though "the Metropolitans" were a state agency, the governor had no power over them. The Republican-dominated legislature had put the police under the control of a board that strongly backed Superintendent Kennedy.

In office since 1860, Kennedy was a big, rugged man, scrupulously honest, with a strong sense of duty. Anyone who approached him to ask for a favor did so at his peril. He was likely to stand up, shouting, "You ask me to let you commit a breach of the law! Get out! Get out at once!" Though an Irish Catholic himself, Kennedy was a strong supporter of the Union cause. Even before Fort Sumter was fired upon, he issued orders forbidding arms shipments from New York to the South and personally journeyed to Washington to investigate reports of threats to assassinate President-elect Lincoln. In size and prestige, the New York Metropolitans were far and away the country's premier police force. In 1862 the secretary of war designated them as provost marshals, allowing them to apprehend deserters and citizens guilty of making "disloyal" statements. The New York cops interpreted their mandate broadly. In that year alone, acting as marshals, they made two thousand arrests, ranging as far as Ohio to do so.

As soon as Superintendent Kennedy learned of the situation in the Nineteenth Ward, he began to deploy his twenty-four hundred cops to deal with trouble. He ordered all off-duty officers recalled and on-duty officers held after their shifts ended, and he dispatched reinforcements to the draft offices.

When he had finished issuing orders, Kennedy decided to personally check conditions in the field. At 10 a.m. he started uptown in a horse-drawn cart, alone, unarmed, and wearing civilian clothes. At a draft office on Broadway, he found the drawings proceeding quietly. A quick tour of the West Side was also uneventful. So Kennedy headed toward Forty-Sixth and Third. As he drew near, he spotted smoke. At 10:15, when the lottery drawings commenced, a mob had attacked the office and set it on fire, forcing the sixty officers on duty to retreat. Because of the throngs, Kennedy's cart could not get through, so he dismounted and started walking toward the scene. Suddenly members of the crowd recognized him and begin shouting, "There's Kennedy! Kill him!" Several men began to pummel the sixty-year-old superintendent. When he appeared to have been knocked senseless, he was dumped into a small pond. Somehow he managed to struggle out and get back on his feet. Nearby he recognized John Egan, a popular Irish leader in Tammany Hall, and called to him, "Come and save my life!" Egan managed to hold the mob back while other bystanders placed Kennedy on a passing feed wagon, which transported him downtown to police headquarters. When he arrived he was unconscious and so badly mauled that the president of the police board didn't recognize his own superintendent. (Despite his injuries, Kennedy was back at work on Thursday and remained head of the force for another seven years.)

The attack on the draft office ignited a conflagration. Angry Irishmen roamed through the streets looting and burning, and attacking blacks. Some blacks had to jump from the rooftops of burning buildings. The fury of the rioters was maniacal. After a mob hanged a crippled black man, a sixteen-year-old boy dragged the corpse through the streets while onlookers cheered. Even children were ruthlessly attacked. Rioters torched the Colored Orphan Asylum on Fifth Avenue, burning one little girl to death. Police fought their way through and evacuated two hundred of the others. Seven hundred of the city's estimated twelve thousand blacks took refuge at police headquarters on Mulberry Street. The cops, half of whom were Irish Catholics, performed valiantly, often against great odds. One mob began marching on police headquarters. Instead of waiting for them to arrive, an inspector took two hundred men to meet them at Broadway and Houston. With clubs drawn the police charged, and in ten minutes the rioters were routed.

For four days the battle of New York raged, with the fighting in the streets more vicious than at Gettysburg. U.S. soldiers, rushed to the city, fired artillery at rioters. An army colonel caught by a mob was tortured to death. Some policemen's lives were saved by civilians. The wife of John Egan, the man who rescued Superintendent Kennedy, managed to do so for a fallen patrolman by prostrating herself across his body to shield him from kicks and blows. For three days a police station on East Thirty-Fifth Street was besieged by local gangs. A woman who ran a family bakery while her husband was away serving in the Union Army smuggled bread in to the cops through her young son. Several times local toughs threatened to burn down her store and the living quarters above it, but she won a reprieve by paying them off. Finally, soldiers broke through the gangs and lifted the siege. After five days, the city was secured. Various accounts have placed the number of riot deaths at anywhere from a hundred to several thousand.*

The uprising might not have been spontaneous. During the disturbances unknown persons cut telegraph wires so that police spies could not keep headquarters informed of the mobs' movements. At some locations mysterious individuals assumed leadership roles. After one of them was killed, it was found that under his rough workman's clothing he wore a well-tailored suit, and his grooming suggested he was a gentleman. During the course of the Civil War, Southern agents frequently operated in the North. On several occasions they sought to cause uprisings in other parts of the country. The draft riot was not the only rebel assault on New York. The following year, on a single night, a series of fires broke out in hotels and other public places shortly after men with Southern accents had left the premises.

Had the Metropolitan police failed in July 1863, the city might have been taken over by rebel sympathizers. In 1885 a historian of the police would write:

> The Police had saved our city; the mob was vanquished and dispersed. Had the rioters succeeded in overpowering the Police and military, and gained possession of the city but for one hour, there is no calculating what irreparable calamities might have, as a consequence, befallen the city and the Nation. . . . But happily all this was averted. Had it not been so, who can say how the war would have terminated?[1]

Despite the stakes, it was only by chance that the police were controlled by a pro-Union board. The Metropolitan force had not been created for reasons of domestic security; it was formed to strike a blow at the corrupt administration of Democratic mayor Wood (who was out of office in 1863). A few years

---

* The lower figure is undoubtedly an underestimate, because it is reasonable to assume that some families of individuals killed by security forces buried their dead secretly for fear of official retaliation. Indeed, for a generation afterward many New Yorkers appeared to suffer from amnesia about their activities in July 1863. On the opposite end of the scale, modern researchers have concluded that the higher number of deaths is grossly exaggerated. Therefore, a figure in the low hundreds probably comes closest to the mark.

after the war, when the political winds in Albany blew in a Democratic direction, Boss Tweed was able to have the police returned to municipal control.

━━━━━

The Union victory in the Civil War accelerated the process of changing America from a rural, agricultural society to an urban, industrial one. With this came European-style domestic security problems, particularly in New York. Until the 1870s, disorders in the city arose primarily out of ethnic rivalries, not political or class conflicts. In 1849 protests against a British actor appearing at the Astor Theatre led to a riot in which twenty-two people were killed. In 1857 a battle between an "American" gang from the Bowery and an Irish gang from the Five Points sparked two days of disorder in which eight people were slain. The Draft Riot had a political and class basis, but it was largely a rebellion of Irish Catholic immigrants who targeted blacks. In 1870, when Irish Catholics attempted to disrupt a parade of Irish Protestant "Orangemen," five people lost their lives. The next year, even though the Orange parade marched under military protection, thirty-seven people were killed.

By the end of the 1870s, though, the perceived security threats began to come from radicals espousing ideologies calling for the overthrow of the American political and economic system. In 1871, after France was defeated by Prussia and the other German states, leftists seized a portion of Paris in defiance of the provisional French government. The rising and subsequent administration, known as the Paris Commune, was ruthlessly crushed by government troops, often with the summary execution of rebels. Afterward some of the survivors fled to America. Another seminal event was the formation of the International Working Men's Association, or First International, in 1864. Eight years later, when adherents of Communist Karl Marx began to be outnumbered by anarchist followers of Michael Bakunin, Marx moved the International's headquarters to New York City to avoid a takeover by the rival faction.

In 1877 America was disrupted by a railroad strike, the first nationwide work stoppage in its history. With trains not running, the economy was severely affected. Business suffered, and workers lost their jobs or had their wages cut. If the railroads sought to move trains, massed strikers blocked them. When police and National Guardsmen attempted to disperse the mobs, violence ensued. In Baltimore, ten people were killed; in Chicago, twenty; in Pittsburgh, twenty-five. New York suffered along with the rest of the country. In July a coalition of radicals asked the mayor for permission to hold a meeting in Tompkins Square, on the Lower East Side, to urge support for local strikers. Three years earlier, when protesters had requested a permit to hold a meeting in the square to demand the creation of public works projects to alleviate unemployment, the mayor had refused to give them one. When they assembled anyway, mounted police charged the crowd and scores of people were injured. This time a new mayor agreed to allow the meeting. Seven hundred police were mobilized, and four regiments of the National Guard stood on alert in their armories.

Leaving the frontline duties to the police and keeping the National Guard on reserve represented a wise move. National Guardsmen were essentially civilians in uniform and were often commanded by wealthy men who had purchased their commissions. When deployed for riot control, they were likely to panic and begin shooting wildly. In dealing with mobs, National Guard regiments were not adept at using formations such as a line to move a crowd back, a diagonal to turn it, or a wedge to break it up. In many situations the primary tactic was for an officer to command, "Ready, aim, fire!" At Astor Place, the twenty-two people killed by guardsmen's bullets included one police officer. In the Orange riot of 1871, the guardsmen were responsible for most of the thirty-seven deaths. One of the regiments on duty that day was commanded by the infamous Wall Street buccaneer Col. Jim Fisk. When the shooting started, the gallant colonel jumped off his horse and ran from the scene—not stopping until he reached the Hudson River, where he hired a boat to take him to New Jersey.*

Five thousand people showed up at the Tompkins Square rally, where speakers in French, German, and English addressed them. With the memories of the Franco-Prussian War still in their minds, some of the speakers were more afraid of each other than they were of the massed security forces. The police were commanded by Union Army veterans, who had drawn from

---

* Fisk frequently used his regiment to protect him from enemies and process servers. Unfortunately for him, on the night when he was fatally shot by a rival for the affections of the actress Josie Mansfield, his regiment was not at hand.

their experience the lesson that rebellion must be crushed as soon as it rears its head. Around 9:15, as the crowds started to leave the park, about three hundred "roughs," as the *New York Times* described them, attempted to stage a march. When Insp. William Murray, who had fought at the First Battle of Bull Run, ordered them to disperse, they ignored him. Without further parley, Murray commanded the police to charge. Scores of heads were broken by officers' clubs, sending the marchers fleeing into the night. When the news from New York was flashed across the country, strikers everywhere lost heart. "Murray's Charge," as it came to be known, was credited with causing the railroad strike to collapse. Murray himself won such acclaim that a few years later he succeeded to the post of superintendent of police.

Radicals in the United States never constituted a single group with a coherent program. Anarchists scorned all forms of governments as oppressive; Communists favored one controlled by workers. Some extremists wanted to launch an immediate revolution. Most Socialists believed that a better society could be achieved by making gradual progress. The press tended to lump all radicals together as "anarchists," and cartoonists invariably portrayed them as sinister-looking individuals with hats pulled down over their eyes and bombs concealed under their coats. Some American leaders and influential publications took to warning them to behave, lest they be made to answer before America's most powerful jurist, "Judge Lynch," whose courtroom was the nearest tree or lamppost. Leftist doctrines had little appeal to the mass of Americans, most of whom were basically pragmatic. Optimism about the future had brought them or their parents to the United States. Now they were too busy carving out better lives to pay much attention to the philosophical arguments that consumed the time of European intellectuals. Even if all radicals had joined hands, there were too few of them in the United States to seize New York, much less the whole country. Their greatest use was in fending off attacks on the robber barons of the Gilded Age who controlled the nation's economy and much of its politics. Anyone who proposed such measures as a graduated income tax could be dismissed as a far-out leftist. In the 1890s, when Congress did enact an income tax, the Supreme Court declared it unconstitutional, and Joseph Choate, the New York lawyer who argued the case against the tax, was hailed by many prominent Americans as "the man who blocked the march of Communism."[2]

Occasionally a more informed perspective on radicalism was offered. At the turn of the century, New York City police commissioner Mike Murphy observed that "there are only about 200 anarchists in [New York] . . . on the whole they are a harmless lot. The majority . . . are Socialists. This class has among its numbers some great minds."[3] Murphy's tolerant views may have been influenced by the fact that he was personally linked to Irish nationalist revolutionary groups.

In the late nineteenth century, the most prominent foreign radical in the United States was German-born Johann Most. Originally a Socialist and for a time a member of the Reichstag, he had been jailed in Austria, Germany, and England for his radical activities, in the last country for publishing an article celebrating the assassination of Czar Alexander II in 1881. When he arrived in New York the following year, he started a newspaper, *Freiheit*, in which he carried on propaganda for Socialism and anarchism, mostly the latter. With his hideously scarred face (the result of an accident at birth), bushy hair and beard, and shabby attire, he fit the popular image of an anarchist. In 1886 he was given a year in prison for making a speech deemed an incitement to riot. In 1887, when he denounced the trial of the eight men charged in the Haymarket bombing, in which seven Chicago policemen had been killed (and one died later of his wounds), he was arrested in New York and received a year in jail.*

Most was also an advocate of "free love," and he became part of a ménage à trois with two young Russian immigrants, Alexander Berkman and Emma Goldman. While Most was largely a fighter with the mouth and pen, the revolutionary anarchist Berkman preferred direct action—"the propaganda of the deed," as it was called. In 1892, after thirteen people were killed in a battle between striking workers and hired guards from the Pinkerton National Detective Agency at the Carnegie steel plant in Homestead, Pennsylvania, Berkman decided to assassinate the man in charge at Homestead, Carnegie's

---

* On the night of May 4, 1886, a meeting was called in Chicago's Haymarket Square to protest police clubbings and shootings of strikers. When a detachment of officers advanced to disperse the gathering, a bomb was hurled into their midst. Although it was labeled "the first anarchist bomb thrown this side of the Atlantic," the culprit was never identified. Eight radicals were charged with murder for inspiring the crime through their speeches and writings. One committed suicide in jail, four were hanged, and three were imprisoned. Even in conservative circles, there was criticism of the prosecution's broad theory of criminal responsibility.

partner, Henry Clay Frick.* Berkman first attempted to make a bomb by using directions in a book on revolutionary warfare authored by Most, but he was unsuccessful, probably because the dynamite he used had gotten wet. So he decided to shoot Frick. To do this he would need a gun, and a decent suit in order to gain access to Frick's office.

Neither Berkman nor Goldman had the necessary funds, so Emma, influenced by heroines of Russian novels, decided that she would earn some money by becoming a prostitute. On a hot July night, in a flashy outfit of the type worn by streetwalkers, she went down to the bright-light district on Fourteenth Street. Only twenty-three and retaining the bloom of youth, she was not unattractive, though at five feet tall and 120 pounds, she was a bit on the plump side. Goldman made overtures to several men, but because of her nervousness she was unable to close a deal. After she had spent several hours walking, an elderly man took her to a saloon, bought her a beer, and convinced her she had no knack for prostitution. Then he handed her ten dollars and told her to be on her way.

With the money earned from her foray on Fourteenth Street and a loan from her family, Emma provided the funds to equip Berkman with a pistol and a suit. In Pittsburgh he was able to gain admission to Frick's office and shoot the tycoon twice. While one of Frick's managers grappled with him, Berkman followed up with a knife, stabbing Frick. The struggle ended when a carpenter, who had heard the shots, ran into the room and hit Berkman over the head with a hammer. Frick did not die, so Berkman got off with serving thirteen years in a Pennsylvania state prison.

Goldman received considerable publicity from her association with Berkman and was invited to address various groups. At one public meeting, Most denounced Berkman's action because it had turned public opinion against the Homestead strikers. In retaliation, Goldman mounted the stage with a horsewhip and proceeded to beat Most. Not until her whip broke did she stop; she then threw the pieces on his head and ran out of the hall.

---

* Andrew Carnegie was in Scotland at the time. As was his fashion, after the strikers were killed, he issued a number of pious statements but never suggested improving the pay and working conditions of his employees. While he was a leading advocate of international peace and disarmament, his mills supplied the steel for battleships and other weapons. In present-day New York, the two steelmakers are memorialized by Carnegie Hall and the Frick Museum.

The world of domestic radicals was small, and New York, the immigrant capital of America, was their principal headquarters. Usually they lived or worked on the city's Lower East Side and could often be found hanging out at Justus Schwab's saloon on First Avenue near Tompkins Square. This made it easy for Det. Sgt. Charlie Jacobs, the NYPD's "Red expert," to keep an eye on them. After Goldman spoke at a gathering of four thousand unemployed people in Union Square, the meeting was declared an unlawful assembly and Sergeant Jacobs filed charges against her. She fled to Philadelphia, where she was held for New York authorities until Jacobs went down to fetch her. On the train returning to New York, he adopted a friendly, sympathetic attitude toward his prisoner. He told Goldman that if she would become a police informer and report on radical activity, charges against her would be dropped and she would be given a regular stipend. In response, she hurled a glass of ice water in his face.

Charlie Jacobs was no ordinary cop. As a detective sergeant, he was one of the "forty immortals" who worked out of headquarters under the direction of the famous inspector Thomas Byrnes, who in 1880 created the first modern detective bureau in the United States. Byrnes was known for his ability to cultivate informers and obtain confessions from suspects. So powerful and well connected was he (especially on Wall Street) that he could operate as a virtual law unto himself. In 1892 he had risen to superintendent, the top job in the NYPD. Jacobs brought Goldman in front of Byrnes, hoping he could break her. However, the usual tactics did not work. When Byrnes threatened to put her away for many years, she stood up to him, and for a moment it appeared that he was going to resort to the physical force he sometimes applied on other prisoners. Instead, he simply ordered her taken back to her cell. Goldman was convicted and sentenced to a year in jail. In private, Emma was not as strong as she was in her political life. Despite warnings from other radicals, she allowed herself to be exploited by one of her lovers, Ben Reitman, a Chicago physician who made money booking her lectures. More a poseur than a revolutionary, he occasionally served as a police spy.

In September 1901 President William McKinley was fatally wounded at the Pan-American Exposition in Buffalo, New York. His killer, Leon Czolgosz, proclaimed himself an anarchist and said he had been inspired by the speeches of Emma Goldman. Chicago detectives, who since the Haymarket affair had paid close attention to anarchists, seized Goldman and strove to prove her complicity in McKinley's murder. The Chicago police chief, Francis O'Neill, another strong Irish nationalist, disapproved of the detectives' action. Finally, after six days, he compelled them to release her.*

Other American leaders demanded that the "Red Queen" be tried as an accomplice in McKinley's murder, under the same legal theory used in the Haymarket prosecution—her speeches had incited others to violence. However, the New York State authorities did not embrace that notion. Czolgosz was executed, while Goldman's star rose even higher. After Berkman got out of prison in 1905, he became her costar on the radical circuit. Their appearance at any leftist event put a seal of approval on it and guaranteed that it would receive publicity.

———

As the twentieth century dawned, the United States assumed the status of a world power. Its victory over Spain in 1898 brought it a modest colonial empire. In 1900 U.S. troops were part of an international force that suppressed the Boxer Rebellion in China. McKinley's successor, Theodore Roosevelt, did not hesitate to wield a big stick to acquire the Panama Canal. Recognition of America's status as a world power led to a strengthening of U.S. military forces; the peacetime army was increased from twenty-eight thousand in 1898 to a hundred thousand in 1914. In 1903 a European-style general staff was formed. President Roosevelt was able to obtain congressional approval for the construction of a larger navy.

Domestic security did not receive a similar build up. A glaring example of America's unwillingness to recognize that it had the same security problems as other nations was its failure to deem the protection of its president a national responsibility. In April 1865, just after the bitter Civil War had ended, President Lincoln attended Ford's Theatre with only one bodyguard—

---

* The day before McKinley was shot, Johann Most, too drunk to properly edit his newspaper, put in filler, including a reprint of a fifty-year-old article by a German radical urging the assassination of government leaders. When he heard the news about McKinley, he attempted to recall copies of the paper, but one had already landed in the hands of police. Most was arrested for disorderly conduct and given a year in prison. He died in 1906.

a man who had been discharged from the Washington police force for drunkenness. Predictably, the guard wandered away from his post outside the president's box to have a drink, allowing John Wilkes Booth to slip in and shoot Lincoln. James A. Garfield, who took office as president in 1881, had been a Union general with responsibility for police and intelligence work in the fifty-thousand-man Army of the Cumberland. That experience and the fate of Lincoln gave him an awareness of security problems. Yet in June 1881 he went unescorted to Washington's Union Station, where he was fatally wounded by Charles Guiteau, a disappointed and deranged office-seeker.

Despite two presidential assassinations in just sixteen years, no provision was made for official protection. Congress felt that it smacked too much of royal guards (though sometimes Secret Servicemen were informally assigned to watch over the president). In the 1890s European assassins murdered the Spanish prime minister, the French president, and the empress of Austria. In 1900 Gaetano Bresci killed Italy's King Humbert using a gun concealed in a bouquet of flowers (a common ruse). Bresci had previously lived in the United States, so the Secret Service had looked into his background and later became aware of the concealed-gun ploy. Yet the following year, the three agents protecting President William McKinley when he was murdered in Buffalo did not challenge Leon Czolgosz when he entered the presidential receiving line with a suspiciously bandaged hand.

In 1898, when Spanish agents established a headquarters in Montreal and dispatched spies into the United States, the government thought to hire the Pinkerton agency to carry out counterespionage duties. But after Homestead, Congress had passed a law forbidding the employment of the Pinkertons by the U.S. government. A popular song of the time, "Father Was Killed by the Pinkerton Men," kept the public's memory of the affair alive, and the law could not be circumvented. Instead, the president assigned the Secret Service to counter Spanish spies, acting under the provisions of an obscure law that permitted the Service to conduct investigations for the secretary of state. To augment its numbers, the Service appointed a number of reserve operatives fluent in Spanish. With its small force, it was able to gather sufficient proof that the Spaniards were using neutral territory as a base and persuade the Canadian government to expel them. It also captured a few Spanish spies operating in the United States. The conflict was brief and brought considerable gain to the United States—"a splendid little war," as one prominent American described it, although had Spain been a major power rather than a second-rate one, its agents might not have been so easily defeated.

At the beginning of the twentieth century, U.S. domestic security forces comprised three elements: big-city police departments, the Secret Service, and national private detective agencies. The work of the NYPD, by far the largest and most skilled police force, was typified by Sergeant Jacobs's handling of Emma Goldman. The operations of the last two can be summed up in the career of one man, William Burns, whom the New York Times described in 1911 as "the only detective of genius whom this country has produced."[4]

William Burns was born in Baltimore in 1858, and shortly afterward his Irish Catholic immigrant father moved the family to Ohio. As a boy growing up, he shone in his school's debating club and dreamed of becoming an actor, which in the broad sense is what he did become. Burns was one of those men whom Heywood Broun had in mind when he remarked, "His career typifies the heights to which dramatic talent may carry a man in America if only he has the foresight not to go on the stage." Burns's father was a successful tailor who for a time was the elected police commissioner of Columbus, Ohio. Taking advantage of his father's position, Burns hung around police headquarters and took a keen interest in detective work. When he reached adulthood, he quit work in his father's tailor shop to take a job as a private detective with the Furlong Agency of St. Louis.

In Burns's day private detectives were the most important component of criminal investigation work. Outside of a few places such as New York City, municipal police departments did not have the resources or skills to combat the professional burglars, bunco artists, embezzlers, and other thieves who preyed on the rich pickings of a booming economy. The top private detective agency in the country had been organized by a Scottish immigrant named Allan Pinkerton, who began his career in Chicago. In 1861 Pinkerton supposedly foiled a plot to assassinate Abraham Lincoln in Baltimore while the president-elect was en route to his inauguration in Washington (a claim now questioned by historians). For a time during the Civil War, Pinkerton headed the Union Army's principal intelligence service. Successful as a detective, Pinkerton was a total failure as an intelligence chief, consistently producing vastly inflated estimates of Confederate strength. After the war, he built up a national agency that was available to public and private clients for investigative work and guard service. Pinkerton wrote (or had ghost-written) numerous books about his exploits and those of his agents. Today most are regarded as somewhat imaginative. When he died in 1884, his sons William and Robert ran the agency from dual headquarters in Chicago and New York. It was their guards who fought the strikers at Homestead.

From a distance of more than a hundred years, it is easy to deride the Pinkertons. But they filled a need for a national detective force to pursue criminals, who moved from state to state, and to work complex major cases. Only Pinkerton had enough skilled investigators to accomplish both tasks. His agents were also hired on a merit basis, and he did not hesitate to employ women and minorities, whereas regular police forces drew their detectives almost exclusively from among white males.

As Burns entered his thirties, he seemed to have settled into a career. His family was growing, and his work was satisfying. It was likely he would have become a partner in the Furlong firm or opened his own agency. But he did not like the aura that surrounded detectives, public or private, who were frequently referred to contemptuously as "gumshoes." So in 1891, at age thirty-three, he joined the Secret Service as a three-dollar-a-day assistant operative. Because the U.S. Constitution reserved general policing authority to the states, federal officers were limited to enforcing only laws Congress specifically authorized them to enforce. Every port had customs officers to ferret out smugglers trying to avoid payment of duties on imports—the tariff being the chief source of federal revenue. Postal inspectors handled cases of mail fraud or theft. The Secret Service, an arm of the U.S. Treasury, was in theory largely confined to apprehending counterfeiters. In practice, though, it handled a wide range of federal cases, such as illegal lotteries and frauds. In one instance the service was able to foil a plot to steal the body of President Lincoln from his tomb in Springfield, Illinois.* When assigned to non-Treasury duties, operatives were loaned out to other government agencies, which would pay their salaries and carry them on their own books. The Service itself also hired temporary employees, who were not counted

---

* The plotters expected to return the body in exchange for the release of one of their gang members from prison.

as part of the regular staff. Thus, while the authorized number of operatives rarely exceeded a hundred, the actual complement was larger.

In his early years with the Service, Burns handled routine cases and rose to the rank of special operative at four dollars a day; after five years' service he became a full-fledged operative at six dollars. His big break came in 1898 when, with the assistance of a thirteen-year-old temporary operative named Larry Richey, Burns made a counterfeiting case against two prominent Philadelphia politicians.[*]

After Philadelphia, Burns's career took off. He brought about the conviction of the superintendent of the San Francisco Mint for theft, and the political boss of that city for graft. In his most controversial investigation, he arrested a senator and congressman in Oregon for land fraud. In that case he was accused of rigging the outcome by having his colleagues research the panel and ensuring that the jurors chosen were ones who would support conviction. As one of his detectives wrote in a report regarding a prospective venireman, "He would convict Christ."

In 1909, by then a national celebrity, Burns quit the Service to open his own agency. In a shrewd move, he established his headquarters in New York, the center of the country's economic and social life. By 1898, when Manhattan, Brooklyn, Queens, the Bronx, and Staten Island were merged into a single municipality, New York was already a world metropolis. Early in the twentieth century skyscrapers began to rise high above the ground, and subways were built to run beneath them. In the streets motor vehicles rapidly replaced horses. New York's financiers supplied the capital that fueled the U.S. economy. The city set the tone in fashion and culture. What New York women decided to wear, the whole country would soon be attired in. A hit Broadway play or musical would spawn touring companies. New York was the news center of the continent. If Burns wanted to be in the swim of things, he would have to be based there. Like Pinkerton, he knew the value of public relations and astutely used the city's entertainment and publicity organizations to promote himself and his agency. He appeared in

---

[*] At sixteen, Richey (né Ricci) was given a regular appointment in the Secret Service and dispatched to New York to help battle the Mafia. Later he conducted investigations throughout the country. After working in journalism and in other branches of the government, in 1929 he was appointed principal secretary (chief of staff) to President Herbert Hoover. During and after Hoover's presidency, Richey was always the man closest to him.

Broadway plays as a detective and was never too busy to help a writer turn out a story on his exploits. His son George, also a Secret Service operative and who helped his father on cases, was a close friend of Broadway impresario George M. Cohan. The Burns Agency quickly catapulted to the top of the investigative field, surpassing the rival Pinkertons. It acquired the ultimate vote of confidence from the business world when the American Bankers Association dropped the Pinkertons and retained the Burns Agency.

At the state and local levels, governments continued to hire private detectives to handle cases of major public significance. In 1905, after the former governor of Idaho, Frank Steunenberg, was killed by a bomb attached to his front gate, the Pinkertons were brought in to investigate the crime. Their suspicions fell on the leader of the Western Federation of Miners, a one-eyed giant named William "Big Bill" Haywood, and two of his lieutenants. The Federation had a grudge against Steunenberg because, as governor, he had used troops to police a violent miners' strike. When the state of Colorado refused to extradite the suspects, Pinkerton men kidnapped them off the streets of Denver and brought them to Idaho for trial. After defense attorney Clarence Darrow gave an eleven-hour summation, in which he appealed to populist sentiment against eastern money interests, the jury brought in an acquittal. Haywood went on to become leader of the Industrial Workers of the World (IWW) and preached the anarchist doctrine of overthrowing governments and capitalism "by any means." Known by the nickname Wobblies, IWW recruits came mainly from the hardscrabble mining and logging areas of the West, although it also drew some educated people attracted to its program of violence.

In 1910 the Burns Agency was retained to investigate the bombing of the offices of the *Los Angeles Times*, in which twenty-one people were killed. Burns immediately focused on the International Association of Bridge, Structural, Ornamental and Reinforcing Iron Workers union, which he learned was carrying on a bombing campaign against employers who refused to negotiate with them. During the course of the investigation, Burns removed two suspects from Detroit to Chicago and held them for two weeks in a private home until he obtained their confessions. Ultimately, he charged James McNamara, the head of the union, with arranging the crime, and his brother John McNamara as one of the bombers. Because the *Los Angeles Times* was one of the most vociferous anti-union publications in the country, union men in California had brought in bombers from the Iron Workers in the belief that they would not be suspected because their union had had no dealings with the *Times*. Clarence Darrow, recently triumphant in the Idaho IWW case, was engaged as defense attorney. To the shock and dismay of their supporters, the defense entered a guilty plea to save the McNamaras from the death penalty. Darrow himself was charged with attempting to bribe a juror. At his trial he secured a hung jury by delivering a summation in which he tearfully pleaded for mercy because he had been ruthlessly pursued by "Burns and his pack of hounds." Finally, after Darrow promised in writing not to practice law in California again, the charges against him were dropped.

In reaction to Burns's arrests of the senator and congressman for land fraud, Congress passed a law in 1908 forbidding Secret Service men to be used on investigations other than those that pertained to their Treasury duties. The congressional action was a slap at President Theodore Roosevelt, who had authorized the land fraud investigation. Roosevelt struck back by proposing to create a Bureau of Investigation in the Department of Justice.* Attorney General Charles Bonaparte led the fight to obtain congressional approval.† During the debate, some congressman denounced "French spy methods" of the type employed by Bonaparte's relatives.‡ When Congress refused to authorize the bureau, Roosevelt waited until it had adjourned and then established one by executive order. Initially it was composed of a

---

* Not until twenty-seven years later would it become known as the Federal Bureau of Investigation (FBI). Because the bureau did not really resemble the agency we know today until the 1930's, I will not refer to it before then as the FBI.

† Charles Bonaparte was a grandnephew of Napoleon I. In 1803 Bonaparte's American society belle grandmother, Elizabeth Patterson, had married Napoleon's youngest brother, Jerome, a nineteen-year-old naval officer, while he was visiting Baltimore. After his ship departed she followed him back to Europe, where she gave birth to a son. The Bonaparte family was outraged by the marriage and demanded that the Pope annul it. The pontiff refused because it had been a proper Catholic ceremony performed by the Bishop of Baltimore. Instead, Emperor Napoleon dissolved it himself. Eighteen-year-old Elizabeth Patterson Bonaparte took her son home and resumed her place in society, living to the age of ninety-four. Her grandson Charles was an eminent lawyer who spent most of his career trying to reform Maryland's corrupt politics. Theodore Roosevelt named him secretary of the navy and later attorney general.

‡ France, though not a police state—unless war or a state of siege was declared, individuals could not be incarcerated without trial—was a garrison state where military and police security officers blanketed the country and passed on to the government derogatory information about its opponents. Everything went into thick dossiers, which were kept permanently on file.

Sometimes the security system made huge mistakes. In 1894 a French cleaning woman who worked at the German Embassy and was on the payroll of her own country's army counterintelligence section brought in a paper

handful of Secret Service operatives transferred over and some miscellaneous federal investigators. In a country where private detectives and guards
routinely carried firearms, which they used freely in crushing strikes, the
U.S. government chose not to arm its new detective force, and Bureau of
Investigation agents were given no more arrest authority than a private citizen. When it became necessary to apprehend someone, the usual procedure
was for the agent to obtain the assistance of local police, U.S. marshals, or
the Secret Service. This led to moments of Keystone Kops comedy. It was
not unusual in arrest situations that, while regular police with guns drawn
stormed through the front door of a suspect's house, the bureau agent was
relegated to standing at the back door with a brickbat in his hand. In the
police world, a cop without a gun was no cop at all, and in parts of the
South and West, where men often went about armed, a lawman who didn't
tote a pistol appeared as odd as a man who did not wear trousers.

Initially the bureau lacked an overriding mission, such as the Secret Service task of combating counterfeiting. In 1910, in response to lurid stories
about women forced into prostitution as "white slaves," Congress passed
the Mann Act, which made it a crime to transport females across state lines
for immoral purposes. Enforcement of the law was assigned to the Bureau
of Investigation.*

In the Washington bureaucratic world, an agency composed of empty-
holstered cops whose chief task was chasing pimps was likely to be overlooked
at budget time. To bolster its place in the law enforcement hierarchy, the
bureau played up white slavery, resorting to exaggerated claims that ordinary
women were in constant danger of being kidnapped by white slavers—

(continued)

she had retrieved from the military attaché's wastebasket. The document contained information on a new French
artillery piece, which counterintelligence officers suspected had been filched by a member of the general staff.
Their suspicions quickly focused on Capt. Alfred Dreyfus. When Dreyfus, the only Jew on the staff, was interrogated,
he denied any involvement. Nevertheless, he was court-martialed, convicted, and sentenced to life imprisonment
on Devil's Island. Half the country believed he should have been shot, while the other half came to believe he had
been framed. It took five years to obtain his release from the island and seven more to prove that the evidence
against him had been forged. In the meantime, the real spy, Maj. Ferdinand Esterhazy, decamped to England.

* The Act's sponsor, Congressman James Mann of Chicago, meant it to put a crimp in the operation of his
city's notorious red-light district, the Levee. The first man slated for arrest under its provisions was a well-
known Levee brothel-keeper. The district was a rough place. A few years later, three Chicago detectives were
shot there in a battle with gunmen working for the vice lords. The bureau agent assigned to make the apprehension had to call on Secret Service operative Larry Richey and his partner for assistance.

invariably portrayed as Latinos, Jews, or blacks—and forced into whore-houses, where they were held as prisoners.

The creation of the Bureau of Investigation would ultimately have major negative consequences for federal law enforcement. Before 1908 there was little reason for rivalry among Uncle Sam's agencies. U.S. marshals, customs officials, and postal inspectors each had their own sphere. The Secret Service operatives, either as Treasury agents or on loan to other government depart-ments, handled most other matters. After 1908, with the Secret Service authority curtailed by Congress and the Bureau of Investigation taking on some of its former tasks, the two agencies would become competitors.

No agency had much competence in the area of domestic security. The Secret Service received legal authorization to protect the president, but as late as 1914 only five operatives were assigned to the White House detail. In 1909 President Taft met with President Porfirio Díaz of Mexico along the U.S.-Mexican border near El Paso. At the time, Mexico was seething and revolution was in the air. The following year revolution would break out, compelling Díaz to flee into exile. There were rumors that attempts would be made to assassinate both presidents. While the Bureau of Investigation and the Secret Service battled over who would have charge of protective arrangements, White House aides stuck their oar in at every opportunity. When a meeting between Taft and Díaz did take place, U.S. troops were present in force and nothing untoward happened.

———

In 1911 the man who would teach Americans the rudiments of domestic security operations arrived in the United States to spy on some prominent Yanks. On a November day, a thirty-seven-year-old Englishman, Claude Dansey, arrived at 55 Wall Street, headquarters of the National City Bank, to be interviewed for a job by the bank's president, Frank Vanderlip. The bank was one of the big three of American finance, along with the First National Bank and J.P. Morgan & Co.*

* The last, known more regally as the "House of Morgan," held the premier position. Until his death in 1913, J. Pierpont Morgan was the titan of American finance. His firm functioned as America's de facto central bank, because the United States did not have a government-designated bank. In the panic of 1907, Pierpont's nod or frown determined whether a corporation in distress went under or was saved.

Dansey was not seeking a banking job. He was being vetted for the post of residential secretary at the Sleepy Hollow Country Club situated along the Hudson River, north of New York City. Newly opened, it was a playground for the super rich such as the Astors and Vanderbilts. While the job paid $300 a month and provided luxurious accommodations, socially it was just a notch above being a butler in the mansion of one of its rich members—English butlers being preferred because they not only knew how to care for their masters, but they also did not have the American trait of thinking themselves as good as the next man. Vanderlip, chairman of the club's executive committee, decided Dansey fit the bill, and he was hired. Ironically, Dansey was of higher social status than the men he worked for. Any one of them would have jumped at the chance to link themselves with the British aristocracy.

Born in 1876, Claude Edward Marjoribanks Dansey was the son of a colonel in the most senior and elite unit of the British army, the Life Guards cavalry regiment, which protected the sovereign. Only men from the old landed aristocracy could be commissioned in it. Dansey's mother was the daughter of a lord. Dansey Senior assumed his son would follow him into the regiment and the comfortable country house, club, and turf circles in which a Life Guards officer moved. When Claude was eighteen, however, personal indiscretions with his teacher, a member of Oscar Wilde's circle, led his family to ship him abroad. It was standard practice in upper-class British families to send a black sheep off to the colonies so he could make a fresh start, and Dansey was appointed to the British South African Police (BSAP), a mounted constabulary force that patrolled Rhodesia. Its personnel were not like "coppers" at home, who were drawn from the lower orders of society. The BSAP were a sort of cadet corps for men of quality looking to obtain administrative posts in Britain's colonial empire.

In 1895 Cecil Rhodes—premier of the Cape Colony, South Africa's richest man, and proponent of an expanded British Empire—dispatched a force of BSAP officers, under the leadership of Dr. Leander Starr Jameson, to seize the Transvaal Republic from its Boer rulers. Their foray was a disaster. Some of the officers were killed, while Jameson and the rest were thrown in jail. Rhodes himself was compelled to resign the premiership in disgrace. Luckily for Dansey, he had still been in training, so he was not selected to participate in the coup.

Next, Dansey took up a position as a commissioned officer of the British colonial police in Borneo. In 1899, when the Boers, still smarting from the Jameson raid, went to war with Britain, Dansey returned to South Africa as an army intelligence officer. There he acquired a reputation by slipping into Boer camps at night and bashing sentries over the head. After the war he secured an appointment as a political intelligence officer in Somaliland. Despite his upper-class background, Dansey was regarded by many who knew him as a bit of a thug and possibly dishonest. In 1909 he was cut adrift by the Colonial Office. Angry and fearful for his future, Dansey returned to England just in time to benefit from a newspaper-generated spy scare.

In the early years of the twentieth century, the British public was deluged with warnings that German spies were operating in England as part of the advance guard of an invasion force. According to some of the wilder estimates, there were already thousands in the country working as clerks, waiters, and hairdressers. Cheap thrillers spun tales of a sudden German descent on Britain. A leading newspaper ran a series of articles describing how a German army had landed on the English coast and fought its way to London.*

At the time, it was generally believed that Britain had the most efficient spy service in Europe. In fact, it had no formal espionage corps; information it received came from diplomats, military attachés, and occasional excursions by individuals sent out on special missions. In essence, it had spies but no spy service, so the government established a full-time foreign intelligence agency and a counterespionage force. Later they came to be called, respectively, the Secret Intelligence Service (SIS), or MI6, and the Security Service, or MI5.†

Dansey was offered an appointment in the new intelligence/security services. However, his initial assignment was to check up not on German spies, but on an Irish American. Thomas Fortune Ryan was a Virginia-born Irish Catholic who rose from being a Baltimore store clerk to become a Wall Street

---

* Militarily, the route the newspaper outlined was unsound because it ran through heavily populated towns, which would have served as barriers to the advance. From a circulation standpoint, however, it was desirable that the daily battles be fought in places where the paper had many readers.

† MI stood for military intelligence, though both the British army and navy had their own intelligence departments.

tycoon and leading fund-raiser for the Democratic Party. The British suspected Ryan of supplying funds to Irish rebels. At the time, Ryan was also moving in on the mineral rights of the Belgian Congo in conjunction with a consortium of U.S. investors, including a Guggenheim, a Whitney, and U.S. senator Nelson W. Aldrich, Republican majority leader.* To keep an eye on Ryan, Dansey was sent to New York. British security operations in the United States were an old story. In the 1860s British operatives, working undercover in New York City, had spied on Irish rebels. A British agent who infiltrated one of the rebel groups managed to sit in on a meeting with President Andrew Johnson at the White House.

Frank Vanderlip had Secret Service experience himself. In 1897, when William McKinley became president, he named a Chicago lawyer, Lyman Gage, to be secretary of the treasury. Gage brought Vanderlip, the financial editor of the *Chicago Tribune*, the voice of midwestern Republicanism, along as assistant secretary. Among Vanderlip's responsibilities was the supervision of the U.S. Secret Service. He named as its chief John Wilkie, a former crime and financial reporter on the *Tribune* who would head the agency until 1911. Despite his background, Vanderlip did not tumble to the fact that Dansey was, in effect, a British spy set among the Wall Street elite.

After nearly three years of observing him, Dansey concluded that Ryan was not interested in helping Irish rebels, only in making money. When World War I broke out, Dansey returned to England to take up a position with MI5. In 1917 he would be sent back to the United States to teach Americans the great game. It was the beginning of the relationship between British and American intelligence agencies that would be both productive and troublesome for both sides.

At the turn of the century, the British Empire had two contrasting models of domestic security. In England, where for two hundred years governments had been overturned by ballots and not bullets, police did not even carry guns. In the colonies, where the inhabitants did not welcome foreign rule, the British maintained both military garrisons and powerful police forces to suppress uprisings. Even in Ireland, legally a part of the United Kingdom

---

* Lincoln Steffens, in his exposés of American boss-run political machines, dubbed Aldrich "Boss of the United States."

with representation in parliament, Britain supplemented its military forces with an armed fifteen-thousand-man Royal Irish Constabulary (RIC) that lived in barracks ready to crack down hard on rebel activity.

In the 1880s, when Irish revolutionaries began a bombing campaign in London, RIC detachments were sent into the capital to protect government buildings. The arrival of the carbine-carrying, green-uniformed troopers was an affront to the English police. In response, Scotland Yard created a corps of detectives known as the Special Irish Branch to keep track of rebel activity. One of the first men assigned to it was an Irish Catholic police sergeant named Patrick Quinn. In 1873, at age nineteen, he had left his home in County Mayo to join London's Metropolitan Police Force. He was made a sergeant in just five years. Quinn would spend the rest of his career with the Branch, serving for a time as bodyguard to King Edward VII. When he retired as a superintendent in 1918, he became the first police officer who had risen from the ranks to be knighted. As the Branch began to deal with general political crimes, loosely labeled anarchism, "Irish" was dropped from the title.*

After 1909, Special Branch and MI5 worked the same territory, though MI5 officers were not given the power of arrest. When a suspect had to be taken into custody, the job was assigned to the Branch, which also carried out surveillance of suspects and other support tasks for MI5. A better-educated group than the police, MI5 tended to employ more sophisticated methods. Police detectives followed a case-by-case approach, concentrating on individual crimes and defendants. In military terminology, they were tactically oriented: locate the enemy and defeat him, or in policing, snap the cuffs on the crook and book him. Good intelligence work required a more strategic approach, such as analyses of what the Germans or some anarchist group were likely to do in the future. Instead of having a spy arrested, MI5 was more likely to keep watching him. A spy who was jailed would inevitably be replaced by one that the Security Service did not know. Better then to keep the known one operating, with the possibility of locating accomplices, feeding him false information, or turning him into a double agent. Whereas the police measured success in terms of favorable news stories citing the good work of the arresting officers,

---

* A literary work on pre–World War I British security policing is Joseph Conrad's 1907 novel *The Secret Agent*, which describes the pursuit of anarchists by the "special crimes" section of the Metropolitan Police Force.

MI5 believed that its activities should be kept secret. Under the law, the press was forbidden to write about the work of the secret services.

—————

As America entered the fateful year of 1914, its security forces were still muddling along. There was no equivalent to MI5; Congress would never have permitted it. The Secret Service and Bureau of Investigation, with a combined total of fewer than five hundred detectives, spent most of their time chasing counterfeiters and pimps, not security threats. Private detectives performed tasks that were rightly the responsibility of government.

From an administrative standpoint, America's failure to create a British-model security system could be severely criticized. But there were compelling reasons for not doing so. Americans tended to value freedom over security. Protected by three thousand miles of ocean, the founding generation, with memories of the excesses of British officials, promulgated a Bill of Rights that left police authority in the hands of the individual states.* The later immigrants who arrived from continental Europe came from countries where gendarmerie, constabulary, or carabiniere bared the sword of the king before people's eyes, and where secret police spies were everywhere. The newcomers had no desire to see such forces established in this country. Under the American flag lived the freest people in the world.†

———————————

* On one occasion law enforcement problems inherent in a federal system almost propelled the United States into war. In 1840 a Canadian deputy sheriff named Alexander McLeod, relaxing in an upstate New York saloon, boasted that three years earlier he had been part of a raiding party that attacked an American ship in American waters near Niagara Falls. The vessel, the *Caroline*, had been hired to bring supplies to Canadian rebels. The raiders captured it, set it afire, and killed an American crewman. McLeod was immediately arrested and charged with murder and arson. The British government dispatched a note to the American government demanding McLeod's release on the grounds that his actions had been undertaken as a member of Crown forces. The U.S. State Department replied that it had no jurisdiction over a New York State criminal trial. When the British sought to make their appeal directly to the state, the United States pointed out that diplomatic relations with a foreign power were exclusively reserved to the federal government. The British then declared that if "a judicial murder" of McLeod were carried out, it would mean war. With the prospect of the powerful British navy bombarding New York and other American harbors, every criminal defense tactic known was employed to secure his acquittal. McLeod repudiated his alleged confession; an alibi witness placed him five miles from the scene of the attack, and his lawyers claimed that the actual offender was his brother (who was safely beyond New York law in Canada). Important people carried on ex parte conversations with New York State criminal justice officials. The governor of the state, William Seward, promised that in case of a conviction, he would pardon McLeod. After just twenty minutes' deliberation, the jury came in with an acquittal, and the United States did not have to refight the War of 1812.⁵

† If they were of European heritage. For blacks, Mexicans, Native Americans, and Asians, it was not the same.

In New York City, the security forces still regarded the leading threat as the activities of bomb throwers and radical agitators. In the first decade of the century, the NYPD's Italian squad, headed by Lt. Giuseppe "Joe" Petrosino, had been charged with handling bombings. It was a logical decision because many Italian Black Handers used bombs to intimidate their victims.* After Gaetano Bresci killed Italy's King Humbert in 1900, Petrosino was assigned to check out Bresci's activity during the time he had lived in the United States. In 1909 the police commissioner sent Petrosino to Sicily to investigate Mafiosi on their home grounds. As might have been anticipated, he was murdered in Palermo. The case was not solved, and the Italian squad was essentially disbanded. Its bomb and anarchist work was picked up by another special service squad, headed by Capt. Thomas Tunney.

In honor of Bresci, New York radicals formed the Bresci Circle, which included as many as six hundred people. The group held meetings in the basement of a shabby house on 106th Street in East Harlem, where famous radicals such as Alexander Berkman and Emma Goldman often spoke. It also had an alliance with the IWW. Out in Colorado, the Wobblies were striking the Rockefeller-controlled Colorado Fuel and Iron Company and conducting a guerrilla war against local police and militia. Testifying before Congress, John D. Rockefeller Sr. vowed that he would never give way to their demands. In Ludlow, Colorado, miners and their families, evicted from company housing, established a tent camp. On the night of April 20, 1914, state troops set it on fire, and shooting broke out. By the time it ended, forty-seven people, including women and children, were dead from bullets or suffocation. In New York, Alexander Berkman called for the assassination of Rockefeller. Because Berkman had shot Frick at Homestead, the authorities took him seriously.

In May, Carlo Tresca assumed the leadership of the New York anarchist forces protesting against Rockefeller. Ten years earlier he had immigrated to the United States from Italy, eventually settling in New York. Since then he had made a national reputation as a firebrand by leading major strikes in Lawrence, Massachusetts, and Paterson, New Jersey. By 1914 he and his girlfriend, Elizabeth Gurley Flynn, were second only to Berkman and Goldman

---

* While often used as a synonym for Mafioso, Black Handers were Italians who sent extortion notes to fellow Italians. Usually they contained symbols such as a black hand or a dagger.

on the radical circuit and the security police watch lists. Tresca organized demonstrations at the Rockefeller estate in Tarrytown. On the first day, he was arrested for holding a meeting without a permit. On the second day, police moved in with clubs, arresting and forcibly dispersing the demonstrators. One of those seized was Arthur Caron. On July 4 Caron and two other men were making a bomb in an apartment at 104th Street and Lexington Avenue in Upper Manhattan when it exploded and killed them.

The story received less news coverage than might have been expected, because six days earlier the heir to the Austro-Hungarian throne and his wife had been assassinated during a visit to the obscure town of Sarajevo. As a result, Europe was plunged into one of its periodic crises. However, in the previous ten years, flare-ups in the Balkans or over Morocco had eventually been smoothed out. In any event, Americans did not see European conflicts as relevant to their lives (although in New York, which was the link between European and American commerce, a continental war could have had severe economic repercussions).

It was Tunney's squad that conducted the investigation into the Lexington Avenue bombing. He planted one of his detectives in the Bresci Circle, and eventually the undercover agent was able to learn that the conspirators were planning another explosion—at St. Patrick's Cathedral, seat of the Catholic archdiocese. In March 1915, while the Archbishop was conducting Mass, Tunney and his detectives staked out in the pews and seized several men with bombs. By that time, though, the challenge from the Bresci Circle was nothing compared to the one Tunney's squad was facing from Imperial Germany.

2

THE MANHATTAN FRONT

The Undeclared War, 1914–1917

In the late nineteenth century, German chancellor Otto von Bismarck predicted that the next general European war would arise out of "some damn fool thing in the Balkans." In 1914 his prophecy came true. On June 28 the heir to the Austrian throne and his wife were murdered in Sarajevo. Because the killers were Serbs, it was expected that Austria would demand atonement from the Serbian government. Still, the consensus among European leaders was that the murders would not result in war. As late as July 23, Nathan Rothschild, First Baron Rothschild, head of the continent's premier banking house, expressed the view that "the various matters in dispute will be arranged without appeal to arms." Rothschild's comments reflected the common opinion of European financial leaders. They believed the economies of the great powers were so intertwined that even if a war broke out, the combatants would quickly run out of the money necessary to finance it. It would not be the last time wise men of the financial world were disastrously wrong. The generals and war ministers also shared the notion that any conflict would be of short duration—which is why their war plans were designed to produce a quick victory. It was not the last time, either, that the warlords would be proven wrong—for the troops they commanded, dead wrong.

On July 29, with the Austrian forces bombarding the Serbian capital and the other powers mobilizing, all the European financial markets closed down. In New York, as foreign investors rushed to liquidate securities, prices on the stock exchange fell precipitously. By July 31, it was on the verge of a complete collapse. The situation was reminiscent of the panic of 1907, when a number of banks and brokerages had teetered on the edge and the New York City government faced bankruptcy. Then one man saved the day: seventy-year-old J. Pierpont Morgan Sr., the titan of American finance, organized a pool that provided the funds to rescue most of the threatened institutions. Morgan senior had died in 1913, and his son J. P. Jr., or "Jack," was not as dominant a figure as his father had been. Nevertheless, the House of Morgan was still the place the Wall Street community looked to for direction.

When Jack convened a meeting of financial leaders on the morning of July 31, the immediate question was whether the market should open that day. At 9:30 a.m., half an hour before the bell would sound to commence trading, Morgan decided to consult with Secretary of the Treasury William Gibbs McAdoo. It was a sign of changing times. Other than a few spats during the presidency of Theodore Roosevelt, the New York financial community had always counted on the federal government to favor its interests. Now, though, McAdoo represented an administration less friendly to Wall Street. Alongside him in the cabinet of President Wilson sat Secretary of State William Jennings Bryan. Three times the unsuccessful Democratic candidate for president, he was still a hero in the South and West. In his famous speech at the 1896 convention in Chicago, he had accused the Eastern money interests of trying to "crucify mankind on a cross of gold." At the 1912 convention in Baltimore, his ringing denunciation of J. P. Morgan Sr., Thomas Fortune Ryan, and other Wall Street leaders had swung the convention away from the leading candidate, House Speaker James "Champ" Clark, to Wilson.

William Gibbs McAdoo was a man with a foot in both camps. Like President Wilson, he was a Southerner who had built his career in the North. Born in Georgia, he practiced law in Tennessee and then moved to New York City where he worked as a marketer of bonds. Before the war, he hit the big time when he led the corporation that accomplished the engineering feat of digging tunnels under the Hudson River to provide a railroad connection between New York City and New Jersey. His success then had won the applause of the financial giants. But as treasury secretary, against their overwhelming opposition, he had managed to secure the establishment of a federal bank. By doing so, he moved the center of financial power from the House of Morgan to a government agency, at least in theory. (Under Republican administrations in the 1920s, the bank was a virtual Morgan subsidiary.) In addition to the clout afforded by his cabinet post, the fifty-year-old widower had recently married the president's twenty-four-year-old daughter, Eleanor, giving Wilson a son-in-law only seven years younger than himself. McAdoo did not grovel before Wall Street. He told Jack, "If you really want my judgment, it is to close the exchange." At five minutes to ten, with the man whose job it was to ring the opening gong already at his post, it was announced that the market was shutting down. It would not reopen until December.

A few blocks from Wall Street, at New York's ornate 102-year-old City Hall, another new administration was making itself felt. At the beginning of 1914 a reform mayor, John Purroy Mitchel, had taken office. Only thirty-four, he was the youngest chief executive in the city's history. The "Boy Mayor," as the press dubbed him, was not a WASP gentleman like most reformers. He was the grandson and namesake of an Irish Catholic revolutionary leader. However, he had been educated at Columbia and was enamored of high society, frequently being photographed in such haunts of the rich as Newport, mingling with the Vanderbilts and their kind. It was not the type of publicity that endeared a New York mayor to his blue-collar constituents. Mitchel was also possessed of a hot temper and an erratic nature. Some people speculated that this was a result of an incident early in his career. While he was working in South America, an enemy slipped him poison, the effects of which made him prone to severe headaches.

Mitchel's ascent to the mayoralty was the result of a gigantic police scandal. In July 1912 a gambler named Herman Rosenthal had begun squealing to the New York County district attorney about payoffs to Lt. Charles Becker, commanding officer of a squad operating out of the commissioner's office. In the midst of the inquiry, Rosenthal was shot to death outside a Times Square hotel, allegedly by gangsters acting for Becker. Over the next few years, Becker and the four killers were electrocuted at Sing Sing, the police commissioner was fired, the mayor dropped dead from a heart attack, and the Tammany overseer of organized crime supposedly went insane, escaped from his keepers, and was run over by a train.*

---

* The circumstances surrounding the death of "Big Tim" Sullivan were mysterious. For example, though he was one of the best-known men in New York, for some reason he lay in the morgue at Bellevue Hospital unrecognized for ten days, until a cop who happened to glance at the corpse let out a scream and went running through the halls, shouting, "Lord God, it's Big Tim."

When Mitchel entered City Hall in January 1914, his choice for police commissioner had been Col. George Washington Goethals, the man who had built the Panama Canal. At the time, there was no trouble obtaining someone of that quality for the post. Who would not want the job that, two decades earlier, had propelled Theodore Roosevelt from president of the Board of Commissioners to national prominence? In 1900 as governor, Roosevelt pushed through a law transferring the control of the force from a board to a single commissioner. Since then the post had been filled by former judges, generals, and congressmen. A few years earlier the NYPD had moved from its historic headquarters on Mulberry Street, with its memories of the draft riots and hundreds of other dramatic events, to a new building at Centre and Broome Streets. To preserve tradition, commissioners continued to use Teddy's old desk, as commissioners still do today at the current police headquarters, 1 Police Plaza. When the legislature refused to amend the law to grant Goethals virtually czar-like powers over the police department, he refused the appointment. So Mitchel turned to his secretary, Arthur Woods. The handsome, dashing Woods was a Harvard graduate who had studied at German universities before becoming an English instructor at the preparatory school Groton, where he taught President Roosevelt's sons. Woods was the kind of well-educated, red-blooded WASP gentleman that Teddy Roosevelt admired, so the president began assigning him to carry out official missions.

In 1906, when Roosevelt's military aide, Gen. Theodore Bingham, became police commissioner, Woods was appointed deputy commissioner in charge of detectives. Today, naming an English teacher to head the country's largest police detective bureau would be regarded as absurd. Columnists and TV comedians would have a field day. In those times, it was the practice in New York and elsewhere to place educated gentlemen in charge of the largely uneducated and sometimes ungentlemanly career cops.* Woods spent seven weeks in Europe studying policing and, upon his return, modeled New York's sleuths on their more advanced Continental counterparts. As deputy commissioner, he was no white-gloved administrator; he liked to go out on

---

* At the time of Woods's appointment as deputy commissioner, the chief of the U.S. Secret Service was a former reporter for the *Chicago Tribune*; the commissioner of the Boston police and the superintendent of the Washington force were also ex-journalists.

the street with detectives and get his hands dirty. In 1909, when General Bingham was pushed out, Woods resigned and became a cotton broker. When he returned as police commissioner, he had not changed. Once, when he was reprimanded by the counsel representing the state in an investigation regarding authorizing detectives to tap phones, he burst forth in the spirit of Inspector Byrnes, declaring:

> You know that you cannot do detective work in a high hat and kid gloves. We have got to use the methods of the crook and speak the language. There is too much snappy talk about the rights of the crook. He is an outlaw and defies authority. Where do his rights come in? If people spent less time talking about the dear criminals and more time helping the police to run them down, we would have fewer criminals.[1]

Like Mitchel, Woods moved in the orbit of the super rich and in 1916 would marry Jack Morgan's niece. In the next three years, Morgan, McAdoo, Mitchel, and Woods would play key roles in the war, even though the United States was not yet officially a participant.

When the conflict began, President Wilson was attending to his terminally ill wife, who died on August 6. He did not get around to issuing a proclamation of U.S. neutrality until two weeks later. His action did not stop some Americans from taking sides. Members of the eastern elite, such as the House of Morgan, were outspokenly pro-Allied. Morgan partner Thomas Lamont later acknowledged, "We wanted the Allies to win, from the outset of the war. We were pro-Allied by inheritance, by instinct, by opinion."[2] England was still the place rich Americans looked to for social acceptance. A branch of the New York Astors, the country's most prominent family, had given up its U.S. citizenship to accept a British peerage. Their social rivals, the Vanderbilts, had a daughter married to the Duke of Marlborough, first cousin of Winston Churchill, who was himself the grandson of a New York tycoon. On the other side, many German Americans openly supported their Fatherland, while some Irish Americans hoped for the defeat of their ancient enemy, Britain. German and Irish Americans drew severe condemnation from Theodore Roosevelt, who declared, "There is no room for the hyphen in our citizenship. . . . He who is not with us is against us and should be treated as an enemy alien. . . . We have room in this country for but one flag. We should . . . crush under our heel any movement that smacks in the slightest of playing the German game."[3]

Among Morgan's leading rivals on Wall Street were such German Jewish bankers as Jacob Schiff, head of the Kuhn, Loeb firm. German Jews felt a natural sympathy for their homeland, and they despised czarist Russia for the pogroms it had carried out against their coreligionists. In 1912 Samuel Untermyer, a prominent Jewish lawyer, had led a congressional investigation of the Morgan bank's financial dealings. During the war, Jack Morgan rarely missed an opportunity to question the patriotism of his Jewish rivals and critics.

Initially most Americans were not partisans of either side, preferring that the United States remain neutral. Then, in May 1915, U.S. opinion was inflamed after a German submarine sank the British luxury liner *Lusitania*, killing 1,198 people, including 128 Americans, among them the prominent socialite Alfred Gwynne Vanderbilt. In the aftermath, many U.S. citizens moved from being neutral to being pro-Allied. Had the German government not promised to stop sinking passenger vessels, President Wilson might have been compelled to ask for a declaration of war.

From 1915 on, the policy debate in the United States was between those who favored "peace" and those who advocated "preparedness." The Peace Party included such pacifists as Jane Addams of Chicago's Hull-House and Lillian Wald of New York City's Henry Street Settlement. Other members were prominent clergymen, educators, social reformers, and politicians, often of populist or progressive views. Among them was Secretary of State Bryan, who resigned in protest at Wilson taking a strong line against Germany after the *Lusitania* incident. Preparedness advocates were led by Teddy Roosevelt and his close ally Gen. Leonard Wood, America's foremost military commander, and included most of the eastern establishment. The policy debate disrupted former alliances. In 1912, when Roosevelt had received the nomination of the Progressive Party at a Republican rump convention in Chicago, Jane Addams led the crowd in "The Battle Hymn of the Republic." But in 1915 Teddy and Jane were no longer singing the same song. In 1916, when Roosevelt returned to the Republican fold, the Progressive Party died as a national force.

New York was the center of the preparedness movement. In the summer of 1915, Roosevelt and General Wood established a training camp for potential army officers at upstate Plattsburgh, New York. Many members of the eastern elite, including Mayor Mitchel and Commissioner Woods, enrolled in the course. On May 13, 1916, over a hundred thousand people paraded through the streets of New York City in support of preparedness. Starting at 9:30 a.m., they marched north on Broadway from City Hall, accompanied by two hundred brass bands and fifty drum-and-bugle corps. At Twenty-Third Street they turned onto Fifth Avenue, where Mayor Mitchel and General Wood stood on a reviewing stand and nine thousand supporters cheered from a grandstand. Not until twelve hours after the march had begun did the last contingent reach the parade terminus at Grand Army Plaza, off Fifty-Ninth and Fifth. So successful was the demonstration that other major cities held their own parades. In Washington, President Wilson himself marched in the parade.

More tangible support for the Allies came from the House of Morgan. When Britain, France, and Russia sought loans and supplies in the United States, it took the lead in raising the funds and serving as purchasing agent for the Allies. Soon shiploads of munitions and other materials began flowing out of New York harbor, bound for Europe. The Central Powers argued that it was a unneutral action, but American businessmen were not about to pass up the profits that could be made. The official U.S. government response to German and Austrian protests was that its factories stood ready to fill their orders, too. Of course, with British cruisers patrolling just outside the three-mile limit—"Two inches outside," the Germans would claim—any vessel of the Central Powers attempting to enter an American harbor would have been captured or sunk. So the Imperial Government retaliated by extending the war to the United States.

═══════

After their victory in the Franco-Prussian War of 1870, the Germans enjoyed a reputation for military prowess that endured until the defeat of Hitler in 1945. In most respects it was deserved, but Germany's intelligence work was always a weak spot. David Kahn, the historian of World War II German intelligence, has explained this phenomenon. Their military doctrine emphasized an opening offensive aimed at bringing quick victory. Thus an enemy nation would be forced to react to German initiatives, leaving it no time to implement its own plans. In 1914 the general staff counted on knocking out France in six weeks, before Russia could mobilize its vast army or Britain could build up its meager one. Following the defeat of France, Germany would throw its full weight against Russia. As it turned out, the offensive against France failed, and Germany was left to fight a protracted war on two fronts.

Because the general staff had counted on a quick victory, before the war the Germans had paid no attention to distant America, with its tiny army. In addition, the Prussian Junkers, like most other European aristocrats, looked down on the United States as a nation filled with what even the Statue of Liberty described as "the wretched refuse of [Europe's] teeming shore." Many had left their homeland to avoid military service: hardly promising material for an army. The U.S. government was seen as beholden to avaricious businessmen who put dollars ahead of national honor. Yet, since 1898, the United States had acquired Hawaii, the Philippines, Puerto Rico, and the Panama Canal by force. Its troops had intervened in China, the Caribbean, and Central America. In 1908, President Theodore Roosevelt had sent the U.S. fleet on a world cruise to demonstrate its strength, especially to the Japanese. With a population of a hundred million and a vast industrial capacity, the United States was quite capable of creating a war machine equal to that of any major power. Half a century earlier, when the population was only thirty million, the North and South both raised mass armies that, once they had gained experience, displayed considerable skill on the battlefield. Had German intelligence engaged in a systematic, long-term analysis of American potential, the Imperial Government might have modified its view of the Yankees.

When the war began, no European army had sufficient munitions to carry on a prolonged, large-scale conflict. For the Allies, the shells they received from American factories were manna from heaven. By 1915 this ordnance began taking a heavy toll on the German ranks. Desperate to stop the American arms shipments, the German high command ordered a sabotage campaign against factories turning out munitions and the vessels that transported them. They also commenced a propaganda drive to keep America out of the war. The best place to stop munitions shipments was New York Harbor, and to keep America neutral, Germany would have to influence opinion in the media capital of the country.

Given the prewar view that America could make no significant contribution to a European war, Col. Walther Nicolai, chief of the Imperial Army's Secret Service, had only one part-time spy operating in the United States. Since 1893 Dr. Walter Scheele, a Brooklyn pharmacist and a reserve artillery officer in Kaiser Wilhelm II's army, had been performing industrial espionage on a part-time basis—chemical engineering being one of the few areas in which Germany thought it had anything to learn from America. So it was necessary for the German diplomatic staff in the United States to take the lead in the very undiplomatic sabotage efforts. The ambassador, Count Johann von Bernstorff, had achieved considerable popularity since his arrival in the country in 1908. He was married to an American and spoke perfect English; he also had an American mistress. Bernstorff managed to pick up nine honorary degrees from U.S. universities, including one from Princeton when Woodrow Wilson had been its president. Yet his prewar relationship with American social leaders proved of no value. As he would later write: "When the war broke out the [New York] 400 deserted in a body."[4] Following the usual practices of an ambassador—a job often defined as "a man paid to lie for his country"—Bernstorff sought to avoid direct involvement in the sabotage campaign, leaving that to his top assistants. The military attaché was Franz von Papen, a thirty-five-year-old captain of cavalry who possessed the most prized skill a pre-1914 officer could have: he was an excellent horseman who garnered many prizes at equestrian events. Colleagues snidely referred to him as "the gentleman jockey." His marriage to the daughter of a wealthy manufacturer had provided him with the income an attaché required to maintain a lavish lifestyle in a foreign capital. In Papen's case, it also allowed him to keep a string of mistresses.

The naval attaché, Capt. Karl Boy-Ed, son of a Turkish father and an aristocratic German mother, was known as the Beau Brummel of the Officer Corps. Like Bernstorff and Papen, he had an eye for the ladies. If an ambassador was a man who lied for his country, a military attaché was one who spied for his—though as officers and gentlemen, they did so in a genteel way, receiving official briefings from the host country's armed forces, attending maneuvers, and reading publicly available documents and reports. The dirty work of actual spying was done by social inferiors, such as Gus Steinhauer, a former Pinkerton detective who headed the German navy's foreign espionage operations, which concentrated on Britain.

Bernstorff, who had been on vacation in Germany when war was declared, quickly hurried back, arriving in the United States on August 6. Accompanying him was a middle-aged bureaucrat, Dr. Heinrich Albert, who was named the commercial attaché of the embassy. Albert controlled the purse strings for the various clandestine operations Germany would mount. His government placed $30 million (today the equivalent of at least twenty times that amount) at his disposal. Recognizing where the battle would be fought, all three attachés set up headquarters in New York City. Papen opened an intelligence center disguised as an advertising agency at 60 Wall Street; Boy-Ed located his command post in the German Consulate at 11 Broadway, overlooking the harbor, where he could observe ship movements. Dr. Albert operated out of the Hamburg-America Shipping Line building at 45 Broadway.

The first act of sabotage was a fire set at a manufacturing plant in Trenton, New Jersey, on New Year's Day, 1915. Marine sabotage did not get fully under way until Franz von Rintelen, a naval reserve officer, entered the United States in April 1915 using a Swiss passport made out to him in the name of Emile Gasche (the brother of a fellow officer's Swiss wife). Before the war, Rintelen had spent several years in New York City as a representative of a leading German bank. Wealthy, charming, fluent in English, and at that time a bachelor, he had been a big hit in American society, managing to obtain membership in the exclusive New York Yacht Club, where the only other German members had been the kaiser and his brother, Prince Henry.

For many successful German lawyers, bankers, and other professionals, the ultimate social cachet was to have on their calling cards the notation that they were officers in the reserves. Busy men of high standing were thrilled when they could don the uniform, complete with sword, and go off for a short period of training. In Rintelen's case, because he was a yachtsman, he had chosen to join the naval reserve. At first he served on the staff of naval headquarters in Berlin, where he utilized his many highly placed friends to convey unsolicited advice to the chancellor. Rintelen's excellent connections in New York made him an ideal man to carry out a mission in

America. It might also have occurred to some of his superiors that it would be a good thing to be rid of the pushy reserve "kapitan."[*]

Rintelen conceived of his assignment to what he called "the Manhattan Front" in grandiose terms. He was furnished funds to purchase American munitions plants, proclaiming to his superiors, "Whatever I can't buy up I will blow up." Upon arrival in New York, he opened an import/export firm on Cedar Street under the name of E. V. Gibbons (initials corresponding to those of E. V. Gasche). After several attempts to buy U.S. munitions businesses, he realized that the supply was so great that there was no way he could make a dent in the market. So, as Frederic Hanse, he leased an office on Wall Street from which he directed the sabotage campaign. In doing so, he was able to call for assistance from the crews of ninety German ships that had been trapped in New York Harbor when the war broke out and were now being blockaded by British cruisers. Also at his disposal were several thousand German army reservists who were unable to book passage out of the United States because the military attachés could not secure enough fake passports for them.

Rintelen established a factory on board the interned liner *Friedrich der Grosse*, which turned out fifty bomb containers a day. The devices were then taken to be armed at a workshop established by Dr. Scheele in the predominantly German American town of Hoboken, New Jersey, where the North German Lloyd Line maintained its docking facilities. Afterward, officers from the Hamburg-America or the Lloyd Line distributed them to English-hating Irish American stevedores, who planted them in the cargo holds of Allied ships. To facilitate the operation, the Germans purchased an employment agency that furnished ship loaders. When a munitions vessel required cargo handlers, the agency sent prescreened Irishmen, who would smuggle bombs on board with the regular cargo. Cultural differences marred the working relationship between Germans and Irish, however. The former were mostly stiff-necked, aristocratic officers who believed in keeping military business secret. They constantly complained that the free-spirited Irish dockworkers drank and talked too much.

---

[*] Rintelen was not a full captain (a rank equivalent to an army colonel). In the naval service, an individual qualified to captain a ship often holds a lesser rank. In German, Rintelen's title was *Kapitanleutnant* (captain lieutenant). Before his departure for America, he was advanced to lieutenant commander (equivalent to major).

At first the devices employed were time bombs, but these often failed to explode. So a long, slim metal tube known as a "pencil bomb" or "cigar bomb" was developed, with a copper disk that bisected it vertically. The upper compartment contained a chemical that had a rapid corrosive effect on copper. When it had eaten through the disk, it came into contact with another chemical in the lower compartment that produced a flame. The British stationed guards armed with carbines on their vessels. Adequate to prevent a gang of Irish nationalists or interned German sailors from trying any funny business, they were useless at detecting tiny explosive devices concealed in cargoes. To avoid diplomatic repercussions, Rintelen forbade his agents to target American ships. Nor were they allowed to plant explosive devices in passenger vessels. The usual scenario was that a cylinder would explode at sea, causing a fire. This would compel the captain to flood the hold, thereby destroying the cargo. In most cases, it would also require the crew to abandon ship. At the least, the vessel would have to be towed to port for extensive repairs. Thirty-five ships were eventually sunk or damaged in this way. While Allied intelligence officers were suspicious of the fires, at first they could not be sure the origin was sabotage.

The principal safe house for German agents in New York City was a four-story brownstone at 123 West Fifteenth Street, presided over by a dark-haired, buxom, middle-aged German opera singer, Baroness (from a forgotten marriage) Martha Held, alias Martha Gordon. Neighbors suspected the house of being a bordello because of the furtive men and unescorted ladies who entered through a basement door at all hours of the day and night. Using money supplied by the German government, Held had leased the house as a "recreational center" for German sea captains, military officers, and other official visitors. The attachés and Rintelen used it to meet their agents. On occasion, Ambassador Bernstorff himself would put in an appearance, his arrival invariably drawing a standing ovation. Normally, though, it was Papen who lorded over the proceedings. After dinner he usually departed with a beauty or two on his arm. From time to time, tough-looking Irishmen in dockworker clothing arrived with bombs. The Irish did not find Held's establishment a congenial place—mostly because the evening's festivities never concluded until the fat lady sang. Men whose tastes ran to sentimental ballads about sweet colleens back in Tipperary or

Tralee found it hard to listen to some heavyweight, middle-aged woman bellowing her way through Wagner.

In addition to Martha Held's establishment, there were other safe houses, including a German American club on Central Park South, suites in the Manhattan Hotel on Forty-Second Street (where the drink of that name was invented), and the McAlpin, at Thirty-Fourth and Broadway. German American bars and restaurants also served as convenient rendezvous for stranded German sailors and reservists waiting to obtain false passports. Rintelen and the ringleaders of his ship-bombing ring often gathered at a restaurant in the Woolworth Building in Lower Manhattan. The Irish bombers preferred to hang out at a place known as "the Spanish Club," located on the top floor of a midtown hotel.

Rintelen knew no bounds. Anyone not aware that he was only a reserve lieutenant commander might have assumed that he was a high-ranking nobleman or distinguished statesman acting as the direct emissary of the kaiser. He used a half-million dollars to create the Laborer's National Peace Council, which fomented strikes and slowdowns among longshoremen and munitions workers. He made contact with exiled former Mexican president Victoriano Huerta, who blamed the United States for his downfall, and suggested that, with German military assistance, Huerta could be restored to office and lead a campaign against the Yankees.

On the American side, the security forces were as unprepared to defend the country as the Germans were to attack it, although the NYPD was the first to understand the problem. On August 1, 1914, the day before Germany presented an ultimatum to Belgium, Commissioner Woods changed the priorities of Captain Tunney's squad from anarchists to foreign agents.[*] Tunney was an outstanding officer, one of a cadre of "Roosevelt men" who had joined the force while Teddy was running it and the standards for admission were high. For example, under Tammany rule, police recruits had frequently been drawn from among bartenders and bouncers, but Roosevelt would not appoint anyone who worked in a place where liquor was served.

---

[*] First known as the Bomb Squad, it was renamed the Neutrality Squad in 1915.

The challenge to Tunney's squad was far different than dealing with fuzzy-minded radicals of the Bresci Circle or petty Black Hand criminals. Agents of Imperial Germany were supplied with millions of dollars and had thousands of sympathizers to call on. Given the limited resources and skills of U.S. security forces, the squad had to rely heavily on Allied intelligence, particularly the British. Since this violated America's officially proclaimed neutrality, it had to be kept secret.

Though upper-class Americans fawned over the British ruling elite, the feeling was not mutual. King Edward VII had once commented that he only felt comfortable with one American. Not surprisingly, it was J. P. Morgan Sr. The American ladies who married British aristocrats were never fully accepted. Even wealthy, educated Yanks were seen as provincials. Diplomatic relations between Britain and the United States were often tense. In 1895 the two countries were on the verge of war over a Venezuelan boundary dispute. During the 1899–1902 South African War, U.S. sympathies lay with the Boers, who were seen as embattled farmers reenacting America's own revolutionary struggle.

Before 1914 the British government always preferred that America play a very small role on the international scene. Not only were the Yanks commercial rivals, but they also tended to raise embarrassing questions, such as why the British occupied India, Egypt, and especially Ireland. After 1914 the British sought to bring the Americans into the war as an ally (though a decidedly subordinate one). Consequently, they were willing to share intelligence. Capt. Sir Guy Gaunt, Royal Navy attaché in the United States, took personal charge of British operations in New York. Just as the Germans drew support from the anti-English Irish, Gaunt secured the service of Slavs from the Austro-Hungarian Empire. Chief among them was Emil Voska, a stocky, middle-aged native of Bohemia who had been expelled from his homeland for anti-Austrian activity. Owner of a marble quarry in Kansas, he devoted his time and money to the cause of Czech independence. In 1914 he had gone to London to establish a relationship with British intelligence. Back in New York, he began recruiting some of his countrymen to serve as spies. Among them was a mail clerk at the Austrian Consulate who provided a list of German and Austrian reservists who, with passports bought from unemployed seamen, were planning to sail home to join their regiments. Voska would claim that his ring of informers eventually comprised eighty-four people. Voska's primary allegiance was to a provisional government established by Czech revolutionaries.[*] In a 1940 as-told-to book, he detailed his various exploits in World War I. By no means a modest man, according to him he functioned on the same level as prime ministers and presidents, conducting operations throughout Europe and the United States, and was a major figure behind half of the Allied victories in the war.

When Captain Gaunt received derogatory information about the Germans and Austrians, he would pass it on to the Australian-born editor of the *Providence Journal*, John Rathom. By prearrangement, the *Journal's* exposés appeared simultaneously in such papers as the *New York Times* and *New York World*. Rathom, too, owed his loyalty to a foreign power, the British Empire. Like Voska, he was prone to exaggerate his own importance. Later, he was compelled by the U.S. government to officially retract claims he had made about his wartime exploits. Men like Voska and Rathom illustrate that while certain individuals may provide useful services, their information may be colored by their affection for a foreign nation, and their advice on policy may not always coincide with the interests of the United States.

Anti-British Indian nationalists operating in the United States were also targets of British intelligence. Sometimes the two sides fought gun battles in the streets of San Francisco and other American cities. The New York revolutionary contingent maintained a headquarters on 125th Street near Riverside Drive, where they were watched by the NYPD. In one instance, while a New York detective interrogated an Indian revolutionary, a British intelligence officer who had served in the Indian Police sat behind a screen, handing the American questions for him to ask. So impressed was the Indian with the extensive knowledge the New York cop seemed to have acquired about the revolutionary movement that he broke down and confessed.

In another instance of Allied cooperation with the U.S. authorities, the French military attaché in New York City notified Captain Tunney that an informant had been asked by a German to purchase TNT and deliver it to

---

[*] After the war, he settled in Czechoslovakia while retaining his U.S. citizenship as an insurance policy. It was a wise move because in 1939, when the Nazis marched in, Voska was able to flee back to America.

an address in Weehawken, New Jersey. Tunney assigned German-speaking Lt. George Barnitz to accompany the informant when he delivered the explosives. The occupant of the house, a man named Faye, requested the informant to help him test the explosives in the nearby woods. With the assistance of the U.S. Secret Service, Faye and an accomplice were seized. A search of the house turned up explosive devices and four fully assembled bombs. Faye was revealed to be a German lieutenant who had been sent to New York to assist Rintelen. He and three of his confederates were sentenced to imprisonment in the Atlanta federal penitentiary.

An even bigger break came when Allied intelligence sources notified Tunney that a man named Rintelen was directing the German sabotage campaign. The person they identified turned out to be a waterfront hustler who moved around in a small boat peddling liquor to ships' crews. When he got drunk, he identified himself as "the German captain who blows up ships." For a while, detectives followed the phony Rintelen whenever he went out in his boat, in the expectation that they would catch him climbing on board a ship carrying a bomb.

Rintelen's downfall did not come from American or Allied efforts but because of the jealousy of colleagues. In sending him to the United States, the high command was seeking to place its own representative over the diplomatic attachés, but Papen and Boy-Ed resented being superseded by a mere reserve officer and continually forwarded unfavorable information about him back to Berlin. German officers also placed great stock on social status, and one thing that especially rankled them was their belief that Rintelen was not entitled to the use of the aristocratic "von." In August 1915, Boy-Ed had the pleasure of personally handing Rintelen an order from Berlin recalling him from his mission. Rintelen sailed for home on a neutral ship, using his false Swiss passport. As required, the vessel put in for inspection at a British port. Unbeknownst to the Germans, the British had broken their radio code and were aware that Rintelen was a passenger. When a Royal Navy boarding party, with rifles and fixed bayonets, banged on his door, he refused to leave his cabin, so he was taken by force and held in custody in Britain until the United States entered the war. In 1917 Rintelen was returned to New York, where he was treated as a civilian criminal. He was initially lodged in New York City's notorious Tombs jail, and after conviction he was sent to the Atlanta Federal Penitentiary. Released in 1920, when he returned home to a defeated Germany, he found himself criticized for the sabotage activity he had carried on in America.

With Commissioner Woods solidly behind him, Captain (after 1916, Inspector) Tunney was able to operate almost unchallenged within his own sphere. Despite jurisdictional boundaries, he assigned German-speaking detectives to infiltrate the bars, beer gardens, and restaurants of the Hoboken waterfront where the saboteurs congregated. Det. Henry Barth pretended to be a German secret agent himself—a ruse that led him to a seventy-year-old retired sea captain, Karl von Kleist, who had been born into one of his country's great families. As a young man, instead of accepting a commission in the Guard Cavalry, he ran away to sea. In New York, his job was to deliver empty containers to Dr. Scheele and, when they were filled with explosives, to take them back to German ship captains on the waterfront. In the course of his work, Kleist ran up $134 in expenses that Scheele failed to pay, so the captain wrote to Papen at 60 Wall Street to complain. The letter was intercepted by the police, and Detective Barth, in his guise as a German intelligence officer, arranged a meeting at which Kleist was arrested. During questioning by Captain Tunney at police headquarters, a light fixture failed and an electrician was summoned to repair it. Then Tunney was called from the room. The electrician, a German American, took advantage of the detective's absence to strike up a conversation with Kleist in his native tongue. The captain asked if the electrician (actually Det. Henry Senf) would do him a favor and take some warning messages to his confederates. Kleist wrote out the notes and they were delivered by detectives—resulting in additional prisoners for American jails.

Other German agents were more difficult to snare. Paul Koenig was a detective for the Hamburg-America Line. When the war started, he was engaged to furnish bodyguards for the ambassador and the attachés. Then he began recruiting spies. Koenig knew the police were watching 45 Broadway, so he decided to meet his agents elsewhere. To foil wiretappers, he used a safety block system and code words. A street number in Manhattan named over the telephone meant that he would meet someone five blocks farther uptown. The Hotel Belmont was the bar at the Pabst, a German restaurant in Columbus Circle. Periodically he changed the designations, so that instead of meeting five blocks up, the conspirators would meet five blocks down, and Brooklyn's Borough Hall became the Pabst. Finally, a disgruntled spy whom Koenig had done out of $2.57 was overheard calling him "a bullheaded Westphalian." The police contacted the caller, and when he talked, they had enough information to raid 45 Broadway, where they seized much valuable information. Because the United States was not at war, they were unable to charge Koenig. Later, when America entered the conflict, he was interned for the duration.

At the federal level, President Wilson had two police agencies available to him. The U.S. Secret Service, which reported to the secretary of the treasury, was the stronger of the two. It had a half-century of experience, and its operatives were full-fledged cops. The unarmed agents of the six-year-old Bureau of Investigation, who were responsible to the attorney general of the United States, were not. Between the two organizations, they had approximately five hundred investigators, including a sizable number enforcing the Mann anti–white slavery act.

Like the NYPD, the federal sleuths had to learn counterintelligence methods on the job. The Secret Service chief, William Flynn, a burly New York Irishman, had started his career as a jail official. At the turn of the century he was appointed head of the New York office of the Secret Service. Afterward he briefly served as deputy commissioner in charge of the NYPD Detective Bureau. Flynn's position was strengthened by the fact that his boss was the powerful treasury secretary, William McAdoo. Alexander Bruce Bielaski, chief of the rival Bureau of Investigation, was a career civil servant with a degree from a Washington night law school.

Even though both Treasury and Justice had investigative responsibilities, President Wilson did not place Flynn or Bielaski in control of U.S. security. If someone with the status of Harvardian Arthur Woods had been the head of the Secret Service or the Bureau of Investigation, he might have done so. Woods, with his German postgraduate education and close study of Continental detective work, possessed excellent qualifications to head American security. Unfortunately, he was so closely identified with Teddy Roosevelt that Wilson would never have considered him. Instead, in 1915, the president appointed Frank Polk, counselor of the State Department (a job later designated undersecretary), to coordinate U.S. security operations.

State was traditionally the premier U.S. government department, with a staff composed of men from the social elite, and its culture was genteel. The Secret Service and Bureau of Investigation had a middle-class ethos, and its operations smacked too much of gumshoe methods. Polk, a descendant of America's eleventh president, was a graduate of Groton, Yale, and Columbia Law, and a partner in a prestigious law firm, the kind that handled the problems of Wall Street and large corporations. Polk also moved in the world of New York society and reform politics and had served as Mayor Mitchel's corporation counsel. In April 1914, while he was riding in a car with the mayor and Arthur Woods, a deranged man had fired on them and wounded Polk.

Another prominent New Yorker in the Wilson administration was the number-two man at the Navy Department, Assistant Secretary Franklin D. Roosevelt, whose purview included intelligence. The Harvard-educated Roosevelt was also a lawyer, reform politician, and member of the highest stratum of society. Though he was a cousin of Teddy Roosevelt, he was a Democrat. With Woods, Flynn, Polk, and Roosevelt occupying key posts, U.S. domestic security was largely in the hands of New Yorkers.

In an attempt to come to grips with his new responsibilities, Frank Polk asked the British ambassador, Sir Cecil Spring-Rice, to introduce him to the head of his country's intelligence organization in America. As might be expected, the diplomat was unwilling to admit that his government carried out espionage on the soil of a neutral nation, so he replied that there was no such person. A few days later, Sir William Wiseman, whom Polk had met casually in New York society, dropped by unexpectedly at the State Department. Annoyed that Wiseman would interrupt his busy schedule for a social call, Polk was prepared to utter a few pleasantries, followed by the diplomatic equivalent of, "Here's your hat; what's your hurry?" However, to Polk's astonishment, Wiseman smilingly announced, "I understand you expressed a desire to meet the head of British intelligence in the United States. Well, to the extent that such a position exists, here I am."

Early in 1915, after having been gassed on the western front, Sir William and Norman Thwaites, a former executive of the *New York World*, the country's most influential paper, with close ties to President Wilson, were sent to the United States to represent MI6. Wiseman, barely past thirty and looking even younger, was a champion boxer from Cambridge with a title that had been in his family for three centuries. In the prewar years he had tried his hand at journalism and playwriting, without much success. Eventually he secured a position with New York's Kuhn, Loeb banking house. Thwaites's and Wiseman's duties went beyond espionage. They were expected to persuade prominent Americans of the necessity of helping Britain. Early on, Wiseman established a backstairs channel to President Wilson and his intimate adviser, the shadowy Col. Edward M. House.* Given their influence and background, two more New Yorkers could be counted as key figures in U.S. security.

It was the Secret Service that scored the federal government's first major victory against the Germans. On July 24, 1915, operatives Frank Burke and W. H. Houghton trailed Dr. Heinrich Albert and a German American newspaper editor, George Sylvester Viereck, onto a Sixth Avenue elevated train. Viereck, whose job was to plant German propaganda in U.S. publications and, when possible, obtain ownership of American newspapers, got off at Thirty-Fourth Street. Houghton followed him while Burke remained with Albert. Though youthful in appearance, Burke was forty-five and had been in the service for sixteen years. Before that he had been chief of police of Tampa, Florida. During the Spanish-American War, he had worked with the Secret Service chasing spies. Afterward he was offered a job in the Agency. It was a hot, muggy day, and Albert dozed off. When the train pulled in at Fiftieth Street, he suddenly awoke and started to get off, leaving his briefcase behind. On an impulse, Burke decided to snatch it. When Albert realized what had happened, he ran after Burke, who jumped on a streetcar shouting that a madman was chasing him (while urging the motorman to "step on it") and escaped. The briefcase, marked *streng vertraulich* ("strictly private"), contained papers revealing Germany's campaign of subversion and hinted at the sabotage activities. When McAdoo, who was vacationing in Maine, was notified, he ordered the papers brought to him immediately. The material provided an inferential case that the Germans were conducting unlawful activities in the United States, but not a solid legal one. In any

---

* House was not a military man. His title of colonel was an honorary post bestowed upon him by a governor in his native Texas.

event, Albert's diplomatic status made him immune from arrest. Indeed, under a strict legal interpretation, it was Burke who had broken the law.

Albert could have been expelled, but that might have led to retaliation against U.S. diplomats in Berlin. The American ambassador there was James Gerard, a member of the Knickerbocker elite (the New York equivalent of a Boston Brahmin, but richer) who did not conceal his Allied sympathies—though he was not as unneutral as the U.S. ambassador to Britain, Walter Hines Page. So pro-British was Page that the U.S. State Department treated his dispatches as though they were notes from the British foreign minister, Sir Edward Grey. The shrewd McAdoo realized that the best way to strike against the Germans was to leak the contents of Albert's briefcase to the administration's favorite newspaper, the *New York World*. Not until the papers were published did Chief Bielaski of the rival Bureau of Investigation learn of their seizure. Such was the state of cooperation between federal law enforcement agencies.

Dr. Albert became known among his countrymen by the derisive label "the minister without portfolio." The befuddled bureaucrat had even been foolish enough to place a newspaper ad offering a reward for the return of his briefcase. By doing so, he foreclosed the option of claiming that the papers found in it did not belong to him. Albert was further embarrassed when it was revealed that he had paid some Americans to write German propaganda. One distinguished professor got $20,000 for a book accepted by Yale University Press. Another American obtained financing to produce a film starring an animal. It was to be a sentimental tale of a retired fire horse, purchased for sale to the Allies, that meets its death on the battlefield. At the time, the Germans were busy poisoning horses being shipped to the Allies. Not until the end of 1915 did President Wilson finally order Albert, Papen, and Boy-Ed out of the country. The United States officially accepted Bernstorff's explanation that he was blameless, although the real reason was to avoid reprisal against Ambassador Gerard. Papen also got snagged by the British blockade. When his vessel put in for inspection at a British port, he presented his British government authorization to travel under diplomatic immunity. To his shock and fury, officials pointed out to him that while it covered his person, it did not apply to the steamer trunks he had brought along. They were seized and searched by the British, and among the contents

was a letter in which Papen referred to his American hosts as "idiotic Yankees." Naturally, that soon appeared in U.S. newspapers.[*]

Not all German saboteurs were official agents of the kaiser. Erich Muenter
was a former language instructor at Harvard. In 1915, angry about the
American munitions sales to Germany, he decided to do something about
it. On Friday afternoon, July 2, he slipped into the U.S. Capitol in Washington carrying a package containing three sticks of dynamite. It was the
Fourth of July holiday weekend, so Congress was not in session. Muenter
was able to secrete his package underneath an unmanned switchboard in
the U.S. Senate reception area. To minimize casualties, he set a timing device
for 11:45 p.m., and then went across to Union Station and bought a ticket
on the midnight train to New York. At the scheduled time he was able to
observe the blast. In a letter he mailed to newspapers, Muenter claimed that
he had planted the bomb to show Americans how much damage explosions
could cause.

Muenter was not done. The American most hated by German sympathizers was Jack Morgan, who was held responsible for the flow of munitions
that had killed the kaiser's soldiers. Edward Stettinius was the Morgan partner who actually ran the bank's purchasing program for the Allies, super-
vising a staff of 175 employees. After numerous threats were received
against the House of Morgan, Stettinius's family was moved out of their
Staten Island mansion, while Stettinius himself took up residence on a
cabin cruiser in New York Harbor. There were guards at the Morgan headquarters and Jack's residence in Manhattan but no security at his estate on
the north shore of Long Island. When Muenter arrived in New York from
Washington, he went straight there. On arrival, he managed to brush past
the servants. Morgan himself was in conference upstairs with Ambassador
Spring-Rice. When he heard the commotion, he came down and was shot
twice in the groin by Muenter but helped the butler overpower the attacker

---

[*] Back in Germany, von Papen managed to convince people that he had acted honorably in the United States.
After the war, the playboy cavalry officer went into politics. In 1932 he was named chancellor of Germany
and later vice chancellor under Hitler. In 1942, while serving as German ambassador to Turkey, von Papen
narrowly missed being assassinated by a bomb. Though British intelligence was suspected, the actual perpe-
trators were Nazi Secret Service men pursuing a scheme of their own. Von Papen remained in Turkey, where
he became involved in the "Cicero affair," Cicero being a code name for the valet to the British ambassador
who made copies of top-secret documents and sold them to the Germans.

and survived his injuries. A few days later, Muenter committed suicide in a Long Island jail.

Though the spy chiefs left the country, the rings they established remained. Bielaski's bureau scored a coup in 1916 when its agents raided Papen's headquarters. Papen's successor, Capt. Wolf von Igel, had decided to move the contents of the office safe to Washington so they would be protected by diplomatic immunity. On the morning of April 18, as he and his assistants were loading seventy pounds of material for shipment, bureau men burst in. Igel attempted to throw papers back into the safe but was forcibly stopped. Examination of the documents revealed that they contained the names of every German agent in the United States. The seemingly fortuitous timing of the raid was actually based on intelligence supplied by British wiretappers who had been monitoring the German office.

In July 1916 the Germans were able to pull off the largest act of sabotage in American history. That they could do so was a glaring indictment of U.S. security. In two years of battling saboteurs, the American agents had scored a number of limited tactical successes, but no major victories. Detectives had fooled an old-school gentleman like Captain Kleist or snatched a briefcase from Dr. Albert. They did not penetrate Martha Held's circle. Nor, despite Rintelen's notoriety on the waterfront, did they capture him.

Security efforts were hampered by the fact that the United States was a federal republic. It could not tell cities and states what to do or make them cooperate with Washington or one another. As in the Civil War, only by luck was the NYPD in the hands of the preparedness forces. If Irish-dominated Tammany Hall had been in power, the cops might have been much less aggressive against the Germans. In addition, many security tasks were still left to private agencies, whose bottom line was always financial. They often hired low-paid, poor-quality employees and skimped on their training in order to maximize profit. Some agencies were not choosy about whom they worked for. A few accepted retainers from the Germans or Austrians. Some worked both sides of the street, serving Allied and Central powers alike. All these factors came into play at the ammunition transfer point in New York Harbor, on the New Jersey promontory known as Black Tom

Island.* Most of the ordnance shipped to the Allies arrived by train at Black Tom, where it was loaded onto barges and hauled out to merchant vessels. Safety and security at the site were in the hands of private guards and Lehigh Valley Railroad employees. When work shut down for the night, it was common to leave boxcars and barges loaded with explosives and scattered around the area. In warm weather, to combat the swarms of mosquitoes that infested the island, guards sometimes lit small fires. Given the importance of the munitions to the Allied cause, the British, French, and Russians should have been more concerned about security at Black Tom. Yet none of them took steps to improve conditions there.

It is possible that the Russians contributed to the debacle that occurred. Officials of the czarist government serving abroad were always surrounded by what one observer described as "clouds of secret agents," who were used to spy on exiled revolutionaries. In New York City from 1915 to 1917, the Fox movie studio employed an electrician named Leon Trotsky (né Lev Bronstein) who headed a revolutionary group that received funds from German sources.

The fact that vast amounts of explosives were piled up on a small plot of land in the middle of the most heavily populated and commercially important metropolitan area in the United States should also have been of concern to federal officials and to the New York and New Jersey authorities. An explosion at Black Tom could damage shipping in the harbor, as well as government facilities such as the immigrant reception center at Ellis Island. It might also cause mass casualties in Manhattan or Jersey City.

Among Colonel Nicolai's operatives in America were two adventurous young men. Kurt Jahnke was a twenty-four-year-old who had served as a U.S. immigration guard in San Francisco. In early 1916, when he came under suspicion for bombing a munitions factory in California, he walked into the San Francisco office of the Secret Service and volunteered to become a U.S. spy. The lawmen were not taken in by his bluff, but they did not have enough evidence to arrest him. Jahnke's assistant, Lothar Witzke, was a twenty-one-year-old naval cadet who, after his ship was scuttled off of Chile,

---

* Some researchers attribute the name to the fact that from a higher elevation, the island resembled a black tomcat with its back up. Others claim it comes from the description of a nineteenth-century resident of the island.

was interned. He escaped and made his way through South America to San Francisco, where he was assigned to work for the German Consulate. The two men were told to report to the East Coast for duty under a veteran swashbuckler, Friedrich Hinze, captain of a German merchant vessel interned in Baltimore Harbor who had been ordered by his superiors to destroy Black Tom. To carry out the mission, he teamed Jahnke and Witzke with an Austrian citizen, Michael Kristoff, who had worked at Black Tom.

On Friday, July 28, 1916, a group of German agents including Jahnke and Witzke met in the formal dining room of Martha Held's house in Manhattan. Suitcases filled with dynamite and other explosives had been stored in her bedroom closet. Photos and maps of New York Harbor and Black Tom Island were spread out on the dining room table. When the briefing was completed, the Germans broke into patriotic songs such as "Deutschland über alles" and "Die Wacht am Rhein."

In the early-morning hours of Sunday, July 30, Jahnke and Witzke rowed out to Black Tom while Kristoff, who was known to the guards, walked onto the island using its causeway to await them. The team was able to plant explosives at three different locations without any interference from security guards. At 2:08 a.m., a huge explosion rocked the New York area. All over Manhattan and Brooklyn windows fell from buildings, and people ran into the streets in panic. The Brooklyn Bridge swayed, terrifying motorists driving across it. The shock from the blast was felt as far south as Philadelphia. An even larger explosion followed half an hour later. Shells and shrapnel rained down on Ellis Island; the immigrants there had to be evacuated to the mainland. Hundreds of New York policemen, in fleets of commandeered taxicabs, were dispatched to downtown Manhattan, where they found burglar alarms ringing on every block and the sidewalks filled with broken glass. Thousands of New Yorkers rushed to the Hudson River, where they gazed in awe at huge fires burning on the New Jersey side. At least six people, including an infant hurled out of bed in Jersey City and the chief of security for the Lehigh Valley Railroad, were killed.* So efficient was the operation that officials were not sure whether the explosion had been deliberate. Some suspected that the conflagration had been triggered by fires the

---

* Investigators later concluded that many itinerant workers who slept outdoors near Black Tom were also killed.

guards set to combat mosquitoes. Chief Bielaski told his Justice Department superiors that it was undoubtedly an accident. Later there would be allegations that some of the guards were on the German payroll. The munitions that exploded had been earmarked for shipment to Russia, raising the possibility that traitors among its secret agents had contributed to the disaster. For over fifty years after the war, extensive civil litigation filed against the German government by U.S. claimants would drag on. Even after the case was finally settled, many issues remained unresolved.*

It was the British who were the professionals in the security wars. In 1910, when Kaiser Wilhem II attended the funeral of King Edward VII, he brought along a retinue. One of them, a German naval officer, was trailed by a detective from Pat Quinn's Special Branch to a barbershop in a seedy section of London. Quinn and the head of MI5, Capt. Vernon Kell, persuaded the thirty-five-year-old home secretary, Winston Churchill, to authorize a mail cover on the place. Through it they learned that the barber was receiving regular reports from workers with access to naval facilities whom Gus Steinhauer was paying to spy. Instead of hauling them in, which would only have meant that the authorities would soon have had to track down a replacement network, they let the operation go on. On August 5, 1914, the day after Britain declared war on Germany, twenty-one members of the ring were rounded up.

---

* After World War I, American corporations that had suffered damages in the Black Tom explosion sued the German government. The plaintiffs' case was brought before a joint German-American commission composed of distinguished jurists, including some Supreme Court justices. In pressing their case, the plaintiffs' lawyers relied heavily on information provided by Mrs. Mena Reiss (née Edwards). In the period before the Black Tom explosion, the then-unmarried Edwards was known as the "Eastman Girl" from her appearances in advertisements by the Eastman Kodak camera company. Pretty and popular, she frequently served as an escort for German officers. In her statements to the American legal team, she claimed that blowing up Black Tom had been discussed in gatherings at Martha Held's house. The German legal team sought to discredit her as a courtesan, claiming that her own testimony "pictures herself in a most compromising manner, as a frequent visitor to a house of entertainment of the most dubious type." In 1930, after eight years of litigation, the commission rejected the U.S. charges.

In the 1930s the Americans managed to reopen the case. Among the U.S. legal team was John McCloy, later U.S. High Commissioner in Germany, chairman of Chase Manhattan Bank, and a man who reportedly refused more cabinet appointments than anyone in U.S. history.

Because of the ascension of the Nazis, World War II, and the unsettled postwar conditions, not until the 1950s did the German government agree to compensate victims of Black Tom. Even then the final payments were not received until 1979.

In those days, Scotland Yard put educated gentlemen in charge of their detective branch. Basil Thomson, who took over the Criminal Investigation Department (CID)—which included Special Branch—in 1913, was a son of the Archbishop of York and an old boy of Eton and Oxford. At twenty-eight he had served as prime minister of the British South Seas colony of Tonga, where he counted headhunters among his friends. After the Germans lost their agents in the August 1914 roundup, they had to dispatch hastily trained replacements to England. When they were captured, Thomson would personally interview them. According to him, each began by sticking to his cover story, including a false name. Then, at the right psychological moment, Thomson would say something like, "I put it to you that you are really [the correct name of the prisoner]"—whereupon the suspect would usually snap to attention, click his heels, admit his identity, and make a speech about German superiority and the certainty that his country would win the war. The dramatic posturing would shortly be followed by a trial and, in the case of eleven of the prisoners, execution by a firing squad, usually at the Tower of London.

The key British clandestine agency in World War I was not MI5, MI6, or Special Branch. It was the Naval Intelligence Division (NID), headed by Adm. William Reginald "Blinker" Hall (his nickname the result of an eye tic), whose father had been the first director of NID when it was founded in 1883. The Navy had always swung great weight, and its word was virtually law. MI6 was headed by a naval officer, Cdr. Mansfield Cumming,* but neither he nor his agency were anywhere near equal to Hall and NID. In 1914, when the British were seeking passage for their warships through the Dardanelles, Hall informed Churchill (by then First Lord of the Admiralty) and Adm. John "Jacky" Fisher (First Sea Lord) that he had offered the Turks four million pounds to allow the British ships through. It was a sum equal to a third of a billion in American money today. Churchill, taken aback, asked Hall, "Who authorized this?" To which the admiral coolly replied, "I did." Churchill turned to Fisher and said, "Do you hear what that man has done? . . . Four millions. . . . On his own!" Yet they did not overrule him.[5]

---

* Who, according to legend, initialed his memos with "C" for his last name, thereby providing a designation that continued to be used by chiefs of the service (although there are other versions of the origin of "C").

Hall assembled a staff of civilian scholars who were able to break German code messages. (It was one of their intercepts that led to the capture of Rintelen.*) Working out of Room 40 at the old Admiralty building, they kept their superiors informed of the enemy's top secrets. In 1917 Room 40 intercepted a message from the German foreign minister, Alfred Zimmerman, proposing an alliance of Germany, Mexico, and Japan in a war against the United States. In return, he promised to help the Mexicans recover Arizona, Texas, and New Mexico. Zimmerman had unknowingly given the British the key they had been searching for since 1914—a means by which to bring America into the war. Hall saw his opportunity and turned the telegram over to the Americans on the promise that they would not reveal how it was obtained. Instead, a cover story was developed that they had procured it via their own sources. The coup brought Hall a knighthood and proved to be a godsend to President Wilson.†

In early 1917, when Germany threatened to resume unrestricted submarine warfare, Wilson broke off relations, sent Ambassador Bernstorff home, recalled Ambassador Gerard from Berlin, and asked Congress to authorize the arming of merchant ships—a step that undoubtedly would have led to naval encounters and war. However, antiwar senators staged a successful filibuster to prevent passage of the necessary legislation, so Wilson decided to make the Zimmerman telegram public. At first, many Americans refused to believe that it was genuine. Senator James O'Gorman, an antiwar New

---

* Rintelen, too, was put through interrogation by Thomson, accompanied by Hall and others. At first the German aristocrat took it lightly and tried to bluff his way through. He was taken up short when Thomson asked him sharply, "Do you know where you are?" Rintelen got the drift of the question (i.e., "You are in front of men who can send you to your death.") and he became more cooperative. Luckily for him, it was still a gentlemen's war, and because he had not committed espionage on British soil, he was simply locked up. In one instance, a German spy about to be executed turned to the prison commandant and asked, "I suppose you will not shake hands with a spy?" The officer replied, "No, but I will with a brave man," and extended his hand. Honor and chivalry were still important values among Europe's officer class.

† After his retirement, Hall was elected to Parliament. There he kept his hand in intelligence work and is believed to be the individual who furnished the Zinoviev letter to the press. Generally regarded by historians as a forgery, the letter was from a Soviet official, addressed to Communists in England, advising them to support the Labour government in the 1924 election. Its release contributed to Labour's defeat. In the 1930s Hall's old adversary Rintelen settled in England, and the two men became friends. In 1933, when the former German officer published a book on his activities during the war, it contained a friendly letter from Hall and an effusive introduction by A. E. W. Mason, a well-known British novelist (among his works was The Four Feathers) who himself had served in British naval intelligence. In 1939 Rintelen offered to become a spy for the British but was rejected and, along with other enemy aliens, incarcerated on the Isle of Man.

York Democrat, argued that it was a British forgery. Even the most pro-Allied people were skeptical. Capt. Guy Gaunt reported that at a New York City dining club, composed of members of the social and professional elite, such anglophiles as Teddy Roosevelt's former secretary of state Elihu Root and former ambassador to the United Kingdom Joseph Choate openly voiced suspicion that the Zimmerman note was a fake. However, when a journalist asked Zimmerman about it, for some inexplicable reason he admitted having sent the telegram.

The Zimmerman telegram pushed America over the edge. The shock and anger it caused were almost equal to what occurred twenty-four years later after Pearl Harbor. The Germans had proposed to launch an invasion of the United States, letting loose Mexicans and Japanese on the civilians of the Southwest, a particularly frightening prospect in an age when even enlightened citizens spoke of maintaining racial purity and warned of the "yellow peril." On March 21 President Wilson summoned Congress (then in recess) to reconvene on April 2 to hear a message of national importance. There was little doubt what the message would be. On the night of the 2nd the president, escorted by a troop of cavalry, was driven down to the Capitol to ask for a declaration of war against Germany. The Capitol itself was surrounded by cavalry; inside, it swarmed with Secret Servicemen and police.

When news of the president's speech was received in New York, Ambassador Gerard was in the lobby of the Metropolitan Opera waiting for the curtain to rise on act three. The Met, which then occupied a full block of Broadway between Thirty-Ninth and Fortieth, was a temple of New York's social elite. When Gerard was informed of Wilson's call for war, he approached one of the directors of the company and urged that the news be read from the stage and the national anthem played.* "No," the director said. "The opera is neutral." The aristocratic Gerard was not a man to be put off. He raced back to his box as members of the audience were resuming their seats, stood up, leaned over the rail, shouted to them what had happened, and asked that they cheer for President Wilson. At first his listeners were stunned; some thought that Gerard was drunk or deranged. Then, as his words sank in, the whole

---

* At the time "The Star-Spangled Banner" was not officially the national anthem, but it was generally regarded as such.

house broke into yells and applause. The conductor, on his own initiative, ordered the orchestra to play "The Star-Spangled Banner." Margarete Arndt-Ober, the German lead singer, collapsed in a dead faint. In a harbinger of days to come, she was unceremoniously toted off the stage, and the performance went on with no mention of what had happened to her.

It took four days for Congress to act on the president's proposal, and the vote was not unanimous: 373 to 50 in the House and 82 to 6 in the Senate. But with the support of a large majority of the American population, as expressed by their elected representatives, America was in the war. Even before Congress acted, New York City was prepared. The Navy posted a destroyer in the Hudson with its guns trained on the interned German ships. As the war clouds loomed, Nicholas Biddle had been appointed deputy commissioner in charge of NYPD security operations. The Harvard-educated Biddle was a member of a famous Philadelphia family* and, as a New York banker, had been trustee of the Astor properties, the largest landholdings in the city. Commissioner Woods mobilized 12,000 men, placed guards on all the bridges, and activated a flying squadron of 180 motor trucks equipped with machine guns and sharpshooters. At 5 a.m. on the morning of April 6, when Dudley Field Malone, collector of the Port of New York, received official word that Congress had forwarded the declaration of war to the president for signature, he dispatched six hundred U.S. customs officers, backed up by soldiers, to seize the interned German vessels. Malone personally led the contingent that was assigned to take over the great German liner *Vaterland*. At the gangway he was met by Cdre. Hans Ruser. The two men had become acquainted during the long period of the vessel's internment, and they smiled at each other. "We are ready," the German officer announced, and he promptly handed over his ship to the boarding party. The crew was marched off to incarceration for the duration. After the war, a heavier blow awaited some of them. Rintelen had told the merchant ship officers who assisted him that they would be honored by the Fatherland. Instead, when they returned to a defeated Germany, they were dismissed from the shipping companies for which they had worked for many years.

---

* In 1861 the Prince of Wales wrote to his mother, Queen Victoria, telling her that in Philadelphia he had met members of a distinguished family named "Scrapple" and enjoyed a delicious breakfast of a local dish called "biddle."

All over the city, New Yorkers were coming to grips with the fact that America was at war. Since the incident four days earlier, when the director of the Metropolitan had rebuffed Ambassador Gerard, the management had reconsidered the matter. Undoubtedly the wealthy patrons of the company had talked to them. That night, just before the performance was due to start, the reigning queen of the opera (and glamorous enough to star in early Hollywood films), Geraldine Farrar, stepped out from behind the curtain carrying a huge American flag. The audience responded with a thunderous ovation. On cue the orchestra struck up and Farrar led the company and patrons in singing "The Star-Spangled Banner."* Like the United States of America, the Metropolitan Opera was no longer neutral.

---

* Farrar's patriotic demonstration was possibly motivated by the fact that it was well known she had been an "intimate" friend of the German crown prince. Given the circumstances it was a very good career move.

3

THE STORM CENTER OF AMERICA

New York at War, 1917–1918

In April 1917 President Wilson had to decide whether he would fight the war with a volunteer army or a conscripted one. American tradition favored the former. During the Civil War, President Lincoln's government did not impose a draft law until two years after Fort Sumter had been fired upon. It did so out of necessity when it was no longer able to obtain recruits. Despite vigorous attempts to enforce it, the law was largely a failure. Drafted men refused to report or deserted after being inducted. The more affluent citizens hired substitutes, many of whom also deserted at the first opportunity. Wilson's arch political foe, Theodore Roosevelt, favored creating a volunteer army and offered to personally raise a division (approximately twenty thousand men) and lead it to France.

When Wilson had entered the White House in March 1913, the United States was involved in a crisis with the Mexican revolutionary government. A few weeks earlier, after rioting mobs in Mexico had killed some Americans, the outgoing Taft administration considered dispatching U.S. troops. In the circumstances it might have been expected that the new president would place strong men at the head of the Army and Navy. Instead, he offered the post of secretary of war to a Pennsylvania Quaker, Congressman A. Mitchell Palmer, who declined because of his pacifist views. The president's next choice was an obscure New Jersey judge, Lindley M. Garrison, who had no discernible qualifications for the post but who accepted regardless. Wilson's designee for secretary of the navy was a North Carolina newspaper editor,

Josephus Daniels, who had been of great assistance to him in securing the presidential nomination. Daniels, whose views also leaned toward the pacifist side, was an ardent prohibitionist. His most notable contribution to the running of the Navy was to forbid alcohol to be served on U.S. ships.

In 1916, facing a tough reelection campaign, Wilson chose Cleveland mayor Newton Baker to be secretary of war. Like many members of Wilson's cabinet, he was of southern background. Raised in West Virginia, the son of a Confederate veteran, he earned his law degree at Washington and Lee University in Virginia. Baker's views also tended to be pacifist, which was helpful to a presidential candidate running on the slogan, "He kept us out of war." Five feet six and 125 pounds, the bespectacled Baker was not a very fierce-looking warlord. Cartoonists portrayed him as something of a milquetoast. In office, though, Baker was to prove a very competent military administrator.

Wilson accepted the advice of the generals that a conscript army was necessary and asked Congress to enact a draft law. Baker personally dealt with the unpleasant task of telling Teddy Roosevelt that he was not going to be permitted to lead a volunteer force or go anywhere near France. To add to the anguish, he passed over Roosevelt's friend Gen. Leonard Wood for commander of the American Expeditionary Forces in favor of Gen. John J. "Black Jack" Pershing.

Though the Democrats controlled both houses of Congress, they could find no one to sponsor a draft law. The Speaker, the majority leader (who had voted against the declaration of war), and the chairman of the military affairs committee all refused. Senator James A. Reed of Missouri, a Democratic stalwart, told Baker, "You will have the streets of our American cities running with blood on registration day." It was the ranking Republican on the military affairs committee, Julius Kahn of San Francisco, a Jew born in Germany (the type of person reviled as unpatriotic by Jack Morgan), who piloted the bill through.* A blindfolded Baker drew the first number in the draft lottery: 258. In New York, with its large polyglot immigrant population, including many radicals, there was more than a little fear that the streets indeed would run with blood. If New York experienced a riot, it could only be imagined what would happen in such heavily "German" cities

---

* After Kahn's death in 1924, Gen. Hugh Scott, the former Army chief of staff, wrote, "May he rest in peace with the eternal gratitude of his adopted country."

as St. Louis, Cincinnati, and Milwaukee. Before 1917 Arthur Zimmerman told Ambassador Gerard, "The United States does not dare to take action against Germany because we have 500,000 reservists in America who will rise in arms against your government." For emphasis, Zimmerman repeatedly banged his fist on the table. Gerard responded, "We have 501,000 lampposts in America and that's where the German reservists will find themselves if they try any uprising."[1] If the draft law were to result in blood in the streets and bodies dangling from lampposts, the U.S. Army would probably be too busy fighting in America to go off to France. Much depended upon what happened in New York.

The government ordered men of military age to register for conscription beginning on June 5. In New York a coalition of antiwar radicals scheduled a mass rally at the Hunts Point Palace Auditorium in the Bronx for the night of June 4. Among those scheduled to address the meeting were the "Red King and Queen": Alexander Berkman and Emma Goldman. Wherever Berkman was, trouble inevitably followed. In 1892 he had shot steel tycoon Henry Frick after the Homestead affair; in 1914, after he threatened to kill John D. Rockefeller Sr. over the Ludlow massacre, there were riots at the oil tycoon's Pocantico Estate and explosions in New York City; in 1916 he had been in San Francisco publishing *The Blast* when a bomb went off during a preparedness parade, killing ten people. The public still remembered Emma Goldman from the McKinley assassination. Although no charges had ever been brought against her, many people continued to hold her responsible for the deed. Anytime the two were scheduled to attend an event, alarm bells would ring in law enforcement agencies.

Anticipating that five thousand people would show up, the NYPD deployed a strong force to be present inside and outside. The assignment was considered so important that the highest-ranking police official next to Commissioner Woods, Chief Insp. Max Schmittberger, was placed in charge of the contingent. For twenty-five years he had been the department's expert at handling disasters, riots, mass rallies, and other challenging events, and he was a legend in the city.[*] In addition, a large federal law enforcement contingent, led by the U.S. marshal for the southern district of New York,

---

[*] It was to be Schmittberger's last hurrah. Four months later, he would die at age sixty-five.

showed up, accompanied by assistant U.S. attorneys, federal agents, and a detachment of soldiers.

The first surprise for the security forces was the size of the crowd: fifteen thousand people came to the meeting. Some were just curious onlookers, but many were there to support the antiwar movement. Because the hall could not hold that number, most stood outside, jamming the streets and sidewalks for blocks. Chief Insp. Schmittberger ordered up reinforcements to control the crowds. Inside the auditorium, soldiers managed to occupy the balcony seats, while the antidraft protesters filled the ground floor. Government stenographers were scattered around the crowd, ready to take down the speakers' words. That explained the second surprise of the night. None of the rally leaders urged resistance to the draft law, because under provisions of the act it was illegal to do so. Berkman, Goldman, and the others confined their remarks to standard antiwar, antigovernment rhetoric.

From time to time, the soldiers in the balcony would express disapproval of the proceedings by dropping lightbulbs onto the stage. When Berkman spoke, he was met by cries of, "Go back to Russia!" A speaker of draft age, Joseph Cain, proclaimed, "Give me liberty or give me death!" Immediately a shower of missiles landed at his feet, causing some newspapers to write that apparently the soldiers "wished to satisfy Cain's second choice." Finally, a flustered Emma Goldman brought the meeting to a close. As a parting gesture, she urged the crowd to sing "The Internationale." Every radical in the world was familiar with the story of how, during the Paris Commune, the insurgents had sung it as soldiers shot them down. With troops positioned above them, the audience did not burst forth in song. As the protesters streamed out, some began yelling at a passing detachment of National Guardsmen, leading to a brawl in which police arrested eleven of the demonstrators. The *New York Times* captured the essence of the evening, headlining its story of the event, "Anarchists Awed by Police Clubs."[2]

Eleven days later, federal and local law enforcement officers descended on the anarchist headquarters on East 125th Street. This time the U.S. marshal had a warrant, based on a complaint signed by Lt. George Barnitz of the Neutrality Squad, alleging that Goldman and Berkman had conspired to obstruct the draft. The raiders seized copies of Goldman's publication *Mother Earth* and Berkman's *The Blast*, both of which contained articles urging resistance to conscription. They also confiscated a card index that the officers claimed contained the names of every radical in the United States. When told she was under arrest, Goldman stood up unflinchingly, declaring that she alone was responsible for the contents of her magazine. The raiders showed suitable deference to the Red Queen, allowing her to slip into a gown of royal purple, after which, like a guard of honor, they escorted her to jail. Berkman displayed far less class, snarling at cops and behaving in a distraught manner. When Emma was asked her age, she correctly answered 48, while Berkman snarled that he was 250 years old. Within a few weeks they were tried, convicted, and given the maximum sentence of two years in prison and a $10,000 fine.

There would be no recurrence of the 1863 Draft Riot in New York City. This time the governor, the mayor, and Tammany Hall all publicly supported the war. Over the city hung the shadow of Theodore Roosevelt of nearby Oyster Bay. The immigrant population of Irish, Jews, Slavs, and Italians waved flags and donned uniforms. Most German Americans either proclaimed their patriotism or kept quiet. None of the kaiser's reservists rose in arms.

———

Before April 1917, even though bombs were going off from New York to San Francisco, American law enforcement, which in those days was usually carried on in a rough-and-ready fashion, generally acted in a restrained manner against security threats. Federal and local officers sought to avoid a breach of diplomatic protocol or giving offense to some group such as German or Irish Americans. Detectives did not lean on Bernstorff's or Papen's mistresses for information. The U.S. military did not play any significant role in maintaining domestic security, and there were no mass roundups of suspects. Even after the Black Tom explosion, U.S. authorities were still reluctant to publicly blame it, or forty-two other instances of munitions factory bombings, on German saboteurs. Only radicals beyond the pale, such as the IWW members, were treated like regular criminals.

America's entry into the war changed the spirit and the composition of U.S. internal security forces. The conflict was presented to the public as a holy crusade against the Huns and their leader, the so-called Beast of

Berlin, Kaiser Wilhelm II.[*] The order of the day became to win the war at all costs. Law enforcement agencies supplemented by civilian volunteers were unleashed, and an expanded Army Military Intelligence Division (MID) took center stage in the domestic security arena as part of the War Department. To civilian or military security officers, anyone who opposed the war was regarded as no better than a Hun. President Wilson himself had forecast the change. Shortly before asking for a declaration of war, he told his friend Frank Cobb, editor of the *New York World*: "Lead this people into war, and they'll forget that there ever was such a thing as tolerance. To fight you must be ruthless and brutal, and ruthless brutality will enter into the very fiber of our national life, infecting Congress, the courts, the policeman on the beat, the man in the street."[3]

In June 1917 Congress passed the Espionage Act, making it a crime punishable by twenty years in prison to convey false statements that might interfere with the war effort. It also authorized the postmaster general to bar any mail that, in his judgment, advocated treason, insurrection, or disobedience of U.S. laws. When the statute was legally challenged, Justice Oliver Wendell Holmes, writing for a unanimous Supreme Court, ruled it constitutional and upheld the conviction of a defendant, Charles Schenck, because his words constituted a "clear and present danger" of causing immediate violence. In 1918 the Sedition Act was passed, outlawing the uttering of "disloyal" statements. These included scurrilous or abusive remarks about the flag, the form of government, or the uniform of the armed forces. In the Supreme Court case challenging it, the majority upheld the law, though Holmes dissented, arguing that the plaintiffs were being punished not for their deeds but for their words. Both laws gave security forces wide powers to deal with not only foreign agents but also domestic dissidents. In the wartime atmosphere, anyone who criticized the government was liable to imprisonment.

Before 1917, with President Wilson seeking diplomatic means to avoid war, it was logical for him to make the State Department the primary overseers of U.S. security. After the United States declared war, as happened in

---

[*] By 1917, however, the kaiser had been reduced to a figurehead. The real rulers of Germany were Field Marshal Paul von Hindenburg and his number-two man, Gen. Erich Ludendorff—the former supplying the gravitas, the latter the brains.

every belligerent country, diplomats gave way to soldiers. Before 1917, the Treasury Department's Secret Service was regarded as the federal government's premier law enforcement agency. This, too, was a logical arrangement because most federal crimes dealt with matters of commerce and finance, areas in which the Treasury had the greatest expertise. With the United States at war, it was inevitable that the Department of Justice, which had the final say over who would be prosecuted under wartime statutes, would supplant the Treasury as the country's top cops. In 1917–1918, the struggle for dominance over U.S. domestic security would pit the War Department against the Justice Department, while State and Treasury would have reduced roles.

In 1915 State Department counselor Frank Polk, the government's lead security official, had been thrust into an area he knew little about. In 1917 the War Department's security chief was a man who had been preparing for the job all his life. Col. Ralph Van Deman was a highly educated fifty-two-year-old professional soldier. He had graduated from Harvard in 1888, spent a year at the law school, and then took a medical degree from Miami University of Ohio. As a result, he was twenty-eight before he entered active military service.* Early on, he passed up medical duty in favor of working in the Military Intelligence Division—an unusual choice for an ambitious young professional. MID was a small unit, and its principal duty was preparing maps. In 1898 Van Deman missed action in the Spanish-American War because, with his intellect and commanding presence, he was selected to give President McKinley daily briefings at the White House. Afterward, like his British intelligence counterparts, he learned his craft in the colonies. During the American occupation of the Philippines, he operated against native rebels and Japanese spies. The tall, lanky, craggy-faced Ohioian, who bore a physical resemblance to Abraham Lincoln, became

---

* Van Deman was not the only Harvard graduate who chose the Army. After completing medical school, Leonard Wood became a military surgeon, but in 1886 he joined an expedition pursuing Geronimo. In 1898, while he was serving as White House physician, President McKinley arranged for him to command the 1st U.S. Volunteer Cavalry (the Rough Riders). To defuse criticism for giving the appointment to a doctor rather than a line officer, McKinley awarded Wood the Medal of Honor for his Geronimo adventure twelve years earlier. When Wood was promoted to brigadier general, Col. Theodore Roosevelt took over the regiment. Woods went on to become Army chief of staff and in 1920 was a leading contender for the Republican nomination for president. He lost out in the famous smoke-filled Chicago hotel room.

the country's leading intelligence expert. His intense drive to improve the status of intelligence work often led to clashes with superiors, as a result of which his career suffered. Finally, in 1916, he was appointed head of MID. After the outbreak of war, he was able to expand his staff from 2 officers to 427.

In organizing U.S. military intelligence, Van Deman benefited greatly from the assistance of Lt. Col. Claude Dansey of Britain's MI5. Van Deman organized his personnel into negative (domestic) and positive (foreign) sections, based on the British model. After three years of war, the Allies had accumulated voluminous intelligence, and the British, usually reluctant to share information, generously agreed to furnish it to their American allies. This not only helped to bring the Yanks up to speed but also was a way of keeping them from establishing their own foreign intelligence network. If they had, they might have learned about such things as the secret treaties regarding the postwar disposal of German and Turkish possessions. The British argued that it would be a waste of manpower to send spies abroad (though the AEF in France did have frontline intelligence personnel). Most members of Van Deman's staff were assigned to domestic security duties. Dansey also called on his high-level contacts (garnered during his days at Sleepy Hollow Country Club) to help Van Deman win battles against his American superiors. After the armistice, Van Deman recommended Dansey for the U.S. Distinguished Service Medal, noting that he "probably did more than any one man in getting a hearing for those officers of the general staff who were struggling for an opportunity to bring this most important matter [the needs of MID] to the attention of the War Department." Van Deman also enlisted the superintendent of police of Washington, D.C., a close friend of Secretary of War Newton Baker, to lobby on behalf of Army intelligence.

MID's largest field office was located in New York City. There, cooperation between the police and the military became so close that it was often difficult to determine where one agency left off and the other began. On the recommendation of Commissioner Woods, Van Deman had appointed Deputy Commissioner Nicholas Biddle a colonel in charge of the MID office at 302 Broadway. His staff of twenty-five officers was composed of Ivy League graduates with impeccable social credentials. He also supervised a contingent of fifty "intelligence police"—New York City cops who were given the military rank of sergeant and the title of inspector—operating out of police headquarters on Centre Street.

The Office of Naval Intelligence (ONI) also expanded its operations. By the time of the armistice, it had 438 officers on duty within the United States. Under the direction of Assistant Secretary of the Navy Franklin Delano Roosevelt, the roster of those getting commissions resembled a Harvard alumni directory. The head of ONI's New York office, Lt. Cdr. Spencer Eddy—Harvard man, former career diplomat, noted tennis player, grower of rare orchids, member of the best clubs, and, incidentally, a personal friend of Roosevelt—helped recruit other blue bloods to the organization. His naval office on Wall Street was also closely aligned with the NYPD.

Sometimes Roosevelt could not resist playing spy catcher. He suggested that ONI check up on the German American community living near the Portsmouth, New Hampshire, Navy Yard, because they might purchase an airplane to bomb the facility. When ONI looked into it, they found that the fear was baseless. Roosevelt's secretary, Louis Howe, whose personal untidiness and flippant attitudes offended Navy brass, was accused of trying to organize an espionage ring that reported directly to Roosevelt.[*]

The new security laws, which the Department of Justice would enforce, projected the Bureau of Investigation into the forefront of counterintelligence work. Before 1917, A. Bruce Bielaski had been virtually unknown to the American public. Afterward he received a strong buildup from government publicists. He was described as "an excellent amateur baseball player, boxer and rower."[4] (His transfer from the Bureau of Printing and Engraving in 1907 was thought to have been arranged to strengthen the Justice Department's baseball team.) With "a fighting smile, a low crisp voice, [his] unending, everlasting persistence make him the most feared man in America by the German spies."[5] Early on it was apparent to observers that Bielaski's bureau would supersede the Secret Service as the principal domestic security agency. On the night of June 4, when federal and local police blanketed the

---

[*] Howe had worked for Roosevelt in a personal capacity back in New York and was fervently devoted to making his boss president. He would remain with FDR after the war through his recovery from polio, election to the New York governorship, and the 1932 presidential campaign. When Howe died in 1935, he was serving as secretary to the president.

antiwar rally at Hunts Point Market, though Chief Inspector Schmittberger and the U.S. marshal were in overall command, some reporters noted that Capt. William Offley, superintendent of the New York office of the Bureau of Investigation, seemed to be directing operations.

When the war began, a number of civilian groups volunteered to serve as spycatchers. The Justice Department felt it would have more control if it worked with one large organization, and the task was given to the American Protective League (APL), headed by a Chicago advertising executive named Albert Briggs. Though its leadership came from conservative elements, it attracted Americans of various political shades who wished to assist in winning the war. The membership quickly rose to 250,000, with about 65,000 assigned to security work. In the postwar years, it became fashionable to denigrate the civilian volunteers as bigoted vigilantes. Some may have been, yet viewed in the context of the time, they could be seen as patriots. Three years of propaganda about babies mutilated and nuns raped in Belgium had inflamed American passions. Even those who were initially skeptical about German atrocities believed them after they were vouched for by James Bryce, First Viscount Bryce, a distinguished scholar and former ambassador to the United States who was well known and highly regarded in prewar America.* The 1915 sinking of the *Lusitania* was seen as proof of German barbarity. At the time, very few people were aware that the ship also carried munitions and Canadian soldiers. The German acts of sabotage in the United States before 1917 also helped to confirm many Americans' belief that the war was a struggle to preserve civilization.

In the prevailing climate, it was natural for those who were beyond military age to regard assisting a law enforcement agency against threats to domestic security as a way to do their bit. In addition, Anglo-American literature had long glorified the amateur secret agent or sleuth. Every educated American was familiar with the exploits of Sherlock Holmes, who

---

* James Bryce—Regis professor of history at Oxford, former member of Parliament, and cabinet minister—served as British ambassador to the United States from 1907 to 1913. His classic 1888 book, *American Commonwealth*, lavishly praised the U.S. system of government. Though Bryce was an upper-class Englishman, a type many Americans disliked, his sincere admiration for the United States made him very popular. Ennobled as Viscount Bryce, he headed a commission that looked into allegations of German atrocities and confirmed most of the charges. After the war, when the atrocity stories were shown to be mostly false, his reputation sustained a severe blow.

invariably had to guide the bumbling regular police to the correct solution of a crime.

With only three hundred agents, it would have been impossible for the bureau to make much impact. So Bielaski gave many of the APL volunteers credentials identifying them as members of the "Secret Service Division"—angering the official U.S. Secret Service. Bureaucratic turf battles meshed with larger policy disputes. Treasury Secretary McAdoo and Secret Service chief Flynn proposed to centralize security under their own control and to allow only professionals to exercise law enforcement authority. McAdoo wrote to his father-in-law, the president, "[It is unfortunate] that a miscellaneous corps of so-called secret service operatives be loosed upon the country to pry into the business of peaceful citizens."[6]

Attorney General Thomas Gregory backed Bielaski's use of the APL, though both men would later have second thoughts about the decision. Treasury Secretary McAdoo might have used his clout to win the struggle for the Secret Service, but he had his hands full elsewhere: in addition to running the financial affairs of the government, with further responsibility for foreign loans and the sale of Liberty Bonds, he was appointed controller of all U.S. railroads. The last post alone was a job of monumental proportions. By 1918 he was the virtual czar of the U.S. economy. Flynn, unwilling to play second fiddle to the Bureau of Investigation, resigned and returned to New York to head his own private detective agency, which assisted McAdoo in guarding the railroads.

The shrewd civilian businessmen who directed the APL recognized where the principal battlefield of American domestic security lay. As its official history would note:

> [New York] was the storm-center of America in the war. The heart of the great and intricate system of German espionage, the controlling financial body of Germany's spy Army. . . . Our shipments of men, munitions and supplies largely centered there, and that was the general point of departure of our troops bound overseas. . . . Literally, it was plot and counterplot in New York; war and counterwar; espionage and counterespionage. . . . It was imperative that the vast protective agencies of

the national Government focus here at the gateway to the Atlantic. . . .
[So] every force was rushed to the danger line in New York.[7]

From an office on Manhattan's Nassau Street, the APL established a parallel law enforcement agency with its own chiefs, captains, and lieutenants. It also promulgated its own rules of engagement. In their search for spies or the disloyal, the APL developed standard methods of operation. A typical tactic involved using private business connections to enlist the services of building superintendents who would let APL teams enter offices of individuals suspected of disloyalty. Once in, they photographed papers and records and then turned them over to Bureau of Investigation agents, who used the information to obtain search warrants to seize the files. The official history of the organization described its illegal break-ins as "done 1,000 times in every city in America," claiming that because they were "after the guilty alone," the innocent could not disapprove because there was "no time to mince matters and pass fine phrases when the land was full of dangerous enemies in disguise." In practice, those investigated were not spies, but individuals who were thought to be pro-German or who actively opposed U.S. war policies. People identified as such could be deemed security risks and held in preventive detention. Soon, "off to Oglethorpe" became a common phrase applied to individuals sent to a detention center at Fort Oglethorpe in Georgia.

The APL activities coincided with the mood of the times. Throughout the country, mobs beat up war critics, sometimes compelling them to kneel and kiss the flag. German Americans found life very difficult. If they spoke in their native tongue while riding a streetcar, the other passengers would yell, "Speak American!" Those who failed to do so might be thrown off the vehicle. Before the war, Germans were considered a model minority—hard working, good natured, and scrupulously honest in their business dealings. In 1917 in many cities, Schulz's butcher shop and Mueller's bakery often lost patronage and in some instances were burned down. In New York the posh Germanic Club on Fifth Avenue was demolished by a mob. Musical classics written by German composers were banned from opera houses. German American artists who performed in public risked being booed off the stage. Even poor little dachshunds were kicked on the street.

When some Department of Justice professionals began to have reservations about the tactics of the APL, many of its volunteers gravitated to the MID. Van Deman believed that winning the war overrode concern for legal technicalities, so he was not troubled by the use of irregular procedures. MID's tactics brought complaints from influential Americans, and when Secretary of War Baker began to ask questions, Van Deman was not forthcoming. As a result, he was denied promotion to the brigadier general rank his position called for and was shipped off to France. His successor was Brig. Gen. Marlborough Churchill, another Harvard-educated career officer and distant relation of the Churchills who were dukes of Marlborough. Under his administration, MID carried out the same policies in a less abrasive manner.

The few German spies in the country when war was declared either were expelled with the rest of the Central Powers diplomats or went to Mexico. MID did make one major apprehension, though at the time it did not recognize it. It caught one of the Black Tom bombers. Lothar Witzke had fled south of the border, where, using the name Pablo Waberski, he worked under his old partner, Kurt Jahnke. The MID had undercover operatives in Mexico, and they lured Witzke into crossing the border. In February 1918, carrying a Russian passport made out to Waberski, he entered the United States at Nogales, Arizona. As soon as he stepped onto American soil, a U.S. agent arrested him at gunpoint and hauled him off for interrogation by intelligence officers.* Witzke denied any involvement with espionage. However, he was carrying some coded papers that, when deciphered, included a letter addressed to German diplomatic officials in Mexico, identifying him as a secret agent of the Fatherland. Taken to Fort Sam Houston in El Paso, he was secretly tried and sentenced to death by hanging. The penalty was meant to show disdain for Witzke because only common criminals were hanged; officers and gentlemen were shot. When the findings of the court-martial

---

* The men who tricked Witzke into crossing the U.S. border were a German national who served as a colonel in the Mexican army and a black Canadian who claimed to be an IWW fugitive. The former worked for the U.S. MID and the latter for British intelligence. Other accounts suggest Witzke was lured over by a female U.S. agent. Kurt Jahnke, who was never captured, continued to operate as an intelligence agent. Both before and during World War II, he was involved in several major operations for the Nazi secret service.

were forwarded to President Wilson for review, Attorney General Gregory's Department of Justice raised an objection to the military being allowed to execute civilians within the United States.* President Wilson agreed, and Witzke's sentence was commuted to imprisonment.

Some members of the Department of Justice favored the military approach. Charles Warren was a distinguished attorney and prominent Harvard Law School alumnus who volunteered to serve as an assistant attorney general during the war emergency.† As far as spies or traitors were concerned, his view was that one execution is worth far more in deterrent value than a hundred arrests. While such sentiments seem harsh, the death sentence was the only practical deterrent to foreign spies and saboteurs. Simply locking them up for the duration was meaningless. At war's end they would be sent home, where they would be hailed as heroes. For that reason, military law had traditionally held that, if found behind enemy lines out of uniform, they were subject to execution.‡ In Witzke's case, he was released from prison in 1923 and upon his return to Germany was awarded the Iron Cross.

Witzke actually received a double break. He had been fingered by British agents as a suspect in the Black Tom explosion and had boasted to a U.S. operative that he had been involved in the affair. These leads were not followed up. If they had been, Witzke might have been prosecuted for murder under New Jersey law. If convicted, there is little doubt what the sentence would have been. No thorough criminal investigation of Black Tom ever took place (perhaps because it would have embarrassed important people). Assistant Secretary of the Navy Franklin Roosevelt was in a position to witness the disputes over Witzke between the War Department and the Justice Department. In the next war, as president he would not make the same decision that Wilson had.

---

* Though having been an officer cadet on a warship, who later escaped from a prison camp, he was still a member of the German armed forces.

† A professorial chair at the Harvard Law School bears his name. His 1923 book on the Supreme Court won the Pulitzer Prize for history.

‡ Recollect the executions during the Revolutionary War of British major John André for his role in Benedict Arnold's plot to surrender West Point, and of the American captain Nathan Hale for spying. Both men were captured while wearing civilian dress.

The World War I American spy case that has attracted the most attention from historians of espionage involves the classic ingredients of a cloak-and-dagger mystery, especially the fact that the central character was a beautiful blonde aristocrat, Maria de Victorica. In a 1931 book, Maj. Herbert Yardley, who headed the War Department's code-breaking unit known as MI8, declared her to be "the most daring and dangerous spy encountered in American history." Yardley exaggerated his subjects and his own importance. He claimed credit for Victorica's capture, even though her pursuit and apprehension took place in New York at a time when Yardley worked at a desk in Washington.

Maria de Victorica was described as a tall, strikingly attractive woman of about thirty-five. The daughter of Prussian general Baron Hans von Kretschmann, around 1910 she went to work for Colonel Nicolai, head of the German Secret Service; whether she did so out of patriotic conviction, a desire for adventure, or to support her heroin addiction is unknown. Along the way, she married Manuel Gustave Victorica, an Argentine citizen who was also a German agent. It is not clear what she did for the Fatherland in the early phases of the war, though it can be deduced that she served as a courier transporting messages and currency to German agents. In 1916 she was known to be in Spain and later in Scandinavia. Early in 1917, using an Argentine passport, she sailed on a Norwegian ship for New York. When the vessel was inspected at a British port, she was allowed to proceed. Not long afterward, French authorities notified the British that Manuel Victorica had been arrested for spying. British intelligence officials recollected that a woman with that last name had traveled on an Argentine passport, so they notified Colonel Van Deman to pick up the investigation in New York.

U.S. agents found that a New York financial house had paid her $35,000 on the instructions of a German bank. They also managed to obtain letters that had been sent to her at the firm but remained unopened. The letters were submitted to Yardley at MI8 for examination. His preliminary analysis determined that they contained a coded message written in invisible ink. Yardley, who had broken the code found on Witzke, was able to do the same with Victorica's letters, revealing that they contained instructions for her to hire agents to staff a sabotage ring. This sent American investigators from MID, the Bureau of Investigation, and the NYPD scurrying around New

York to find her. But she was always a step ahead of them. She checked into the Knickerbocker Hotel in January 1918 but left just before her pursuers descended on the place. They picked up her trail at the Waldorf Astoria; again, she had checked out before their arrival. They learned that she was staying at an expensive apartment. When they raided the place, she was gone. They also turned up information that she was using priests to obtain religious statues from a manufacturer in Zurich, Switzerland. Unknown to the priests, the statues were to be filled with TNT.

American agents kept watch on persons whose names had been mentioned in the letters to Victorica. A schoolgirl cousin of a suspect was trailed to St. Patrick's Cathedral. Detectives watched her enter a pew carrying a newspaper and then depart, leaving it behind. Afterward, a man went into the pew the girl had left and retrieved the paper. The detectives followed him by train to Long Beach, Long Island, where he entered the lounge of the Nassau Hotel, lit up a cigarette, and then left without the paper. Immediately a blonde woman went to where he had been sitting and took possession of the paper. When the agents interrogated her, they learned that she was Maria de Victorica. The folded newspaper was found to contain $20,000, which had been smuggled into the country to be used to fund a spy network. After her arrest, cut off from her heroin supply, Victorica broke down physically and was taken to the prison wing of Bellevue Hospital in Manhattan. Too sick to be brought to trial, she died two years later.

———

Despite the cloak-and-dagger stories, there was no major threat from German spies and saboteurs that required the creation of a vast force of security officers. No German agent was ever charged under the Espionage Act. A few hundred trained investigators would have been sufficient to protect metropolitan New York. A few thousand more were all that was necessary to cover the rest of the country. A force of that size could have been recruited from among big-city police detectives, lawyers past draft age, loyal German Americans, and persons like Arthur Woods who had studied at the great universities of Germany and Austria, where they acquired proficiency in the language and an acquaintanceship with German culture. The real reason why the APL and other volunteers were needed was to deal with individuals and groups who opposed the war. These were not just foreign-born radicals like Berkman and Goldman, the wild men of the IWW, or Germans still sympathetic to the Fatherland. Some of the leading antiwar protesters were old-stock Americans who had attended the best schools and belonged to the right clubs. For a while, some of them thought they would not be subject to security crackdowns. After all, they reasoned, they hated the kaiser as much as the most rabid patriots. If they had seen a German agent carrying a bomb, they would have notified the police. Some simply believed that intervening in Europe's quarrels was not wise or that drafting men into the Army was a form of involuntary servitude forbidden by the Constitution.

Roger Baldwin was a proper Bostonian who traced his ancestry to a *Mayflower* passenger. In 1906, after graduating from Harvard with bachelor's and master's degrees, he went to work for a settlement house in St. Louis. On the side, he taught sociology at Washington University. His lifestyle was typical of many well-born young men and women in the Progressive era. They rejected a business or professional career in favor of exploring the underside of life and participating in worthy endeavors. Baldwin took his class on tours of the slums and red-light districts and worked with juvenile delinquents. His political views began moving further left after he met Emma Goldman and was impressed with her rhetoric. Goldman was not equally impressed with Baldwin, and in her memoirs she remembered him as "a very pleasant person though not very vital, rather a social lion surrounded by society girls, whose interest in the attractive young man was apparently greater than in his uplift work."[8] A serious revolutionary like Goldman looked down on what she regarded as dilettantes. According to her, they "impressed me as people to whom Bohemianism was a sort of narcotic that helped them endure the boredom of their lives."[9]

In 1917 Baldwin moved to Washington to work for the American Union against Militarism, an organization formed to counter the preparedness advocates. When the United States declared war, he took a new path. Although he was not an attorney, he organized the National Civil Liberties Bureau (NCLB), which in 1920 became the American Civil Liberties Union (ACLU). Baldwin took up residence in New York and started counseling draft resisters. His organization was not one the U.S. government looked on favorably, whereas Baldwin believed that if he were open about his operations, he could arrive at a mutual understanding with a fellow Harvard gentleman like Colonel Biddle.

In March 1918 Baldwin initiated a visit to Biddle's office to brief him on the work of the NCLB. He explained that, while his group would counsel individuals on their rights under the law, they would not discourage men from joining the armed forces. He also swore that it had no connection with German agents and did not accept any funds from those sources. To prove it, he volunteered to turn over his records for examination by military intelligence officers. Biddle was not about to engage in negotiations with an individual he viewed as obstructing the war effort. On the night of March 6, he personally led a surreptitious entry (sometimes called a burglary) of Baldwin's offices at 70 Fifth Avenue to copy documents. To Biddle's embarrassment, in an official interview ten days later, Baldwin gave him copies of the papers he had already purloined.

One of the agents investigating the NCLB was Archibald "Archie" Stevenson, a Yale-educated attorney who, before the war, had chaired the subcommittee on aliens of the New York City Committee on National Defense, a preparedness group. In 1917 Stevenson volunteered his services to the Bureau of Investigation and, while maintaining a loose affiliation with Bielaski's agency, also went to work for military intelligence as Special Agent 650. Stevenson observed that Baldwin loosened up with men of his own class, and during the course of the investigation, he managed to get Baldwin to speak off the record on a Harvard-to-Yale, Roger-and-Archie basis. Finally, on a Saturday morning in August, Bureau of Investigation agents, accompanied by a squad of volunteers led by Stevenson, raided the NCLB offices. One of the lawyers working there demanded to see their search warrant. After examining it, he claimed it was invalid for "failure of supporting affidavits to show probable cause." Usually lawyers did not dispute the validity of a judicial warrant, "fair on its face" as it was being executed, saving their arguments for judges. But confident of his superior status, he ordered the agents to leave the premises. Instead, the leader of the raiding party pointed a revolver at the learned counsel's head and commanded him to step aside. Confronted with the force of the detective's argument, the attorney quickly shut up and moved out of the way.

When Baldwin himself received an induction notice, he refused to report and was indicted. During the course of the proceedings, Stevenson testified about statements Baldwin had made in their conversations. Baldwin protested, "Archie, you son of a bitch, I said that to you privately at a luncheon. You know I wasn't intending to be quoted." Individuals of high status who run afoul of the law, short of murder, rarely face serious consequences. They always shelter behind their wealth and social connections, confident that fellow members of the privileged class will close ranks around them. But the war spirit was at its height, so Baldwin was locked up in New York's grim Tombs jail. Still, he was taken out daily by a deputy U.S. marshal to the nearby Department of Justice headquarters on Park Row to be allowed to examine the voluminous NCLB papers that were in the custody of the government. The marshal did not even bother to handcuff him. Sometimes he took Baldwin to a burlesque show or allowed him to have lunch with a friend. One day, when the regular guard was not available, a substitute proceeded to handcuff Baldwin. The prisoner told him, "I don't use such things." The marshal was adamant and slapped the cuffs on him. As Baldwin would later recall, "It was a five-block walk from the Tombs to Park Row, and I didn't want to meet anyone I knew while being dragged along by a cop. So I contrived to make him appear to be the prisoner and I the marshal by the simple device of keeping two paces ahead of him—he was short and fat—and dragging him along."[10]

Baldwin was tried before the armistice, found guilty, and sentenced to a year in prison. He was sent to a relatively mild jail in Newark, New Jersey, where the warden was accommodating and permitted Baldwin's friends to drop in regularly for chats. By some mistake, Baldwin was released a month early. When he notified the court of the error, the judge told him not to worry about it.

Most war opponents were not treated as gently as Baldwin. In 1919 a hundred IWW members from all over the United States, including Big Bill Haywood, were rounded up and shipped to Chicago for trial. The officers who escorted the Wobblies did not handle them as though they were socialites. While being transported they were chained together, and armed guards stood ready to shoot them on the spot at the first sign of trouble. The judge assigned to try their case was Kenesaw Mountain Landis, later the commissioner of baseball. Landis was a mercurial man with a somewhat erratic manner whose decisions were frequently overturned by higher courts. The defendants' efforts to turn the case into a show trial were welcomed by Landis because it put him in the spotlight he so dearly loved. The defendants were convicted and given stiff sentences; Haywood got twenty years. The miners' union posted $15,000 bail to obtain his release while he appealed his conviction. In an action that would never qualify as a profile in courage, Haywood fled to Soviet Russia, thereby forfeiting the union's money.

In August 1918, NYPD intelligence detectives arrested six obscure Russian-born radicals for distributing leaflets attacking American intervention in the Russian Civil War. Charged with violating the Sedition Act, twenty-nine-year-old Jacob Abrams, who stood first alphabetically, gave his name to the case. All the defendants received sentences ranging from three to twenty years. The Abrams case was eventually heard by the Supreme Court, becoming the one in which, despite Holmes's dissent, the Court upheld the constitutionality of the law.

Some defendants fared better than Baldwin, the Wobblies, or the Russians. Carlo Tresca and his girlfriend, Elizabeth Gurley Flynn—who were almost as notorious as Berkman, Goldman, or Haywood—were named in the Chicago indictment. Flynn was arrested by federal agents and NYPD cops at her home in the Bronx. While they waited for a train to take them downtown, an uptown train pulled in across the tracks, and Flynn saw Tresca get off. She gave no sign of recognition, but NYPD detective Harry Hand spotted him, ran over, and handcuffed him. Flynn, though from a modest background, had developed many contacts among the upper classes, which she used to secure top legal counsel. She and Tresca were advised to obtain a severance and have their cases heard in New York, to avoid the Chicago show trial. They did, and their lawyers managed to drag out the proceedings and to interest a number of top people in Flynn's fate, including Joseph Tumulty, principal secretary to President Wilson. After the armistice, the government dropped the charges.

The lawyers who worked with the NCLB also faced indictment, so they retained a well-known New York criminal lawyer, G. Gordon Battle. He was not an ideological soulmate; rather, he was counsel to Tammany Hall and an ardent supporter of the war.* The well-connected Battle was able to get the defendants off.

---

* G.(eorge) Gordon Battle Liddy of Watergate fame was named for him.

Based on the cases of Baldwin, the IWW Chicago defendants, the Russian immigrants, Tresca and Flynn, and the NCLB lawyers, several generalizations can be made. Defendants stood a better chance of acquittal, or at least of receiving a soft sentence, if they were members of the social elite, less chance if they were low-status industrial workers or immigrants. Those whose lawyers were competent and offered standard legal defenses, rather than ones designed for political show trials, were much more likely to walk. It was also better to avoid hanging judges like Landis. In essence, security offenses were handled in a roughly comparable fashion to ordinary criminal cases.

In 1918 the cycle of domestic security policing entered its harshest phase. From 1914 to 1917, the operations of the understaffed domestic security forces had often been too little too late. As a result, German saboteurs had a field day. In 1917–1918, the war-expanded security apparatus clamped down hard on radicals and anyone suspected of favoring the German cause. Then people who simply thought that the United States should stay out of war or that the draft law was unconstitutional became targets. Finally, it landed on individuals who appeared to be shirking their responsibilities in the war effort. By 1918 many draft-aged men had been deferred; others had failed to register. The sight of healthy young individuals who were neither working in war industries nor fighting was a source of outrage to those who were, and to their families. A name was coined for them—"slackers"—and it was not just a mild reproach.

In the summer of 1918, the Army provost marshal issued a "work or fight order" designed to force the slackers to do their bit. Police and federal agents, sometimes accompanied by servicemen or APL volunteers, began roaming through American cities, accosting draft-aged men and demanding that they show their registration documents. Those who could not were taken into custody. In September 1918, Bureau of Investigation chief Bielaski planned a huge anti-slacker drive in New York City. To assist his own agents, he obtained 1,750 soldiers and sailors, nearly 1,000 APL operatives, and the full cooperation of the NYPD. On the day of the operation, the security forces were out in force on the streets and in public gathering places such as restaurants and places of entertainment. When they saw a likely offender, they asked for his registration papers. If he could not produce them, he was taken to the nearest police station, where he was questioned further by intelligence officers. If thought to be delinquent, he was shipped to a National Guard armory to be held in custody. Some of the individuals hauled in were not draft eligible, including teenagers who looked older than their years or middle-aged men who, for appearances' sake, had dyed their gray hair. Most of the others seized had papers, but not on them. This category included some off-duty police officers who had also neglected to carry their badges.

According to the APL, 21,402 men were apprehended, of whom 756 were inducted into the service and 2,485 were found "delinquent" from their local boards. Other estimates put the number of men seized as high as 50,000. U.S. senator William Calder of New York complained of men being "taken out of their places of business and crowded into vans, perhaps 50 or 60 packed in like sardines, and sent to the police station houses." One prominent New Yorker, with two brothers in the armed forces, was having dinner with a young woman in a Brooklyn restaurant when the military police appeared and demanded to see his papers. Though he had signed up, the draft board had not sent him a confirming document. He was arrested and hauled to a station house, where he stood for five hours in a lockup without food or water. He was then taken to a National Guard armory. Finally, a business partner tracked him down and arranged his release.

On this occasion the security forces had gone too far. In the climate of the time, radicals, aliens, German Americans, or U.S. citizens opposed to the war could be locked up. But the ill-conceived slacker drive had bagged people who were none of the above, including a number of individuals with sufficient stature that their complaints would be heard. Much of the criticism landed on Bruce Bielaski.

During the war, there were few opportunities for antiwar forces to present their views to the public. In some cases, if they had tried to do so they would have faced criminal charges. In New York City, though, there were two public referendums on the war—the first indirect and inconclusive, the second direct and indicative. In November 1917 the city held a mayoral election. With America at war, it might have been expected that the ardently pro-Allied John Purroy Mitchel would be reelected. However, his aloof, often abrasive ways offended some voters, and his support for the war turned many of the city's Irish and Germans against him. He also faced the usual problem of most New Yorkers voting as Tammany or the other political machines told them, unless a huge scandal temporarily gave them the urge to "turn the rascals out." The Democratic nominee was an undistinguished Brooklyn judge, John F. "Red Mike" Hylan. He had begun his career as an elevated motorman but was fired for reckless driving when he nearly ran over his superintendent. As a politician he carried on a perpetual war against transit interests, making him a favorite of newspaper tycoon William Randolph Hearst. By 1917 Hearst was a bitter man. The New York City voters had rejected him in 1905 when he ran for mayor. The state's voters did the same twice when he sought the governorship. In both contests Tammany Hall played a major role in bringing about Hearst's defeat. As a result, the Hearst papers constantly attacked Tammany boss Charles Murphy. Yet, in a cynical deal, Murphy agreed to back Hearst's man, Hylan, for mayor. A strong Socialist, antiwar, mayoral candidate, Morris Hillquit, was also in the field to siphon off anti-Tammany votes from Mitchel. In November Mayor Mitchel was defeated.

Mitchel joined the Army and a few months later was killed when he fell from his plane during pilot training.* He had left his seat belt unfastened because it aggravated the chronic headaches that had plagued him since his South American days. Arthur Woods resigned and went off to the Army, where he rose to lieutenant colonel. The new Tammany police commissioner, Richard Enright, was a bitter enemy of the Mitchel administration, which had passed him over three times for promotion to captain. Inspector Tunney had been a favorite of the reform administration, so naturally Enright disliked him, too. Tunney and twenty of his Bomb Squad detectives transferred en masse to the U.S. Army, which made him a captain and sent him around the country to organize similar units in other police departments. His group is generally considered to be the first members of what became the Army Counter Intelligence Corps.

Although the Hearst papers had vigorously opposed America's entry into the war, Mayor Hylan did not dare cut back NYPD cooperation with military

---

* Mitchel Field on Long Island was named for him—not, as many people believed, for aviation pioneer Gen. Billy Mitchell.

intelligence. Across the river, in Hudson County, New Jersey, Boss Frank Hague opposed the war. So, in 1917, President Wilson ordered the Army to seize the vital port of Hoboken and run it for the duration. If the New York City government had tried to obstruct the war effort, Wilson might well have placed New York under military rule. Colonel Biddle continued to direct NYPD's security operations, and the cops cracked down just as hard on radicals and antiwar people as they had under Mitchel.*

The final New York City referendum on the war took place in the November 1918 election for the House of Representatives in the 14th District. Congressman Fiorello LaGuardia ran for reelection to the seat he had left in 1917 to join the Army. The Lower Manhattan district was home to a multiethnic, heavily immigrant population. In prewar days it had been a Tammany stronghold that also produced a large Socialist vote. LaGuardia was as complex as the district he represented. Born in New York of immigrant parents—an Italian father and an Austro-Hungarian Jewish mother—he had been raised on a western army post in Geronimo country, where his father had been the regimental bandmaster. For the rest of his life, he would favor broad-brimmed Stetsons and claim Prescott, Arizona, as his hometown. His father was poisoned by bad food during the Spanish-American War and invalided out of the Army. Afterward the family moved temporarily to his mother's home in Budapest, where LaGuardia perfected his fluency in several languages. While there he secured an appointment as a U.S. consular aide at posts in Austria-Hungary. Upon his return to New York, he became a lawyer representing labor unions. His reformist, left-of-center ideas made him unwilling to join Tammany, and his flag-waving patriotic views, molded when he was a child of the regiment, kept him from lining up with the Socialists. He joined the Republican Party. The short, stocky LaGuardia, with his cowboy hat, squeaky voice, and argumentative manner, was out of place among Manhattan's elegant, reserved WASP Republicans. In 1914 he was allowed to run for Congress in the 14th District because it was thought to be a hopeless race for the GOP. He lost but made a good showing, so in 1916 he tried again. Whether

---

* Despite the Hylan administration's cooperation, he was never fully trusted by Wilson. Before the president returned from the Paris Peace Conference in July 1919, Treasury Secretary William McAdoo told an aide to Hylan that soldiers would be deployed in the streets of New York to guard the president. The aide assured him the NYPD would perform the task in fine fashion. McAdoo was not satisfied, but fearing unfavorable publicity, he gave way. On the day of Wilson's arrival, the NYPD handled security without any problems.

it was LaGuardia's ability to speak to people in their own language, his radical ideas balanced by his super-patriotic oratory, or his charismatic personality, he won the seat by a narrow margin. Then, after casting his vote for the war, he abandoned his congressional duties to go off to the Austro-Italian front as a U.S. Army bomber pilot. Decorated and promoted to major, he managed to be furloughed home in time for the election.

The voters' choice was clear. LaGuardia's opponent was Scott Nearing, a well-known intellectual who had been fired from two universities for his radical views. At the time, he was under indictment for obstructing the draft by publishing an antiwar pamphlet, "The Great Madness." After the war, he would become a prominent member of the American Communist Party. When reporters interviewed LaGuardia, he feigned ignorance as to whom his opponent was, but he declared that if it was a young man he would ask him what regiment he had been in. When LaGuardia stumped the district, he always told his audiences not to hold it against Nearing because some people called him yellow or a traitor, thereby reminding the voters of the charges. During the war, the Lower East Side had exhibited considerable patriotism. The notorious gangster Monk Eastman, though overage, had enlisted in the Army. When he came back from France, he was so loaded with medals that the governor pardoned him for his previous offenses. A locally recruited regiment included the Lost Battalion, which had captured the nation's imagination during the Battle of the Argonne. Boss Murphy also helped out by decreeing that in any district where a Republican was opposed by an antiwar candidate, Tammany would not field a Democratic contender. LaGuardia won handily.*

———

A few days after the congressional elections, news of the armistice was flashed to America (prematurely, as it turned out). The country had gone to war singing; "Over There," written by Broadway's George M. Cohan, had become virtually a second national anthem. Its promise that "the Yanks are

---

* The following year he was elected president of the city Board of Aldermen, causing him to be touted as the next mayor. But it was not to be. The sudden death of his wife and newborn baby caused him to temporarily abandon politics. Later he would run successfully for Congress in a predominantly Italian district uptown in East Harlem. In 1933 he was elected mayor of New York City.

coming" raised Allied morale. The war would end on the same high note. Deliriously happy crowds danced through the streets of New York and every other city. America had won the war for the Allies—not by its battlefield accomplishments but by shipping more than 1.5 million men to France, with millions more in the pipeline behind them. The American reinforcements convinced the British and French to hang on and the Germans that it was useless to go on fighting a war that could not be won. From an organizational standpoint, the U.S. military leaders had done a first-class job. Fears about resistance to the draft had proven groundless. When the United States declared war, it had about two hundred thousand soldiers, counting the half-trained National Guard. During the war, 4 million men would serve in uniform, 70 percent of them draftees. Had the war lasted into 1919, the U.S. Army would have become the largest combat force on the western front, and its troops would have spearheaded the Allied offensives.

In 1903 the War Department had created a European-style general staff. Under its auspices, the Army had been transformed from a frontier constabulary to the nucleus of a modern army. In 1917 it quickly became a mass army. In previous wars, regiments had been raised by the states and commanded by amateur officers. In 1917 the federal government controlled the Army and saw that it was led by men who had passed through professional training courses. Even a national hero as prestigious as former president Roosevelt was not allowed to raise a volunteer force. The World War I structure would continue to provide the organizational basis for the Army through World War II, Korea, and the Cold War. The Army also benefited from having Newton D. Baker as its civilian head. Some historians rate him as the greatest secretary of war the United States ever had.

No similar revamping of U.S. domestic security took place. America fought the war with no equivalent of MI5 or MI6. It failed to coordinate the activities of the Secret Service with the Bureau of Investigation and compounded that error by utilizing untrained civilian volunteers. In many respects, it was easier to reform the Army than the security police. The military was a hierarchical body presided over at the top by a cabinet officer, and below him by generals. Most of the senior officers were West Pointers or had at least absorbed the learning and traditions of that institution. The general staff—a German invention—was established to study war scientifically and promulgate doctrines and methods that would guide military officers at all levels. Its officers were rotated in from troop duty and returned to their regiments after a period of time to impart what they had learned. All senior Army officers were required to undergo advanced training.

U.S. security forces did not even have the rudiments of such a system. In World War I, no single cabinet officer directed the security forces. The secretaries of war, the navy, and the treasury; the attorney general; and the undersecretary of state all had a piece of the action. The municipal police forces were controlled by local politicians—although in New York, Colonel Biddle managed to bridge the gap between the Army and the NYPD. There was no law enforcement equivalent of the Army general staff or prescribed career for higher-ranking officers. No common doctrine permeated American law enforcement. Politics, sometimes of the worst type, often influenced decision making.

Given America's inexperience at security matters, it was inevitable that if it became involved in a world war, many mistakes would be made and many excesses would occur. If, as most people believed at the time, the war was to uphold freedom, the excesses were simply the price we had to pay to ensure victory. The real criticism of American security in World War I is that we did not learn from the experience.

4

FROM RED SCARE TO BLACK CHAMBER

1919–1930

In November 1918 anyone witnessing the armistice celebrations might have believed that it presaged an era of national unity. A few months later, the troops began returning from France. However, before the victory parades could be held, the country was in turmoil. A wave of strikes swept the nation. One of the most turbulent areas was the Pacific Northwest, long a center of IWW activity. In February 1919 its principal city, Seattle, faced a challenge new to America—a general strike. Before that, individual unions had struck; now all the city's labor organizations announced that they would simultaneously cease work to show solidarity with striking shipyard workers. The Seattle mayor, Ole Hanson, was a political progressive who had been elected with strong labor support. Confronted with the possibility that the city would be left without light and power, or trucks to deliver food and other essential supplies, he telegraphed Secretary of War Newton Baker: "Will you furnish troops? Wire quick." Baker immediately dispatched soldiers to Seattle, while the mayor began augmenting the security forces by swearing in volunteer policemen. Though sixty thousand workers walked off their jobs, the shutdown was not total: some workers continued to maintain essential services. Across the country, politicians and newspapers denounced the strikers. Some of the most severe condemnations came from leaders of the American Federation of Labor. After five days, the strikers went back to work and life returned to normal.

Mayor Hanson, who resembled Uncle Sam without the whiskers, was hailed as a national hero and flooded with invitations to speak. He began traveling to other cities to warn of the danger to America of the IWW and other "Bolsheviks." On April 28, during one of Hanson's out-of-town journeys, a package wrapped in brown paper and addressed to the mayor arrived at Seattle City Hall. A clerk who handled it noticed that it was leaking fluid. When police examined it, they found that it contained a wooden tube filled with an acid detonator and TNT.

The next day, when a similar paper-wrapped package arrived at the Atlanta home of a former senator it exploded, blowing off both hands of a maid and badly burning the senator's wife. In New York at 2 a.m. the following morning, Charles Caplan was reading his newspaper as he journeyed home to Harlem on the C train after working the late shift at the main post office. When he noticed a story about the bomb that had exploded in Georgia, it rang a bell. The package was described as seven inches long and three inches wide and marked "sample," with the return address of New York's Gimbels department store and an alpine mountaineer logo on the wrapping. A few hours earlier, he had handled similar parcels. Though marked first class, they had lacked sufficient postage, so he set them aside. Caplan got off the train at the next stop and headed back to work, where he located sixteen of the packages. The NYPD bomb squad disarmed all of them. The individuals to whom they had been sent constituted a who's who of prominent Americans, including the super rich Jack Morgan and John D. Rockefeller. Among the judiciary, one was addressed to Supreme Court justice Oliver Wendell Holmes, who had written the court's decision upholding the Espionage Act; another was intended for Chicago federal judge Kenesaw Mountain Landis, who had sentenced the IWW defendants to prison. Three other packages were addressed to members of President Wilson's cabinet. Locally, Mayor Hylan and Commissioner Enright had been targeted. Hylan had issued an order banning the display of a red flag in New York City, and Enright's cops had enforced it. Eighteen more packages were intercepted in various stages of delivery before they could explode.

The timing of the bomb mailings indicated that they were meant to be received around May 1. May Day was the traditional time when radicals paraded, carrying red banners, to celebrate their beliefs. Sometimes the occasion was marked by violence. With headlines screaming about bombs, many predicted that May Day 1919 would witness radical uprisings. In New York an evening rally was scheduled at Madison Square Garden to protest the conviction of Tom Mooney, who was serving a life sentence for setting a bomb at the 1916 San Francisco preparedness parade. Outside the Garden, a group of U.S. servicemen carrying an American flag threw rocks and attempted to enter the building, but they were dispersed by the police. In Boston, when police tried to stop a crowd of radicals parading without a permit, a riot broke out. Two officers were shot, a captain died of a heart attack, and a hundred marchers were arrested. In Cleveland, war veterans disrupted marchers who were carrying a red flag. A melee ensued, leaving one participant dead and more than a hundred under arrest.

In 1917 the Bolsheviks had seized power in Russia. By 1919 Bavaria and Hungary were under the control of Communist regimes. Leftist mobs rioted in the streets of Italian and British cities. One band of protesters hoisted the red flag over the Glasgow City Hall and held it until they were ousted by the Army. In the United States, many people saw the wave of strikes, bombings, and riots as the harbinger of revolution.

In retrospect, it is difficult to understand how Americans could have been so frightened of a Red uprising. American radicals were few in number and, with the exception of fringe groups such as the IWW, confined their actions to rhetorical flourishes. The events in Europe had taken place following four years of total war that left even the victors battered, bloody, and nearly bankrupt. The United States had only been in the war for a year and a half, and its losses were minimal. When it emerged from the conflict, it was the richest country on earth. It went from being a debtor nation to being a creditor one, and New York City replaced London as the financial capital of the world. However, what appears easy to discern in hindsight is not always so clear at the time. The war altered the calculations by which most Americans had lived. The wartime attitudes of "Everything for the boys in uniform" and "Live today, for tomorrow you might die" had erased the sexual mores of the Victorian era. Inflation upset the balance between classes, with blue-collar workers in munitions factories and shipyards earning more than educated professionals. The nation's top political journalist, Mark Sullivan, later would claim that the beginning of many college professors' tilt to the left occurred when their real incomes declined significantly.

A confluence of other events also upset the general social equilibrium. Shortly before the armistice a devastating flu epidemic swept the world, killing upward of 25 million people. In America the death toll numbered well over five hundred thousand. In New York City each morning, health department crews drove their wagons through the streets, calling to residents, "Bring out your dead." In 1920, after national prohibition took effect, the corner saloon, which had been a center of neighborhood life, passed from the scene, to be replaced by illegal speakeasies.

Even before the discovery of the postal bombs, the NYPD had been cracking down on radicals. In March the Bomb Squad, commanded by Sgt. James Gegan, raided the Union of Russian Workers on lower Fifth Avenue and took into custody 162 individuals found on the scene. The cops tore up copies of the union publication, known as "The Little Red Book," because they claimed it urged violence. At headquarters the police released 158 of their prisoners; the remaining four, who admitted to believing in anarchist principles, were held.

Security officers suspected that the guiding force behind the bombing and riots was the Bolshevik government of Russia. In January 1919 it had appointed Ludwig C. A. K. Martens as its representative in the United States. When he presented his credentials to the U.S. State Department, it declined to recognize him or his government. Like the Germans in 1914, Martens knew where the power lay, and he opened up offices in a building on Fortieth Street west of Sixth Avenue in Manhattan. His government might have been Marxist, but it supplied him with $200 million (on the order of $3 billion today) to operate in the land of capitalism. Martens proceeded like a cautious bureaucrat rather than a revolutionary firebrand. While some Bolsheviks openly declared that they intended to seize power in the United States, Martens studiously avoided making provocative statements when he addressed leftist meetings. Instead, he concentrated on the task of securing diplomatic recognition for the Soviet state.

During the war, the MID* had vied with the Justice Department's Bureau of Investigation for leadership of the internal security forces. If Colonel Van Deman had been available, he might have taken a major role in combating

---

* In 1918, when it became the second section of the General Staff, it received the title by which it would henceforth be known, G-2.

the "Red menace" by the sheer force of his knowledge and personality, but he was in France heading U.S. security at the Paris Peace Conference. In that capacity, he again worked with Colonel Dansey, who was performing a similar duty for the British.* Gen. Marlborough Churchill was also in France part of the time. Even when he was in Washington, though, he operated less aggressively. His boss, Secretary of War Baker, did not favor the Army again assuming a major role in domestic security. Not all of the MID got the message. In November 1918, volunteer Bureau of Investigation/MID agent #650 Archie Stevenson had compiled a report on radicals, declaring that "without question . . . there is an organized conspiracy to overthrow the present form of the American government."[1] Of course, he was right, at least in a narrow sense. People like Bill Haywood did not shrink from urging violence to overthrow the existing political system. But did the conspirators number a thousand people in a few scattered fringe groups, or a hundred thousand members of a highly organized force? Did they have fifty guns or fifty thousand? What was lacking was a factual analysis of the threat. In January 1919, testifying before a U.S. Senate Committee chaired by Lee Overman of North Carolina, Stevenson declared that sedition was common among U.S. professors, particularly those in the fields of sociology, economics, and history. He provided the committee with the names of prominent leftists he considered security threats, such as Jane Addams, Morris Hillquit, Scott Nearing, and Stevenson's bête noire, Roger Baldwin. The *New York Times* characterized the list as a "Who's Who in pacifism and radicalism."[2]

It was a long leap, though, to conclude that someone who was a pacifist or radical wanted to overthrow the U.S. government. In 1912 Addams had supported Teddy Roosevelt for president over a strong Socialist candidate, Eugene Debs. In 1919, when the left-wing Socialists went over to Communism, they had to form two separate parties because they could not agree among themselves. The Communist Party was directed by foreign-born individuals, while the rival Communist Labor Party was led by the matinée idol of American radicalism, John Reed. When the then-twenty-four-year-old, clean-cut Harvard graduate first appeared at the 1913 strike in Paterson,

---

* In the postwar period, Van Deman would assume the role of gray eminence of U.S. domestic security. After his retirement as a major general in 1929, he continued to operate a private intelligence network out of his home in San Diego until his death in 1952.

New Jersey, he looked so out of place among men like Carlo Tresca that he was suspected of being a police spy. But he soon convinced them of his bona fides and the following year turned up in Ludlow, Colorado. In 1919 Morris Hillquit remained with the Socialist Party, headed by Norman Thomas. Neither man advocated overthrowing the government. Roger Baldwin never joined the Communists or the Socialists. In later years, he would furnish information on suspected Communists to the FBI and expel Elizabeth Gurley Flynn from the ACLU board of directors because she was an admitted Communist.

Stevenson's testimony brought him a rebuke from Secretary Baker, who denied that Stevenson had ever been associated with MID/G-2. Baker noted that some of the people on the list "were individuals of great distinction, exalted purity of purpose, and a lifetime devotion to the highest interests of America and mankind," singling out Jane Addams for particular praise. Senator Overman fired back that it was G-2 that had suggested Stevenson be called as an expert witness.

The fallout from his testimony ended Stevenson's association with federal government agencies; it did not stop his activities. He was a member of the Union League Club, whose president was Charles Evans Hughes (former governor of New York, former associate justice of the Supreme Court, and 1916 Republican nominee for president). Stevenson persuaded Hughes to name him chairman of a committee to study the activity of "Reds" in New York State. In March his committee issued a report calling on local authorities to take action. In response, the New York State legislature appointed a joint committee chaired by Republican senator Clayton Lusk. The state attorney general was appointed chief counsel, though the guiding force was the associate counsel, Archie Stevenson. The committee decided to strike at what it presumed to be the heart of American radicalism. On June 12 its investigators, accompanied by New York City and state police, executed a search warrant at Ludwig Martens's Soviet Bureau on West Fortieth Street. They seized records and a red flag from his office and took into custody several of those present. Instead of taking the prisoners to a police station, the officers transported them to City Hall, where the Lusk Committee was in session. There, Stevenson and committee investigators questioned Martens and the others about their activities.

The Department of Justice took a different approach to the alleged threats than Baker's War Department. The change was the reflection of the new leadership at Justice. Thomas Gregory was no longer attorney general. In March, President Wilson had appointed A. Mitchell Palmer to the post. Palmer seemed a strange choice to be the country's chief law enforcement officer at such a time. In 1913, as a Pennsylvania congressman, Palmer had turned down the secretary of war post because of his Quaker beliefs. Before 1917 he had been opposed to America's entry into the war. In his first days in office, he did not give a clear indication of what his policies would be. A. Bruce Bielaski, head of the Bureau of Investigation, had incurred considerable criticism for the way the "slacker drives" had been conducted. So when Palmer took over, Bielaski was replaced by William Flynn, former chief of the U.S. Secret Service.* In that job he had objected to the extralegal tactics of the MID and the APL. With the pacifist Palmer and the professional cop Flynn in charge, it might have been thought that the Justice Department would operate with due regard for legality. But with bombs exploding and riots in the streets, the public expected it to act vigorously.

As assistant director of the bureau, Chief Flynn named Frank Burke, the former Secret Service agent who had snatched Dr. Albert's briefcase. The key figure in the department's domestic security operations was a twenty-four-year-old attorney named J. Edgar Hoover, who headed what was at first called the Radical Division and later the General Intelligence Division (GID). Hoover was not a professional policeman or soldier, nor was he one of the Ivy League aristocrats who had performed intelligence work during the war. He came from a Washington civil service family and held a night law school degree. Only twenty-two when America entered the war, and a former captain of his high school ROTC unit, Hoover had not volunteered for military service. Instead he took a job at the Department of Justice alien property section (headed by A. Mitchell Palmer), which gave him a draft deferment. As head of the radical section, Hoover was authorized to coordinate information gathered by G-2, ONI, the State Department, and local police. While attending law school Hoover had worked at the Library of Congress, where

---

* Bielaski did not stop sleuthing. In the 1920s, while conducting a private investigation in Mexico, he was kidnapped by bandits. He demonstrated his athletic prowess by freeing himself from his bonds and escaping.

he learned how to synthesize vast amounts of information. So he went to work compiling a card index file of sixty thousand suspected radicals.*

Attorney General Palmer had been one of the cabinet members to whom a bomb had been mailed. In June he received one by personal delivery. On the night of June 2, he and his family were upstairs in their home on R Street in Northwest Washington preparing for bed. Suddenly they heard a thump at the front door, followed by a huge explosion. A man carrying a bomb up the steps had tripped, setting off the device and blowing himself up. Across the street, Palmer's neighbors, Assistant Secretary of the Navy Franklin D. Roosevelt and his wife, Eleanor, had just entered their home after parking their car in a nearby garage. Had they arrived a minute later, they might have been killed. Roosevelt came out of his house, stepped across mangled body parts that had landed on his porch, and ran over to help Palmer. When he returned to his own residence, the most noteworthy information he thought to convey to Eleanor was that he hadn't realized that Palmer was a Quaker until the shaken attorney general began "thee and thouing me all over the place." That same night, there were seven more bombings across the country. Among the targets were the homes of the mayor of Cleveland and judges in Massachusetts, New Jersey, Pennsylvania, and New York City. The country grew even more alarmed. A New York Times editorial asked, "Has the gift of skill and genius in ferreting out criminals been denied to our present day detectives?"[3]

As the summer of 1919 wore on, there were race riots in Chicago, Washington, and other cities. In September the Boston police went on strike, leaving the streets to mobs of looters and rowdies, who were not brought under control until Governor Calvin Coolidge ordered out the National Guard. Coolidge's action brought him the same acclaim that Seattle mayor Hanson had received. Palmer's seeming hesitancy in dealing with the various threats drew increasing criticism in the press. Unknown to the journalists, the attorney general was ready to act. Mitchell had become convinced that America was in the early stages of a revolution. His operating philosophy became the same one military intelligence had followed during the war—defeat the enemy and don't worry about the legal technicalities. While some writers attribute Mitchell's policy to

* Some accounts credit Hoover with instituting the card index system to keep track of suspects. It had actually been developed by Britain's MI5 and taught to MID by Colonel Dansey. Hoover's contribution was his skill at using the system, which under his direction grew to 200,000 names.

his narrow escape from death, his actions also coincided with his ambitions. He reasoned that a vigorous crackdown on radicals would bring him the Democratic nomination for president in 1920. So he approved a plan, prepared by young Hoover, to strike a major blow at U.S. radicals. It authorized the Bureau of Investigation, assisted by other federal agencies and local police, to round up individuals deemed security threats. Those seized who were aliens would be deported; the rest would be turned over to local authorities for prosecution under state criminal anarchism and syndicalism laws.

The first major target of the Department of Justice was the Union of Russian Workers in New York. It had publicly proclaimed the necessity of a revolution in the United States, though it did not move beyond talk. While many members were activists, others simply attended classes on academic subjects or used its library. November 7, 1919, was the second anniversary of the Bolshevik revolution in Russia, so it was anticipated that the URW would be celebrating. That night Chief Flynn and Sergeant Gegan led a raiding party that swarmed through the building, searching files and asking people, "Are you a citizen?" In the end, two hundred individuals were arrested and taken to Department of Justice headquarters in the city. Similar raids were carried out on the organization's offices in eleven other cities. New York police also arrested a number of people in their homes. Over a period of several days, more suspects were rounded up. Among those seized were Alexander Berkman and Emma Goldman. Of the 750 people arrested, 249 were marked for deportation, including Berkman and Goldman. Those slated for expulsion were held at Ellis Island in New York. Early on the morning of December 20, they began ascending the gangplank of an old troop transport, the *Buford*, which the press labeled "the Soviet Ark." Still exhibiting wear and tear from its wartime services, the vessel could never have been mistaken for a luxury cruise ship. When a reporter called out sarcastically to Goldman, "Merry Christmas, Emma," she thumbed her nose at him. Berkman, standing on the deck, noticed Flynn and J. Edgar Hoover among the crowd on the dock and shouted, "We will come back and when we do we'll get you"; Goldman shook her fist at them. Both lawmen laughed.

After nearly a month at sea the *Buford* landed at a Finnish port, from which the deportees made their way into Russia. Goldman and Berkman did not find the Soviet state to their liking. They were anarchists, not Communists—

rebels against the state whether it was run by capitalists or commissars. In Soviet Russia they were shocked to find that Lenin's government had imprisoned or shot leftists as well as reactionaries. When Goldman complained to him personally, she was ordered to be quiet. Within two years Goldman and Berkman left to start a life of exile in various European countries.

Goldman met further disillusionment in the West. When she began to write and speak about Soviet repression, most of her radical friends condemned her. Even Roger Baldwin, so devoted to civil rights in America, donned rose-colored glasses when viewing the USSR. In the 1920s, in a letter to Goldman, he stated, "I do not protest against them as much as I do against similar evils in other countries, for the simple reason that such protests might be used by the common enemies of us all, the capitalist and imperialist press."[4] Goldman's biographer would later write, "She was all too aware that Baldwin's letters revealed that virulent moral schizophrenia which caused its victims to cry out in righteous rage against oppression in the West and to remain respectfully silent before much worse in the East."[5]

While Goldman was still in the USSR, John Reed, under indictment in the United States for sedition, turned up in the Soviet Union as well. In October 1920 he died of typhus and was buried in a wall of the Kremlin. Bill Haywood also arrived. Goldman rebuked Haywood for sticking his organization with the cost of his forfeited bail, likening him to the captain of a sinking ship who abandons his crew. Haywood claimed that he could help the cause of revolution in America better from Russia, and that the Communist Party would pay the bail. As it turned out, he didn't, and they didn't either. After Lenin's death in 1924, the new rulers of the USSR had no time for Haywood, and he sank into homesickness, depression, and alcoholism. He might have emulated Berkman and Goldman and left Russia, but there was no place for him to go without risking arrest and extradition to America, where prison awaited. After he died in 1928, half of his ashes joined Reed's in a wall of the Kremlin, and the other half were shipped to a cemetery in Chicago where the men hanged for the Haymarket bombing were buried.

With the forced departure of Berkman and Goldman, Carlo Tresca became the leading anarchist in America. Curiously, not only did he escape conviction in the IWW case, but he was not deported in 1919. Many leftists suspected that he had been cut some slack because he had provided information to the government. For the rest of his life, the Communists and some anarchists would vilify him as a police informer.

In general, the public reaction to the deportations of Berkman and Goldman was favorable. They had long been regarded as menaces. After Hoover became famous, many writers, aware of his genius at public relations, suggested that he had put them on the deportation list for the publicity their names would generate. As a practical matter, the American public would never have accepted any list that did not include them.

Hoover's next move was to apply for warrants to arrest three thousand more individuals designated as security threats. His plan was to stage a number of simultaneous raids across the country in order to bag the whole lot in one fell swoop. On January 2, 1920, squads of law enforcement officers carried out raids in thirty-three cities across twenty-three states, seizing as many as four thousand alleged radicals.* In some instances, government undercover agents who held administrative positions in the radical groups had arranged for meetings to be held on the 2nd, to make it easier to seize those on the wanted list. Once again, New York was a center of activity. In a typical incident, federal agents and police stormed a Communist meeting on East Tenth Street shouting, "Hands up!"

Although the initial press reaction was again favorable, some prominent Americans began to question the government's actions. They wondered why, if the arrestees were preparing a revolution, raids carried out in thirty-three cities had turned up only three guns and no bombs. Some criticism came from establishment circles. Charles Evans Hughes chaired a committee of the New York Bar Association, which issued a highly critical report. A group of professors led by Harvard's Felix Frankfurter and Roscoe Pound condemned Justice's tactics. On the other side, the noted legal scholar John Henry Wigmore of Northwestern Law School declared that "Mr. Palmer saved the country."[6] Former president Theodore Roosevelt had died in 1919, but his son, Col. Theodore Roosevelt Jr., just back from frontline service in France, was groomed to replace him. Already he had been elected to the

---

* The precise figure varies because some local police departments, such as the one in Chicago, jumped the gun on January 1 when they made over two hundred arrests. In addition, people not on the arrest list who were found on the raided premises were hauled in. In other places, friends and family of the prisoners who came to local jails to inquire about them were locked up as suspected radicals.

New York State Assembly, where Theodore Sr. had started his own career. To the surprise of the Republican leadership, when the assembly voted to expel five Socialist members, young Roosevelt objected on the grounds that it was unconstitutional to deprive duly elected legislators of their positions. The Speaker then proceeded to read aloud to the assembly passages from the writings of Teddy Roosevelt Sr., which he used to contrast the "Americanism" of the father with the "un-Americanism" of the son.[7]

The Department of Labor, which then controlled immigration matters, refused to approve many of the Justice Department's deportation requests, opening a dispute between the two cabinet departments. The previous September, President Wilson had suffered a stroke and was unable to fulfill his duties, so no one possessed the authority to resolve the intragovernmental conflict. Even before his stroke, Wilson had been too preoccupied with other matters to administer the government. Shortly after the armistice, accompanied by his wife, he went off to make a triumphal tour of Europe and then got bogged down at the Paris Peace Conference. On his return, he stumped the country advocating support for his League of Nations proposal. Wilson's stroke incapacitated him for the last eighteen months of his term. During that time, depending on which version of history one accepts, the country was either leaderless or under the control of Mrs. Wilson, whose education had ended after tenth grade. Despite her lack of experience in government, she was not hesitant about making major decisions. Using the excuse that the president was too ill to receive visitors, including members of his cabinet, she would relay their requests to him. Then she would emerge from the president's quarters and give them his answers. It is widely believed that she simply made the decisions herself, often dictating high-level appointments based on her personal predilections. Anyone who offended her was out, and those who flattered her were in.*

---

* The British ambassador was one of those who ran afoul of the First Lady. In 1918, at a Washington social gathering, a British military attaché had jokingly posed the question, "When the President proposed to Mrs. Galt [Wilson's wife's name from a previous marriage], what is the first thing she did?" To which the punchline was, "She fell out of bed." The attaché was quickly sent back to England. In 1919, when former foreign secretary Edward Grey (now Viscount Grey of Falloden) arrived as the new ambassador, he brought the offending attaché along. The American government asked for his withdrawal. Instead, Grey attached the man to his personal entourage, making him immune from the host country's authority. Mrs. Wilson was infuriated, and thanks to her influence, Grey was not allowed to present his credentials at the White House. Without being able to do so, he could not function as an ambassador; therefore he had no choice but to return home. In a period of world crisis, when British-American cooperation was vital, the First Lady and the noble lord chose to behave like spiteful children.

Palmer, Flynn, and Hoover countered criticism of their operations by claiming that on May Day, 1920, the Bolshevik revolution in America would definitely commence. But despite some disturbances on May 1, nothing major happened. The failure of an uprising to occur and the increasing criticism of the government's heavy-handed tactics should have spelled the end of what came to be known as the First Red Scare. The presidential aspirations of A. Mitchell Palmer, billed by his admirers as "the Fighting Quaker" and by his detractors as "the Quaking Fighter," were not to be realized. In July 1920 the Democratic convention, meeting in San Francisco, decisively rejected his bid for the nomination. Instead, it chose Ohio governor James Cox, a man who even party leaders believed possessed minimal talents. Franklin Roosevelt, who had been named assistant secretary of the navy because Theodore Roosevelt had once held the job, continued to follow in his cousin's footsteps, receiving the nomination for vice president. In June, at the Republican convention in Chicago, a group of leaders meeting in a smoke-filled hotel room had steered the nomination to a dark horse, Ohio senator Warren G. Harding. On the convention floor, there had been a boom for Governor Coolidge, the hero of the Boston police strike, as Harding's running mate. Since vice president was regarded as an unimportant job, the convention managers allowed the delegates to have their way.

The election would serve as a referendum on whether the United States should join the League of Nations, with Cox in favor and Harding basically opposed. In the larger sense, it would resolve the debate between those who wanted it to assume Britain's role as the world's leading power and those who wished America to remain aloof from European politics. In November Harding won in a landslide. As a result, the United States remained outside the League.[*]

---

[*] However, the United States did not retreat to isolationism, as is sometimes assumed. Before 1914 America played a role in world affairs, and its armed forces policed parts of China, Central America, and the Caribbean. It continued to do so after 1920, but it did not occupy the dominant world position. The attempt of weakened Britain and France to do so, through their control of the League of Nations, was a failure. In the 1920s the isolationists were mostly kept at a distance by Republican administrations that were more responsive to Wall Street than Western Populists. Not until the 1930s, when the Depression breathed new life into Populism, did the isolationists exercise significant influence over U.S. foreign policy.

In September 1920, as the presidential candidates campaigned and the Red Scare appeared to be receding, it was revived with a vengeance. The center of the new world financial capital was the corner of Wall and Broad Streets in New York. Located at 23 Wall was the citadel of American finance, the House of Morgan. Across Broad Street was the New York Stock Exchange, the gigantic casino in which hundreds of millions were bet daily and for-tunes made and lost. Across from 23 Wall was the U.S. Sub Treasury, with a statue of George Washington on the steps in front of it, marking the site where the first president had taken the oath of office.

On Thursday the 16th, with the noon bells of historic Trinity Church sounding, a horse-drawn wagon parked across the street from the Morgan headquarters exploded, sending five hundred pounds of shrapnel flying in all directions. Windows fell in at the stock exchange and were blown out as high as the twelfth floor of other buildings. The stock exchange president walked quickly across the trading floor (running was not allowed) to ring the bell, ending operations for the day. It was lunchtime, and the streets had been jammed. Thirty-eight people died as a result of the blast; hundreds were injured. Some were literally blown to pieces. A woman's head, with her hat still on it, was found stuck to the wall of the Morgan building.* If someone wanted to launch an attack against Ameri-can capitalism, there was no more symbolic place to do so. The method and timing indicated that the explosion was also meant to cause the max-imum number of casualties.

For fifty years Wall Street had been denounced by individuals as diverse as Emma Goldman and William Jennings Bryan. The House of Morgan probably drew the most opprobrium of any financial group. In July 1915 the German sympathizer Erich Muenter had shot Jack Morgan in protest against the bank's support for the Allies. Whoever mailed the bombs in April 1919 had included Mr. Morgan on their gift list. Thus, no one should have been surprised at what happened in September 1920. Some preparations had been made for a possible attack against the country's financial center, but they were outdated. In the late nineteenth century, the NYPD drew a "deadline" around the district that criminals were forbidden to cross upon

---

* The dents from the shrapnel were left there afterward as a reminder of the event.

pain of arrest (and often a beating). The deadline had been officially discontinued around the turn of the century; still, cops kept a close eye on the area. However, their emphasis was on conventional crooks, not terrorists. In 1913 the Wall Street powers had persuaded the U.S. government to station soldiers on nearby Governors Island, arguing that it was necessary to protect the financial district from mob violence. On September 16 the regular police complement in the area had been reduced to cover parades and strikes. The officer who normally stood in front of the Sub Treasury had been detailed away (luckily for him, because if he had been at his post, he would surely have been killed or maimed). Following the blast, seventeen hundred cops poured into the area in an ad hoc fashion, arriving in commandeered cars and trucks. The police commissioner and other top brass on the scene did not follow any coherent response plan.

It is not clear that so many officers were needed in one small area, but seventeen hundred were not enough for the official in charge of the Sub Treasury. Whether in fear of looting or the prospect of a Bolshevik army descending on Wall Street, the official put in a hurried call to Governors Island demanding troops. Within forty minutes a regiment of infantry, with loaded rifles and fixed bayonets, double-timed into Wall Street. Legally it was doubtful that a Treasury official had the right to deploy U.S. soldiers into the streets of a city (or to move troops at all). Had the bombers been seasoned practitioners of irregular warfare—a skill that, after six years of war and revolution, was not in short supply—they might have set some secondary devices timed to explode after police and soldiers arrived on the scene. Apparently, no one in the security forces considered that possibility.

The investigative phase of the case began almost immediately. Postal officials found that sometime between the 11:30 and 11:58 a.m. pick-ups, five circulars had been deposited in a mailbox that was a two-minute walk from the blast. Each contained a slightly different message, such as:

> *Remember we will not tolerate any longer*
> *Free the political prisoners*
> *Or it will be sure death for all of you*
> *American anarchist fighters*[8]

Similar circulars had been left at some earlier bombing scenes, including Attorney General Palmer's house. Chief Flynn, who arrived by express train from Washington, declared it was the work of "Red Anarchists," and he and Hoover announced it was finally the signal for the start of the Bolshevik uprising. The next day, editorials all over America took heart in the fact that the statue of George Washington was still standing. Financial districts in other parts of the country were cordoned off, and security was increased at government buildings and corporate headquarters. Many top business figures and public officials began surrounding themselves with armed guards.

The Secret Service, the Bureau of Investigation, G-2, and the NYPD all put forth great effort to solve the Wall Street bombing, usually without coordinating with each other. The NYPD had the local contacts and the most manpower, but it was not playing with its first team. Inspector Tunney was no longer a member of the department. After his return from army service, he had been reduced to the rank of captain and assigned to chasing pickpockets. The man who for four years had fought the top agents of the German Empire now had to spend his time dealing with petty thieves. Only forty-five, Tunney had decided to retire and open a private detective agency. His replacement was Sergeant Gegan. In the hierarchy, an inspector held a position in the police equivalent to a colonel in the army, while a sergeant was just a sergeant. One of Gegan's colleagues in the investigation was the mayor's brother-in-law, Sgt. Irving O'Hara, who had no hesitancy about advising the top brass.*

There were many lines of inquiry for cops to follow. The horse pulling the wagon, an old, dark bay, must have been kept somewhere in the New York area. Some stable owner was likely to notice if a horse of that description had suddenly disappeared around September 16. The horse's shoes found at the scene could have led to the man who made them and in turn to the man who purchased them. A farrier on Elizabeth Street in Little Italy reported that he had made the horseshoes. Another farrier, on Chambers Street, claimed the shoes had come from his shop. A few blocks from the

---

* When Hylan took office in January 1919, he appointed Deputy Commissioner Frederick Bugher as commissioner. Twenty-three days later, he summoned Bugher to his office and summarily fired him. According to department rumor, when Sergeant O'Hara had attempted to tell the commissioner what to do, he had been rebuffed, thereby displeasing the mayor.

bomb site, a street cleaner found a knob from a safe that detectives theorized was used to house the explosives in the wagon. Efforts to link the knob to a safe came to nothing. Federal agents used explosives expert Walter Scheele to assist them in the investigation. A few years earlier, as a reserve major in the kaiser's army, he had been helping Rintelen blow up New York. Someone in the busy Wall Street area—probably several someones—must have seen the wagon being driven to the Morgan headquarters. Various witnesses reported that it had a business address on the side, but they provided half a dozen different companies' names. The driver was described as appearing Italian, Jewish, or Spanish.

Just before the explosion, a crew of government porters had been carrying hundreds of boxes filled with gold ingots from the vault in the Sub Treasury building to the nearby assay office. At noon they had quit for lunch and closed the doors to the Sub Treasury. Investigators looked into the theory that the explosion was meant to cover a robbery, possibly by men disguised as police or guards who could take advantage of the confusion to snatch millions. Detectives did not hear any rumbles from underworld informers, suggesting that professional crooks were not involved. The bomb might have been set by revolutionaries as part of a robbery to obtain money to advance their cause, although, since no one attempted to steal the gold on the 16th, robbery seemed an unlikely motive.

Among the odd characters who always pop up in major investigations like this one was Edwin P. Fischer (aka Edward Fisher), a forty-two-year-old lawyer and former tennis champion who had told friends weeks before the blast to stay away from Wall Street until after September 16 because sixty thousand pounds of explosives were going to blow up. Fischer, a former mental patient, was taken into custody in Toronto and brought back to New York. He arrived at Grand Central Station wearing two complete business suits, one on top of the other, with a white tennis costume underneath; he told reporters that he always wanted to be prepared for a game. As he was being led through the station, he stopped to pick up three discarded cigars, declaring that although he didn't smoke, he would keep them anyway. The escorting officers immediately confiscated them, expecting to find a message to Fischer from his confederates. On examination they turned out to be just cheap cigars. Nothing was found linking Fischer to any particular group, and the only explanation he or his family could give for his prediction was that he possessed psychic powers.[*]

In 1919 the *Times* editorial that asked whether present-day detectives no longer had the gift of skill and genius might well have been titled "Bring Back William Burns." The "Great Detective" had been in his office at the nearby Woolworth Building when the explosion occurred. Within a few minutes he arrived at the scene. Before World War I, he had been much admired. In 1913 when Sir Arthur Conan Doyle, creator of Sherlock Holmes, came to New York, he declared Burns to be the American equivalent of Holmes. After 1914 his reputation had suffered. He was accused of breaking into a prominent New York law firm to plant a Dictaphone. His longtime enemy, the American Federation of Labor, brought pressure that forced the state to hold a hearing on whether Burns's license should be revoked. After a prolonged investigation, he paid a hundred-dollar fine. During the period of American neutrality, Burns's private clients had included the German government. The Wall Street bombing provided an opportunity for him to restore his reputation and a means of promoting his detective business.

Announcing that he had been retained by an unnamed client, Burns posted a $50,000 reward for the capture of the bombers (a fortune in those days, and five times the amount the city of New York was putting up). His offer specifically required that to be eligible for the reward, the information had to be offered to his agency exclusively. It was generally suspected that the client was either the House of Morgan or Burns himself. Another individual who tried to insert himself into the investigation was former New York City police commissioner Arthur Woods, who through his 1916 marriage was now a member of the Morgan family. Woods lined up with Burns and reportedly supplied Morgan funds to the Burns Agency. The various investigators worked from different premises. Flynn and the bureau agents concentrated on anarchists, especially those of Italian background. Burns suspected it was Russian Communists. The NYPD did not propound a consistent theory of the case.

---

[*] In contemporary times, if a man like Fischer had emerged in connection with an investigation of a major terrorist attack, several books would be written about him in which he would be described as everything from a CIA agent to a space alien.

In August 1921, a few months after the Harding administration took over in Washington, Flynn was dismissed as bureau director and Burns was named as his replacement. J. Edgar Hoover was appointed assistant director. As an Ohioian, Burns had excellent connections with the Ohio Gang that dominated the Harding administration and was especially close to incoming attorney general Harry Daugherty. In December 1921 Burns announced that the man responsible for the bombing was a Polish anarchist named Wolf Lindenfeld who, when he was arrested in Warsaw, confessed that he had carried out the act on the orders of the Communist International. Then Lindenfeld repudiated his confession. Eventually, it was disclosed that he had once been an informer for the Burns Agency and was in Poland working on a case for them. Sergeant Gegan of the NYPD was among those who laughingly dismissed Burns's identification of Lindenfeld.

The Wall Street bombing was probably not the work of Bolsheviks because it did not fit their pattern of operation. Instead of planting bombs in the United States, they concentrated on ferreting out American industrial secrets and building disciplined cadres for the day when they could seize power. Most likely it was, as Flynn suspected, anarchists. Though an arrest was never made in the bombing, the consensus among federal investigators was that a Massachusetts group known as Galleanists—disciples of their leader, Luigi Galleani—were behind it, as well as other bombings. Galleani, educated as a lawyer, was a man of high culture who edited a small anarchist paper called *Cronaca Sovversiva* (*Subversive Comment*). Often it ran editorials that proclaimed such things as, "To hell with the Constitution." The U.S. Department of Justice labeled the paper "the most rabid, seditious and anarchistic sheet ever published in this country." In June 1919 Galleani had been deported. The Department of Justice believed that it was a Galleanist, Carlo Valdinoci, who was killed when the bomb he was carrying exploded outside Attorney General Palmer's house. Five days before the September 16 attack, two members of Galleani's group, Nicola Sacco and Bartolomeo Vanzetti, had been indicted for robbery and murder in Braintree, Massachusetts. For many years it was an article of faith among leftists that Sacco and Vanzetti were virtual saints who were framed. In 1977 Massachusetts governor Michael Dukakis issued a proclamation declaring, "Any stigma and disgrace should be forever removed from the names of Nicola Sacco and Bartolemeo

Vanzetti." Critics declared that Dukakis had "disgraced his office and his state by attempting to honor the memory of two convicted murderers." Today, most accounts of the case describe the two men as gun-toting anarchists, and the consensus of opinion is that Sacco was guilty of the murders and probably Vanzetti was, too. Even Carlo Tresca propounded this view, claiming that it had been confirmed by the chief defense lawyer in the case. The current opinion among students of the Sacco and Vanzetti case is that one of their comrades, Mario Buda (aka Mike Boda), set off the Wall Street blast, and then fled to Italy.

In the second decade of the twentieth century, America had received shock after shock. In 1914 it was the outbreak of the war. In 1917 the United States abandoned its historic policy of not becoming entangled in European quarrels and plunged into the conflict. In postwar Europe, Bolshevik revolutionaries sat in seats once occupied by kings and emperors. A weakened British Empire could no longer maintain the Pax Britannica. The safe and comfortable Victorian and Edwardian world that Americans had known was fast disappearing. Mobs carrying red flags marched through city streets, and even the police in staid old Boston went on strike. However, in the 1920s, the crisis appeared to subside. In Germany and Hungary, Communists who had temporarily seized power were ousted. The Polish army sent the invading Soviet army reeling back from the gates of Warsaw. In Italy a former Socialist turned fascist, Benito Mussolini, seized power and crushed the Communists. In Britain, short-lived Labour governments were defeated by the Conservatives.

New York thrived. In the 1920s Broadway replaced London's West End as the musical center of the English-speaking world. A former minstrel show performer named Al Jolson became the most popular singer in America. Despite Prohibition, nightclubs were packed and booze flowed freely. Jimmy Walker, who was elected mayor in 1925, was more likely to be found at the casino in Central Park than his office in City Hall. Clip joints flourished. A former rodeo rider known as Texas Guinan greeted the well-heeled customers in her nightclub with the cry, "Hello, suckers!" and the suckers loved it. With the stock market booming and everybody making money, it was assumed that the good times would roll forever. Along with bread, New York enjoyed circuses. The city was the first port of call for such world celebrities as English Channel swimmer Gertrude Ederle, Atlantic flyer Charles Lindbergh, explorer Richard Byrd, the Prince of Wales, and the beautiful Queen Marie of Romania. Vast crowds would turn out to cheer them as they were driven up Broadway. The majordomo at such events was Grover Whalen, a Tammanyite who served in the administration of Mayor Hylan. Always turned out in a silk hat and morning coat, with a boutonniere pinned in his lapel, the handsome, mustachioed Whalen looked the part of a circus ringmaster. Even if VIPs were in short supply, it did not matter— the show went on. Whalen could turn a ticker-tape parade into a major event no matter how obscure the person being honored. He simply arranged for the festivities to be held at noon, when the downtown streets would be packed with lunchgoers. When Whalen moved on to become general manager of Wanamaker's department store on lower Broadway, he continued to perform his greeter duties.

Radical doctrines ceased to hold appeal for all but a few malcontents. Immigrants became more Americanized. By the late 1920s, the shoeshine man who had come over from Slobbovia was not only playing the stock market but giving tips on it.* For a time, the Sacco and Vanzetti case in Massachusetts provided a focus for radical protest, as did the imprisonment of Tom Mooney in California. But outside of a narrow circle, people were more interested in things like stocks, cars, and fashions. Sacco and Vanzetti were executed in 1927, and Mooney remained in prison until the end of 1939.†

In 1924 William Burns would be caught up in the Teapot Dome scandal, which involved Harding administration officials, including the former secretary of the interior, accepting bribes to turn over government oil lands to

---

* Or such is the legend. According to Wall Street wizard Joseph Kennedy Sr., when his shoeshine man gave him a tip, he realized it was time to get out of the market. So he sold out just before the 1929 crash.

† The guilt or innocence of Mooney was a subject guaranteed to start heated arguments at any gathering of intellectuals. According to journalist Ernest Jerome Hopkins, a partisan of Mooney's innocence: "If you expressed the belief that the real bomber escaped, this brands you as a revolutionary and maybe *particeps criminis*; whereas if you say that Mooney and [his codefendant] Billings set off the bomb, you are thereby and therefore a slave of capital and a rotten log in the path of progress."[9] After Mooney's release from prison, he proved to be such an unappealing character that he was dropped by the Left.

private businessmen. Daugherty and Burns were indicted for using detectives to gather derogatory information on U.S. senators probing the scandal. Though Burns was not convicted, he lost his government post and his career ended in disgrace.

Hoover, who once again claimed to have no involvement in Justice Department excesses, succeeded Burns. The new director was not a man like Flynn or Burns—tough, streetwise cops familiar with the underworld in cities from New York to San Francisco. They even looked the part. One can readily imagine them, pistols in hand, kicking down the door of some thieves' den, shouting to the occupants, "Line up against the wall!" and slapping the cuffs on them. Hoover was a desk man, skilled at compiling card indexes and writing legal briefs. He had never worked a case in the field, much less kicked down a door or handcuffed a thug. Of medium height and build, other than his bulldog face, he would never have been taken for cop. Hoover owed his promotion, in part, to his friendship with former Secret Serviceman Larry Richey (then top aide to Secretary of Commerce Herbert Hoover), who recommended him to Attorney General Harlan Fiske Stone.

As a counterintelligence officer, Hoover had little experience. He had also never served in the military or visited Europe. Given his lack of background, it was not surprising that many of his assessments were often wide of the mark. For example, he reported that Harlem's Black Nationalist leader Marcus Garvey was a British agent. In fact, Garvey constantly urged the African subjects of the British Empire to revolt against their colonial masters.

The United States did not maintain diplomatic relations with the Soviet Union, so the Soviets could not flood the country with spies posing as foreign service officers. Those who did operate in America had to do so as "illegals." In 1925 Werner Rakov, a Baltic German, was sent to the United States to head the local branch of Soviet military intelligence, GRU. As a cover, he enrolled at Columbia University under the name Felix Wolf. The Soviets maintained a trading company, known as Amtorg, on Thirty-Seventh Street in Manhattan. Included in its budget was $2 million for espionage. Rakov used Amtorg as a base for spying out U.S. industrial secrets.

U.S. security agencies responded to the Soviet threat in different ways. The Bureau of Investigation, having been burned by the fallout from the Red Raids, was cautious about undertaking political investigations. Hoover's agents filed reports on Communist activity and forwarded information to state authorities for possible prosecution under anarchist and syndicalist laws.

The most aggressive federal security agency was the Office of Naval Intelligence. It was assumed in many quarters that the United States would eventually go to war against Japan. So the ONI carried out burglaries of Japanese consulates in order to photograph codebooks and spied on meetings of Japanese American groups. On the domestic scene, its agents secretly entered the headquarters of the Communist Party of America, on New York's East 125th Street, ransacking files, throwing papers on the floor, and forcibly opening the office safe. To create even more confusion, they stole checkbooks and bankbooks. Information gathered illegally by naval officers and their informants was kept in a secret file known as "the Red book."

Sometimes ONI's intelligence estimates were as amateurish as J. Edgar Hoover's. In 1919, at the height of the Red Scare, the director of ONI, Adm. Albert Niblack, issued a report that read like a dime novel. He described a nationwide terrorist plot led by Berkman, Goldman, and "several other anarchists." According to Niblack, a terrorist campaign would be perpetrated by a combination of German and Russian Jews, Mexican bandits, IWW subversives, and a Japanese master spy named Kato Kamato. He wrote, "The terror will surpass anything that ever happened to this country and the brains of the plot are already on the Pacific Coast." None of his predictions were borne out.

The capabilities of ONI were sometimes utilized for political purposes at the highest level. In 1930, when President Herbert Hoover sought to obtain some papers that he believed were damaging to him, he turned to Wall Street investment banker Lewis Strauss (later a World War II admiral and afterward President Eisenhower's secretary of commerce). Strauss was a Naval Reserve officer who maintained close contact with the Third Naval District in New York City. The district intelligence officer, Lt. Cdr. Glenn Howell, who had already led break-ins at Communist headquarters and Japanese consulates, reluctantly agreed to undertake the mission, writing in his diary, "I could find myself in a hell's brew of trouble." With the help of a former New York City police officer named Robert Peterkin, Howell made a surreptitious entry into the office of a minor functionary of the

Democratic Party. Based on Howell's report, the president was assured that the man posed no threat.

Following the armistice, high-level intelligence activity was carried out in New York City under discreet fronts. The most important was the American cipher bureau, or "Black Chamber," the organization that broke foreign countries' coded diplomatic messages.* Supported by funds from the War and State Departments, it was headed by Maj. Herbert Yardley, former chief of MI8. He directed a team of nine professional code breakers and sixteen support staff. Special Army phone lines connected the office directly with Washington.

As a young man in Indiana, Yardley had learned railroad telegraphy. In 1913, at age twenty-three, he was hired by the U.S. State Department as a $900-a-year code clerk. He spent his spare time demonstrating how easy it was to break U.S. codes. When America entered the war in 1917, Colonel Van Deman arranged for Yardley to be commissioned in the military intelligence division and put him in charge of MI8 as a captain. Impressed by his work in the Witzke and Victorica cases, Van Deman made use of Yardley at the Paris Peace Conference. Afterward Van Deman recommended that MI8 be maintained on a permanent basis. Because of a law restricting the expenditure of State Department funds in the capital, instead of being located in the District of Columbia, the Black Chamber was set up in Manhattan. Moving it there also kept it out of the sight of Congress and prying bureaucrats.†

During the 1922 Washington Naval Conference, Yardley's Black Chamber broke the Japanese diplomatic code. The decrypts revealed that Tokyo would accept more stringent limitations on the number of capital ships it was allowed, as compared to Britain and the United States. So the United States held fast in the negotiations until the Japanese diplomats caved in

---

* Black Chambers had existed in other countries for generations. The term comes from the curtained-off, candlelit rooms in which early code breakers worked. In centuries past, code breaking was carried on by a small, highly educated elite, usually clergymen or mathematicians, who sometimes passed on their skills from father to son.

† The first New York Black Chamber was located on East Thirty-Eighth Street, but in 1920 it moved to a twelve-foot-wide, four-story, sandstone townhouse at 141 East Thirty-Seventh Street. In 1923 it moved again to the eighth floor of an office building at Forty-Seventh and Vanderbilt. From a historical standpoint it was a fitting location. At Forty-Fourth and Vanderbilt there is a plaque on the outer wall of the Yale Club commemorating the 1776 execution of alumnus Nathan Hale, America's most famous spy.

and agreed to a 5-5-3 ratio. For his work, Yardley was awarded the Distinguished Service Medal and a bonus.

Yardley's salary of $7,000 a year (equal to that paid to J. Edgar Hoover as head of the Bureau of Investigation) allowed him to pursue his recreational activities. A skilled poker player and frequent visitor to New York's speakeasies, with an eye for the ladies, he found life in New York congenial. In 1929, when Henry Stimson, a distinguished New York lawyer, became secretary of state and learned of the Chamber's work, he withdrew his support for it on the grounds that "gentlemen do not read other gentlemen's mail."* The high-living Yardley found himself out of work at the start of the Depression. To earn money he wrote a book revealing the work of the Black Chamber. A bestseller in Japan, it proved extremely embarrassing to the American government. When Yardley tried to publish a sequel, the manuscript was seized by U.S. authorities.

Yardley wrote (or had ghostwritten) a novel about the Victorica case, *The Blonde Countess*, which he sold to MGM. But the resultant movie, *Rendezvous*, starring William Powell as a character based on Yardley, Binnie Barnes as the countess, and Rosalind Russell as Yardley's romantic interest, played down the code-breaking aspects in favor of making him an action hero. Hollywood realized that American audiences would not watch for two hours while some clerk did puzzles at his desk. When Yardley saw the film, he became so angry that he stormed out of the theater.†

The war had given a number of prominent New Yorkers a taste for the great game of spy and counterspy. Some liked it so much that they continued to play at it. There were also business advantages to be gained from having access to foreign intelligence. One group, known as the Room, maintained an apartment on East Sixty-Second Street, where important people met to discuss intelligence matters and to exchange information with Britain's MI6. Its circle, as members or associates, included such prominent

---

* However, Stimson did not actually make that statement until years later, when he did so to a writer helping him prepare his memoirs.

† In the 1930s Yardley strove unsuccessfully to make a living selling real estate in the Queens section of New York City. During World War II, no U.S. intelligence agency would hire him, so he went to work for the Chinese Nationalists and later the Canadians. In both jobs, pressure from the U.S. authorities caused his dismissal. In 1957 he wrote the classic *Education of a Poker Player*, a bestselling book on gambling. Yardley died in 1958.

citizens as Franklin Roosevelt, society leader Vincent Astor, publisher Nelson Doubleday, Theodore Roosevelt's son Kermit, and Rockefeller in-law (and Chase Manhattan banker) Winthrop Aldrich. On one occasion W. Somerset Maugham spoke to the members. Though a world-famous novelist, the topic was not literature but intelligence, based on his wartime services in MI6. After the armistice, MI6 had no reason for keeping a station in New York City other than to spy on the United States. To cover its operations, it closed its previous headquarters and opened a new one at a secret location. This move quickly came to the attention of J. Edgar Hoover and other American officials. While Roosevelt, Astor, and their colleagues from the Room were exchanging information with British intelligence, Hoover was writing memos denouncing the Brits.

The bursting of the Wall Street bubble in 1929 signaled the end of the good times and the onset of a long period of domestic discontent. In New York, within a few months of the crash, the city witnessed its most violent radical protest since the Tompkins Square disorders half a century earlier. As always, the police department was in the forefront. Its leader was Commissioner Grover Whalen, the former city greeter, whose qualifications for the post were minimal. Whalen owed his appointment to a police scandal. In November 1928 the murder of Arnold Rothstein had shaken the politics–organized crime alliance to its foundation. Rothstein, often referred to as the Brain or, more simply, A. R., was the nearest real-life equivalent to a movie version of Mr. Big, a man who bossed gangsters, made and broke mayors, and was always above the law. He functioned as the financial guru of organized crime, providing money for drug dealing, gambling operations, and other illegal activities. The nation at large knew him as the man who fixed the 1919 "Black Sox" World Series. Even then he was never brought to justice. His murder had not been the result of a mob war or political plot, just some messy personal business. A. R., in his arrogant way, had taken his time repaying $300,000 that he had lost in a card game. When the winners appealed to George McManus, the gambler who sponsored the game, it was incumbent upon him to secure payment from Rothstein. But A. R. kept putting him off, claiming that his money was out on bets and he would not pay until he was ready. Unless McManus, a well-respected gambler with a host of political friends, was prepared to abandon his career, there was only one course of action open to him. On the night of November 4, Rothstein walked out of his hangout at Lindy's Restaurant on Broadway, telling an associate, "McManus wants to see me," and headed for the nearby Park Central Hotel. A short time later, Rothstein stumbled out to a side door of the hotel and told an elevator operator, "I've been shot, get me a taxi." Instead he summoned hotel security to the scene, and shortly afterward police arrived. The next morning Rothstein died at the Polyclinic Hospital.

Detectives who rushed to the hotel learned that A. R. had been in room 349 with some other men. In a closet they found an expensive overcoat, which apparently had been left behind by someone in a hurry to leave. Sewn into the lining was the owner's name: George McManus.

When the shooting occurred, Mayor Jimmy Walker and his number-one girlfriend, Betty Compton, were enjoying themselves at a suburban nightclub. On the podium, orchestra leader Vincent Lopez noticed someone whisper in the mayor's ear, after which His Honor turned pale. Lopez, a big celebrity in New York at the time and personally close to Walker, went over to the mayor. Walker told him Rothstein had been shot, and "that means trouble from here on in." The mayor and his girlfriend then made a quick exit.

For a few days McManus could not be found, and police issued confusing statements about the investigation. The press and civic watchdogs were in an uproar. Finally, McManus called a detective and agreed to surrender. The arresting officer allowed him to stop at a barbershop and receive a shave and a haircut so that he would look presentable in his newspaper photos. The spectacle of the police department catering to the accused murderer added to the outcry, especially since McManus had two brothers on the force. If Tammany were to retain control of City Hall, a new police commissioner would have to be appointed—one whom the public would trust but who would not upset the politics–organized crime alliance. Because the cops were under heavy criticism, it was better that he be an outsider. Walker hit on Whalen, whose public image as a greeter was a favorable one and whose $100,000-a-year job at Wanamaker's seemed to confirm his management skills. Whalen agreed to accept the post as a matter of public duty, and Wanamaker's promised to continue to pay his salary while he was on leave.

George McManus was eventually charged with murder, but the case presented was very weak: the district attorney's court papers read like a defense brief. In any event, the public did not want a good guy like McManus jailed for killing a rat like Rothstein. What they wanted was a law enforcement cleanup, and Whalen began taking a number of highly publicized steps to improve the police. He formed a squad known as "Whalen's Whackers" to make high-profile raids. He had the headquarters building sandblasted and its gold dome regilded and illuminated at night by huge spotlights. He created an aviation unit. It was mostly public relations, but for a while it worked.

At the time of Whalen's appointment, it looked like the right move for Tammany. Mayor Walker could hardly be faulted for not realizing that a massive depression was about to hit the country and that a byproduct of it would be public disorder. Whalen, though an intelligent man, was no Arthur Woods. He was good enough for managing ticker-tape parades, fronting a department store, and bringing some good publicity to the NYPD. He was not up to reforming a corrupt department or dealing with massive civil disorder.

In 1930 the American Communists decided that the time was right for disciplined cadres to lead mass actions. Dormant party cells began to prepare for street warfare. One of their targets was organized labor. The more conservative unions were controlled by old-line AFL craft workers, others were led by dedicated Socialists, and some were run by organized crime figures. Arnold Rothstein had been instrumental in increasing the mob's hold on the city's garment trade.

To deal with the Communists, Whalen formed an intelligence unit under a veteran detective commander, Insp. Henry Bruckner. To staff it, he selected fifty recruits out of the police academy who, because they were not known as cops, could be used to infiltrate the party. In January 1930 one of a group of strikers involved in a brawl outside a Bronx cafeteria was shot by a police officer. The wounded man, Stephen Katonis, died a few days later. The Communists decided to hold a state funeral for him at their headquarters. They assigned sixteen of their members as a guard of honor to stand around Katonis's casket. Four of them were members of Inspector Bruckner's special intelligence squad. Finally, after three days, the city government invoked health laws to compel them to bury the corpse.

Next the Communists announced that they would hold a rally at Union Square on Fourteenth Street. Whalen warned the party's leaders that they could not do so without a permit, but they were defiant. At noon on March 6, a hundred thousand people arrived at the Square. There they were directed to form for a march down Broadway to City Hall. Police commanders on the scene again told them that the march would not be allowed without a permit. The protest leaders ignored them. The only change that they made in the plan was to issue orders to the marchers to halt at Ninth and Broadway and break all the windows in Wanamaker's as a salute to Whalen. The NYPD had assembled a thousand foot cops, three hundred mounted men, and a hundred motorcycle officers at the scene. When the march got under way, foot and mounted police moved in and began breaking the crowd up. But the photos of what leftists called "Whalen's Cossacks" charging into the crowd on horseback and swinging clubs appeared all over the world. Shortly after the Union Square affair, Mayor Walker decided he could dispense with Whalen's services as police commissioner and replaced him with an outstanding career cop, Chief of Detectives Edward Mulrooney.

In the mid-1930s, when Whalen was named to head a group that would put on the New York World's Fair in 1939, it was his responsibility to persuade foreign countries to furnish exhibits for the event. Though Whalen had no love for the Communists, he did not hesitate to approach the Soviet Union to build a pavilion. By that time Franklin Roosevelt was president of the United States, and diplomatic relations with the Soviet Union had been restored. Officials at the Soviet Embassy quickly phoned dictator Joseph Stalin and told him of the proposal. While the Communists had no more love of Whalen then he of them, Stalin liked the idea and he authorized five million Depression-era dollars for the project.

5

COUNTDOWN TO WAR

1931–1940

On Saturday night, September 25, 1935, the German liner *Europa* was preparing to depart from Pier 84 on the west side of Manhattan. Bon voyage parties were going on in staterooms, and people were still boarding and departing the vessel. A uniformed U.S. Customs officer, Maurice Joseph, was patrolling the pier when he observed a man carrying a violin case in heated conversation with one of the ship's stewards. Suspecting that he might be witnessing a smuggling transaction, Joseph approached the two men. As he did so, the steward ran up the gangplank and disappeared. The officer asked the second man, who spoke with a German accent, if he could look inside the violin case. Without much enthusiasm, he consented. A quick glance revealed that beneath the fiddle were letters in German and photos of drawings. Joseph decided to take the man to his supervisor, and together they examined the contents of the case. During preliminary questioning the suspect became so upset that when he was asked his identity, he did not give any of his various aliases; instead, he furnished his questioners with his own name, William Lonkowski. The drawings and some letters found on the prisoner persuaded the customs men that this was a matter for military intelligence. When they called Army headquarters on Governors Island, the staff major for counterespionage was not available, so a private was dispatched to the customs office. The enlisted man was so impressed with the material seized that he phoned another major for instructions. When the second officer arrived, he made a cursory examination of the materials. Then he released the prisoner and told him to come back in three days for further questioning.

If an intelligence officer had looked carefully at the materials seized, he might have determined that one of the photos contained drawings of the Navy's newest scout bomber. If he had vigorously interrogated the suspect, Lonkowski would probably have broken down and confessed that he was a German agent. Instead, a confederate arranged for him to be driven to Canada, where he boarded a German freighter about to sail for home.

On Monday the disgruntled customs agents showed the material seized from Lonkowski to ONI operatives, who recognized some of the drawings as experimental planes. When the ONI men learned the suspect had been released, they went ballistic. They called their superiors, who immediately notified the director of ONI in Washington. Within a few hours, Lt. Cdr. Ellis Zacharias, a star of the ONI, had flown up to New York and was on the case. After he had been briefed, Zacharias went to the head of G-2 for the New York area and told him bluntly, "Major, to me this is a pure case of espionage, and I feel that your people should have communicated immediately with Naval Intelligence—especially since the pictures involved experimental Naval planes." The major could only reply, "Well, it did not seem like much to us."[1]

Security officers who attempted to follow up on the case were too late to apprehend Lonkowski or question his wife. She had hastily left the Long Island boardinghouse in which they lived and departed for Germany. The only information the officers were able to turn up was that Lonkowski had made contact with a German American, Dr. Ignatz Griebl, who lived on East Eighty-Seventh Street in Manhattan. Griebl also was a U.S. officer, a reserve lieutenant in the Army Medical Corps. The director of ONI wrote an official letter of complaint to the chief of army intelligence, and a notation was put in the G-2 files at Governors Island about Lonkowski and Griebl. But nothing of substance happened over the next two years.

In the Roaring Twenties, life in New York had been sunny. But after the 1929 crash, Broadway shows and nightclubs folded; clip-joint queen Texas Guinan died in 1933 at age forty-nine. Al Jolson's career went into rapid decline. In 1932 Governor Franklin Roosevelt forced Mayor Jimmy Walker to resign. Facing possible criminal charges, Walker hopped a liner and fled to Europe with his girlfriend, where he spent the rest of the decade. The only flourishing business in New York was organized crime. In 1931, following a series of mob wars, a thirty-four-year-old gangster named Salvatore Lucania (aka Charles "Lucky" Luciano) forged five separate gangs, or "families," into a confederation that carved up the city. Among its prized possessions was the harbor, where nothing moved without payment of tribute to some mobster. Frequently the morning papers that carried an article about the arrival or departure of a VIP on a luxury liner would contain a smaller story about a body found on a dirty dockside street or a gangster who, it was rumored, was at the bottom of the river.

By 1932 in the country at large, 25 percent of the workforce was unemployed. Out in the heartland, which produced the nation's food supply, banks were foreclosing on farmers who could not pay their mortgages. In traditionally conservative Iowa, attempts to auction off repossessed farms drew crowds who intimidated potential buyers into not bidding. When a judge refused to stop signing foreclosure orders, a mob dragged him out of his courthouse and put a rope around his neck, though they did not actually lynch him. The governor called out the National Guard to maintain law and order. If Iowa farmers were rioting, what lay ahead for America? Some men of great wealth began to whisper that the country needed a "man on horseback"—someone like Army Chief of Staff Gen. Douglas MacArthur. In 1932 a contingent of World War I veterans marched on Washington to demand immediate payment of a bonus they were not scheduled to receive until 1945. Military intelligence was assigned to maintain surveillance of the so-called Bonus Army. The undercover agents correctly discerned that the leaders of the march were strongly anti-Communist. However, a counterintelligence officer submitted a report indicating that Hollywood's Metro-Goldwyn-Mayer studio was behind a contingent of marchers. He noted that the studio was "100% Jewish, as to controlling personnel, and possibly funded by the Soviet Union."[2] Apparently the officer was not much of a film fan. MGM was run by Louis B. Mayer, a conservative Republican who insisted that his studio produce all-American, family-values movies such as the Andy Hardy series. When some of the marchers set up a camp and decided to remain in Washington, President Hoover ordered the Army to remove them. Led by MacArthur on horseback, with his staff officer Maj. Dwight Eisenhower following on foot, troops, including Maj. George Patton, forcibly evicted the marchers and set fire to their shanties.

Two years later, former Marine general Smedley Butler, who had been awarded the Medal of Honor twice while "pacifying" Central America and the Caribbean, would claim he had been approached by Wall Streeters to lead a coup d'état against President Roosevelt's administration.

The year 1933 marked a transition in New York, the country, and the world. Reformer Fiorello LaGuardia was elected mayor, Prohibition was repealed, and Franklin Roosevelt's New Deal took over in Washington. In his first hundred days, the president instituted a number of programs to fight the Depression. While not immediately effective, they gave reassurance to millions of people that something was being done to alleviate their plight.

Much of the blame for the crisis fell on the leaders of Wall Street, and the country demanded blood. In 1933 a clever former New York assistant district attorney, Ferdinand Pecora, served as counsel to a U.S. Senate committee probing the financial community. The committee subpoenaed the heads of many prominent institutions such as National City Bank and Chase. Pecora summoned to the hearings the most prominent figure on Wall Street, Jack Morgan. In his cross-examination of Morgan, Pecora revealed that Jack had paid no income tax for the years 1930, 1931, and 1932, and none of the other twenty Morgan partners had paid in the latter two years. During the course of the proceedings, one of Morgan's entourage complained that the hearings were a circus. An alert PR man for Ringling Brothers Circus decided to capitalize on it. During a recess, he placed a female midget on Jack's lap. Instead of shouting for his bodyguards to remove her, Morgan spoke to the woman in a kindly way and won some sympathy.

It was also the year when the United States recognized the Communist government of Russia. The resumption of diplomatic relations meant that the Soviets could send spies into the United States under official cover. In the midst of what appeared to be a collapse of capitalism, possibly of Western civilization, the Soviet agents should have found America, particularly New York, a fertile environment in which to operate. However, Mayor LaGuardia would prove more adept at dealing with disorders than were his Tammany predecessors. When he took office on January 1, 1934, the city was awash in sit-down strikes and unruly protests. The NYPD's traditional response to such tactics was to disperse protesters. When mass rallies were held without a permit, like the one at Union Square in 1930, mounted police were used to break up the crowds. LaGuardia's new police commissioner was a New York lawyer and former World War I Army general, John F. O'Ryan. When the city's reform elements had met to put together a fusion ticket,* O'Ryan and LaGuardia had been the two leading contenders for the mayoral nomination. O'Ryan stepped aside in favor of LaGuardia and in return was given the police commissioner post. O'Ryan saw Communists behind the wave of strikes. LaGuardia, a long-time labor lawyer, believed that the disorders stemmed from economic distress rather than Marxist conspiracies. He also realized that the Communists would like nothing better than pictures of New York "Cossacks" riding down and clubbing people. O'Ryan demanded to be allowed to go on the offensive against the strikers; when the mayor refused to let him, he resigned. His replacement, Lewis J. Valentine, was a tough career cop who was willing to follow LaGuardia's policies. O'Ryan declared publicly that LaGuardia had sold out to the Communists and was destroying a great police force.

The most important world event of 1933 would turn out to be the ascension of Adolf Hitler and his Nazi Party's control of Germany. History would regard this as the beginning of the run-up to World War II. As in the 1914–1917 period, New York would be the principal battleground in an undeclared war.

When Hitler came to power, he forbade his intelligence services to engage in espionage against America. His directive was based not on respect for legality or morality but on hardheaded political reality. The Reich's diplomats argued that if Nazi agents were caught spying, their efforts to win American sympathy for "the New Germany" would be compromised. But even in a dictatorship, intelligence organizations tend to go their own way, regardless of orders from the government. The German army, forbidden by the Treaty of Versailles to possess warplanes, was already filching the secrets of American military aviation. In 1927 its secret service, known as the Abwehr,† had

---

* The New York term for an alliance of disparate groups that would temporarily unite to defeat the machine candidates.

† The word means defense; however, counterespionage—defense against spies—was only one of its functions.

commenced "Operation Sex." While the name suggests that beautiful cour-
tesans were going to seduce U.S. officers into revealing secrets, it actually
referred to Lonkowski, then a thirty-four-year-old aeronautics engineer, who
was given the cover name William Sexton (hence "Operation Sex"). He was
assigned to infiltrate aviation factories on Long Island and to observe the
Army Air Corps bases at Mitchel and Roosevelt Fields.

Lonkowski was not a man in the mold of his countrymen who had spied
and sabotaged in the United States during World War I. Unlike Papen or
Rintelen, he was no aristocrat. He had been an ordinary mechanic in the
German air force. After the armistice, he studied engineering but did not
find a job in industry. So he went to work for the Abwehr, spying on French
aviation. Witzke and Jahnke, the men who blew up Black Tom in 1916,
were swashbuckling adventurers; Lonkowski was a thin, nervous, bespectacled, mild-mannered individual whose chronic ulcers kept him on a diet
of milk and toast. Nevertheless, he was competent. He secured employment
at the Ireland Aircraft Company and quickly rose to foreman. Over time, the
V-man (or agent) Lonkowski built up a small cadre of H-men (subagents)
whom he placed in aviation jobs. At regular intervals he sent the Abwehr
reports on such subjects as new U.S. fighter planes and research on airplane
engine development. His superiors were pleased with his work, paying him
$500 a month from their limited supply of foreign currency.

The chief of the Abwehr, Adm. Wilhelm Canaris, was a career naval officer of Greek descent. Early in World War I he had served on the cruiser
Dresden in South American waters.* After his ship was scuttled and Canaris
interned in Chile, he escaped and joined the intelligence branch. In the world
of espionage, his exploits were legendary; some were even true. Operating
out of Spain, he supposedly delivered funds to Mata Hari and, according to
some (highly unlikely) accounts, became one of her lovers. It was said that
he had escaped from a Spanish jail by strangling a priest who visited him in
his cell, after which he took the dead cleric's garb and walked out past the
guards. In the postwar years of riot and revolution in Germany, he was
involved in the murders of Socialists and Communists. Contrary to his fear-
some reputation, in person he was a short, slim, courteous man with a great

---

* Where one of his shipmates was Officer Cadet Lothar Witzke.

fondness for his two dachshunds. On trips away from Berlin, he would call regularly to check on their feeding and bowel movements. Historians still debate what Canaris's political convictions really were. A monarchist at heart, by the late 1930s he was secretly anti-Nazi and recruited many individuals of similar view to his staff. Some writers have claimed that he was actually a British agent. While that is doubtful, like many intelligence chiefs, he kept a channel of communications open to the opposition, in his case MI6. Nevertheless, in the 1930s, Führer's orders or no, he moved aggressively to gather intelligence for the Third Reich.

With the advent of Hitler, a few German residents in the United States began to openly espouse Nazism, but they did not win much support from German Americans. Some, who might have hailed the reemergence of Germany as a great power, still remembered the opprobrium that had fallen on Americans of German descent during the first war. In addition, Hitler's anti-Semitic policies were deeply offensive, not only to Jews but to other Americans. American Nazis, organized in groups such as "Friends of the New Germany," staged parades and public demonstrations, which drew the attention of the U.S. government. In early 1934 a congressional investigating committee issued a report condemning their activities. To avoid the bad publicity that the American Nazi zealots were drawing, Hitler's government broke off relationships with such groups. Other pro-Nazi organizations continued to operate, though more discreetly.

In the 1930s the most active Nazi spy in New York was Dr. Griebl. He had come to the United States in the 1920s following service in the Imperial Army during World War I. After obtaining an MD degree, he opened up a practice in the German enclave of Yorkville, on the Upper East Side of Manhattan. Comfortably ensconced in his new homeland, he became a citizen and obtained his reserve commission. When Hitler came to power, Griebl sent a letter to propaganda minister Dr. Joseph Goebbels, offering to serve as a spy. Goebbels forwarded it to the Gestapo,* a security police force. In Nazi Germany, Abwehr officers, Gestapo men, Nazi Party counterintelligence agents, and the regular detectives of the *Kripo* (*Kriminalpolizei*) frequently tripped over each other pursuing spies. The Gestapo also had

---

* The name derives from a postal abbreviation for *Geheime Staatspolizei*, or secret state police.

responsibility for keeping an eye on Germans living abroad. Every German liner had secret police watchdogs in its crew. Captains, whose word was normally law on board ship, were often compelled to take "advice" from some pastry chef because he was a Gestapo man. A German traveler in America had to be careful not to criticize Nazis, lest there be repercussions when he returned home. Even Germans living in the United States, including anti-Nazis, were wise to bite their tongues for fear that their families, still in the Fatherland, might be sent to a concentration camp.

Griebl was invited to meet in Germany with a Gestapo official, who passed him to the Hamburg Abwehr station that controlled espionage in Britain and the United States. There he was taken on by Naval Lt. Cdr. Erich Pheiffer. Upon his return to New York, Griebl organized a small spy ring. In late 1934 Commander Pheiffer ordered Griebl and Lonkowski to combine forces into a *Kriegsorganization* (war station), or KO. When Lonkowski was captured, it was Griebl who arranged to spirit him out of the United States. At the time, though Griebl's name was supposedly noted in the G-2 files, he continued to keep right on with his activities. U.S. security forces were small and had their eyes on other targets. The counterintelligence branches of the Army and Navy were focused on Japanese and Soviet agents. In the 1930s a Japanese "Inspectorate of Intelligence" was established in New York City.

In 1936 another volunteer Nazi spy began operating in New York. Twenty-seven-year-old Guenther Gustave Rumrich was a heavy drinker, drug user, and thief who had served in the U.S. Army for seven years. Despite two desertions and the embezzlement of mess funds (which brought him six months in the stockade), he had managed to reach the rank of sergeant. Following a third desertion, he decided to take up a new line of work—espionage. After reading a book by Col. Walther Nicolai, chief of the German Secret Service during World War I, Rumrich was inspired to write a letter to the author offering his services to the Nazis. In it Rumrich described himself as a former U.S. Army lieutenant and asked that a response be inserted in the personal columns of the *New York Times*, addressed to Theodore Koerner. The long-retired Nicolai turned the letter over to the Abwehr. On April 6, 1936, the *Times* carried a notice: "Theodore Koerner—letter received, please send reply and address to Sanders, Hamburg, 1 postbox 629, Germany." Rumrich responded and was assigned to Dr. Griebl's spy ring.

Rumrich's fascination with tales of espionage might explain why he invariably behaved like a character in a B movie. To determine the strength of the garrison at Fort Hamilton in Brooklyn, he posed as an Army doctor and phoned the post to order that figures on the venereal disease rate be delivered to him. Emboldened by that stunt, he planned to call up and order the Army colonel who commanded Fort Totten in Queens to bring secret documents to a meeting at a Manhattan hotel. There Rumrich intended to knock the officer unconscious and steal the papers. When he informed his superiors, they were horrified at the prospect of creating a diplomatic incident and vetoed the scheme.

Nonetheless, in 1937 Nazi spies pulled off a major coup by stealing America's super-secret Norden bombsight—the most advanced such instrument in the world. U.S. experts boasted (with some exaggeration) that it could guide a bomb dropped from a plane into a pickle barrel. With war rapidly approaching, German Luftwaffe (air force) chief Hermann Göring demanded that the Abwehr obtain a copy. The job was assigned to Maj. Nikolaus Ritter. After serving in the wartime German army, Ritter had immigrated to the United States, where for ten years he ran a textile business. During that time he grew so fond of his new country that he took out citizenship papers. When his business became a casualty of the Depression, he cast about for a new source of income. A German air force general serving as military attaché in Washington suggested he join the Luftwaffe. So Ritter returned to Germany, accepted a commission as a major, and was posted to the Abwehr. Ritter, who prided himself on his ability to speak "American" English down to the latest slang expressions, was a natural to go back to New York and steal the bombsight. There he made contact with a German immigrant named Herman Lang, who worked as an inspector at the Norden plant on Lafayette Street in Lower Manhattan. Over several months, Lang secretly took home blueprints and copied them. Ritter turned the material over to an Abwehr courier, who smuggled them out of New York on a liner. Lang's prints enabled German scientists to construct a bombsight that was more advanced than the Norden original. Göring was so grateful that he invited Lang to come to Germany, all expenses paid, so that he could personally thank him. The Abwehr gave Lang $1,500 as a reward for his services.

Unlike Ritter, who kept a low profile, the spies who revolved around Dr. Griebl were indiscreet. V-men and their associates flocked to the bars and rathskellers of Yorkville in the East 80s, places like The Café Vaterland, The Hofbrau House, The Hindenburg Café, and The Yorkville Casino. Dr. Griebl could be found most nights at one of them. Though married, the short, pudgy physician was usually accompanied by his six-foot-tall, blonde girl-friend, Kate Moog. The wealthy, college-educated Moog owned a nursing home and lived in a fourteen-room upscale Riverside Drive apartment, where she was attended to by six servants. On one occasion she had accompanied Griebl on a trip to Germany, where she met Abwehr officers. According to her later account, they offered to set her up in a villa in Washington, D.C., where she could entertain U.S. officials. Another regular was Karl Schlüeter, a steward on the *Europa* who served as an Abwehr agent. To impress his colleagues, Schlüeter claimed to be a high-ranking officer when actually he was just a low-level V-man with little knowledge of espionage tradecraft. He was so careless that he regularly carried a pistol, even though doing so could bring him to police attention. One night at The Hindenburg, he accidentally dropped his piece on the floor. Instead of retrieving it and making a hasty exit, he began showing it off to his drinking companions. One of Schlüeter's couriers, and an intimate friend, was young, redheaded, full-figured Johanna "Jenni" Hoffman, a hairdresser on the *Europa*.

The Gestapo also began operating in New York. Many of its agents were storm-trooper types who had distinguished themselves in street battles during Hitler's rise to power, not officers and gentlemen like Ritter or Griebl. A typical one was Rudy Bittenberg, officially assistant purser on a liner but actually the ship's secret police watchdog. In 1937 he was assigned to organize a Gestapo outpost in New York City. As soon as he arrived, accompanied by two of his thugs, Bittenberg called on the New York superintendent of the German lines and demanded passes to go on board any of the company's vessels in port. After getting the lay of the land and water, Bittenberg appointed one of his assistants, Karl Herrmann, to head the New York Gestapo.

Herrmann was an aggressive security policeman, anxious to make his mark by ferreting out enemies of the Reich. He quickly focused on what he suspected was a major anti-Nazi ring directed by Mrs. Thomas Manville, an

Anarchist Johann Most addressing a meeting in New York City, 1887. Previously imprisoned in three European countries, after his arrival in the United States in 1882, he was regarded by American security officers as the most dangerous radical in the country. In 1901 he published an article urging the assassination of government leaders. The next day President McKinley was fatally wounded. As a result, Most was sentenced to a year in jail.
LIBRARY OF CONGRESS

America's leading security policeman William Flynn, chief of the United States Secret Service (1912–1917) and director of the Bureau of Investigation (1919–1921). Prior to his appointment as chief of the Secret Service, he had headed the New York office of the agency and was briefly a deputy commissioner in charge of NYPD detectives. As Bureau of Investigation head, he played a leading role in the 1919–1920 "Red Raids."
LIBRARY OF CONGRESS

ABOVE LEFT: Sabotage at Black Tom. In 1916 German agents set off an explosion on Black Tom Island in New York Harbor, where munitions—destined for shipment to the Allies—were stored. So powerful was the blast that thousands of windows were shattered in Manhattan, the Brooklyn Bridge swayed, and the noise was heard as far south as Philadelphia. FEDERAL BUREAU OF INVESTIGATION

ABOVE RIGHT: In 1914, at the start of World War I in Europe, NYPD commissioner Arthur Woods formed a police bomb squad to forestall acts of sabotage. Harvard-educated and married into the family of J. P. Morgan, Woods was a vigorous supporter of the Allied cause. COLLECTION OF THE NEW-YORK HISTORICAL SOCIETY

Col. Ralph Van Deman, father of U.S. military intelligence (seated second from left) at the Versailles Peace Conference in 1919. Standing at far left is a young U.S. intelligence agent, Allen Dulles. Later promoted to general, Van Deman was the gray eminence of U.S. security intelligence until his death in 1952. After carrying out further espionage work in World War II, Dulles was director of the CIA from 1953 to 1961. NATIONAL ARCHIVES

"America's premiere detective," William Burns, right, talking to a reporter on the steps of the Morgan Bank shortly after the bomb exploded on Wall Street, September 1920. As head of the country's leading private detective agency, he assigned himself a major role in the investigation of the case. From 1921 to 1924 he was head of the Bureau of Investigation.

Herbert O. Yardley, head of America's code breakers from World War I until 1929. In the 1920s from an office in New York City, he decoded the codes of other countries. After being fired by Secretary of State Henry Stimson, who did not believe "that gentlemen should read other gentlemen's mail," Yardley wrote a book revealing that the United States had been reading Japanese diplomatic messages during the 1922 Washington Naval Conference. From then on the U.S. government regarded him as a pariah.

Special Agent Leon Turrou, the New York FBI's leading spy catcher. In 1938 he uncovered a Nazi espionage ring. Despite his success he was fired from the bureau for revealing too much information to the media. In the 1939 movie *Confessions of a Nazi Spy*, Edward G. Robinson played a character based on Turrou.

Members of the Nazi spy ring uncovered in 1938. It included, left to right, Dr. Ignatz Griebl, a respected physician and U.S. Army reserve officer; Guenther Gustave Rumrich, aka Crown, a reckless Nazi operative; and Johanna Hoffman, a hairdresser on a German ocean liner who was the ring's courier between New York and Germany. FEDERAL BUREAU OF INVESTIGATION

Aftermath of the July 4, 1940, New York World's Fair Bombing. NYPD detective Fred Morlock, right, explains to Mayor Fiorello LaGuardia, seated on auto bumper, and Police Commissioner Lewis J. Valentine how he removed a suspected time bomb from the British Pavilion at the New York World's Fair after an attendant had found it. While detectives were examining it, it exploded, killing two bomb squad officers. ASSOCIATED PRESS

FBI director J. Edgar Hoover talking to movie star/ballerina Vera Zorina (to his left), 1940. Zorina's politics and her provocative costume did not mesh with Hoover's political views or personal morality, which is probably why both appear to be uncomfortable.

FBI agents and U.S. sailors in New York City, December 8, 1941, escorting Japanese through Ellis Island Ferry Gate on their way to detention as part of the nationwide roundup of Japanese nationals. Within the next few days, federal officers and New York police also took into custody German and Italian nationals.

George Dasch, leader of the four-man German sabotage team that landed on Long Island in 1942. Dasch voluntarily surrendered to the FBI, led them to his comrades, and provided information on another four-man team that had landed in Florida. President Roosevelt ordered that the eight saboteurs be tried by a military court-martial. Six of them were sent to the electric chair, and two others, including Dasch, received long prison terms.
FEDERAL BUREAU OF INVESTIGATION

Gen. William J. Donovan, wartime OSS chief, presenting a medal to William S. Stephenson, who from an NYC office directed British Security Coordination in the Western Hemisphere from 1940 to 1945. Though the two men look like ordinary businessmen, they were both veteran swashbucklers. BETTMANN/CORBIS

A rescue worker reaching into a New York police car covered with debris while firefighters spray water on smoldering ruins in the background, following the September 11, 2001, terrorist attack on the World Trade Center. LIBRARY OF CONGRESS

NYPD commissioner Ray Kelly explaining the technology of "smart cameras," which detect such things as packages left too long in vehicles. The cameras, coupled with license plate readers, radiation detectors, and bio-chem monitors, keep a close eye on the downtown financial district, midtown Manhattan, transit hubs at Herald Square, Times Square, Penn Station, and at Grand Central Station. NYPD

extremely wealthy elderly woman whose husband had cofounded the Johns-Manville asbestos company. Mrs. Manville, a regular traveler to Europe on German liners, was noted for giving expensive gifts to crewmembers such as stewards, bartenders, and hairdressers. Not only was she openhanded with ordinary working stiffs, but she invited them to drop in at her deluxe suite in the Savoy Plaza Hotel. Gestapo suspicions were heightened when surveillance revealed that she was friendly with some prominent Jews who had fled Germany to the United States after the Nazis took over.

Herrmann's men could have resolved their suspicions about Mrs. Manville by simply reading the newspapers. Her son Tommy, an aging playboy, had a propensity for acquiring and losing brides. He was married ten or twelve times—no one could keep track. Most of his marriages lasted for brief periods, in one case eight hours. Thanks to the tabloids and radio comedians, he was a household name. Finally, after running around in circles, the Gestapo came to the realization that Mrs. Manville was just a kindly old lady who loved to make people happy by giving them expensive presents. Son Tommy kept up the family tradition by paying large settlements to the cigarette girls and cocktail waitresses he divorced.

In 1937 Britain's MI5 raided the home of a Scottish woman named Jennie Jordan (the widow of a German soldier killed in World War I) who was functioning as a postal drop. German spies abroad, wanting to send information to their chiefs back home without arousing suspicion, would write letters to an apparently harmless lady in Scotland who would then forward them to Abwehr mailboxes on the Continent. Mrs. Jordan received and sent so many letters that she aroused the suspicion of postal authorities, who alerted the security service. Among letters seized were some from agents in New York to their superiors in Berlin, which disclosed that the Nazis were conspiring to obtain plans for the defense of the East Coast, secret codes, maps belonging to the Army Air Corps, and the blueprints of the U.S. Navy's newest aircraft carriers. A high-ranking official from MI5 journeyed to America to personally brief FBI director J. Edgar Hoover on the discovery.

By 1938 Hoover had become the dominant figure in American law enforcement. Like Allan Pinkerton and William Burns, he had created a large national detective force. But where theirs were private, his was a government agency. As with Pinkerton and Burns, his mastery of public relations enhanced the standing of his bureau and his own prestige. Under Roosevelt's New Deal, the FBI had been employed fighting garden-variety street crime, a task normally left to state and local cops. Hoover turned the FBI's hunt for such small-time hoodlums as John Dillinger, Charles "Pretty Boy" Floyd, and George "Machine Gun" Kelly into a war against "public enemies," which ended in victory for Uncle Sam. At first glance it was not clear what made ordinary stickup men worthy of the attention of the national government. A better choice might have been organized crime figures, who were making hundreds of millions of illicit dollars and controlling the politics of many American cities. Probably it was because Dillinger generated more headlines than Lucky Luciano but did not have as much political influence.

In the context of the times, though, the Roosevelt administration could hardly have ignored newspaper headlines about desperados running wild. Some politicians urged that the Army be called out. The reasons for not assigning soldiers to carry out civil policing require no elaboration. Another option would have been to appropriate federal money to strengthen state and local law enforcement agencies. In fact, the reverse happened. After Hoover's G-men came out second best in gun battles with hoodlums like the Dillinger gang, he quietly recruited cops from the police forces of Texas and Oklahoma, where the western frontier spirit was still strong and lawmen were quick on the trigger. Known within the bureau as "the Cowboys," they were the ones who shot Dillinger and other public enemies. Like many of the programs initiated by the New Deal, whatever the reality, the hunt for public enemies made the citizenry feel that the government was doing something about problems, not sitting on its hands. When the FBI gunned down a Dillinger or Floyd, it was a dramatic example of "doing something" that even anti–New Dealers could applaud.

That Hoover was around in the mid-1930s to carry on the war against crime was owed to his political skills, helped by more than a little bit of luck. He had managed to deflect blame for his role in the 1919–1920 Red Raids, the fallout from which had destroyed his big boss, Attorney General Palmer, and contributed to the replacement of his immediate superior, Director Flynn. Hoover repeated this feat during the Teapot Dome scandal, which had sunk Attorney General Daugherty and "America's greatest detective," William Burns, and he managed to end up with Burns's job. Not everyone bought Hoover's protestations of innocence. Senator Thomas Walsh of Montana, who had been a target of bureau agents during Teapot Dome, always held Hoover responsible. In 1933 Walsh was named attorney general by incoming president Franklin Roosevelt. If Walsh had taken office, it would almost certainly have meant Hoover's dismissal. However, en route by train to his swearing-in, the seventy-two-year-old senator, accompanied by his new bride—a vivacious, young Cuban socialite—succumbed to a heart attack in their bedroom compartment.

Though Hoover got a reprieve, he was still not out of the woods. In 1934 Roosevelt's powerful campaign chairman, Postmaster General Jim Farley, pushed to have New York private detective Val O'Farrell named to replace Hoover. O'Farrell, a former NYPD cop, was the investigator to which prominent New York politicians and socialites turned when they needed some sleuthing done. Always a good source for journalists, he became so widely known that when German Social Democrats suspected that President Friedrich Ebert had been murdered by poisoning, O'Farrell was retained to investigate the case. O'Farrell also had a serious negative. He had been very close to Arnold Rothstein and often carried out assignments for him. Had he become FBI director, the bureau might have descended into a political morass, with scandal inevitable. Again, Hoover was lucky. O'Farrell also died suddenly of a heart attack. After some FBI agents were killed by the Dillinger gang, Hoover himself came under criticism for his lack of field experience. While being questioned by a senator, he had to admit that he had never personally made an arrest. From then on he made sure that he was on the scene whenever some public enemy was about to be collared.*

Hoover was also shrewd enough to move cautiously on the always-sensitive domestic intelligence front. His security expert in the New York field office, Leon Turrou, was an agent with a background far different from that of the typical Middle Americans who staffed the FBI. Born in Poland in 1895, he

---

* In 1939 fugitive mob boss Louis "Lepke" Buchalter surrendered to Hoover and columnist Walter Winchell on a New York street. In that instance, while Hoover took the bows, the cases against Lepke for drug dealing and murder had actually been made by the agents of the Federal Bureau of Narcotics and the New York County District Attorney's office, not the FBI.

had been taken by his adoptive parents to Egypt, China, Russia, Germany, and England. In 1915 he quit his job as a dishwasher in New York City to return to Russia and join the czar's army. In the 1920s he did a hitch in the U.S. Marines. Turrou's background alone might have disqualified him for a job in the bureau. Nevertheless, in 1929 Hoover assigned him to New York, where he investigated Communists and handled cases involving foreign nationals. In 1934 he was one of the agents who interrogated German immigrant Bruno Hauptmann after his arrest for kidnapping the Lindbergh baby. From the letters recovered in Scotland, Turrou was able to construct a profile of a German agent referred to by the code name "Crown." He lived in New York, was fairly well educated, was fluent in German and English, had served in the U.S. Army, and was a married man who was chronically short of funds. There the trail ended.

In February 1938 Ira Hoyt, chief of the State Department's Passport Division in New York City, received a call from "Under Secretary of State Weston," who ordered him to send fifty passport blanks to him at the Taft Hotel in Midtown. The caller was actually Guenther Gustave Rumrich. Karl Schlüeter had offered Rumrich $1,000 to obtain fifty blank U.S. passports, which German intelligence required to outfit spies being sent into Poland. Rumrich confused blank passports with passport application blanks, the latter being forms that were available to the public at many government facilities. The passport division head in Washington was Ruth Shipley (née Bielaski, sister of the World War I head of the Bureau of Investigation), who ran her agency as a virtual extension of U.S. intelligence, constantly flagging people she regarded as "subversives" and sometimes denying them visas. State Department security officers alerted the NYPD Alien Squad. The squad was the latest incarnation of the department's security units that had existed in some form since the Civil War era when, as U.S. Army provost marshals, they hunted down rebel agents and sympathizers.*

---

* The popular name for police intelligence units that kept track of supposed subversives (of whatever ideology) was "Red Squads." Generally they were police backwaters and their members worked in the shadows.

Over the years the NYPD version of a Red Squad operated under various titles. Often its functions were carried out by more than one unit. In the World War I era a Radical Bureau existed alongside Inspector Tunney's Neutrality Squad. In the 1920s, the Radical Bureau encompassed three squads: bomb, industrial, and gangster. The second handled labor-management issues and the third, organized crime. In 1931 the Bureau of Criminal Alien Investigations was created. In 1940 Special Squad 1 was established by Mayor

Alien Squad detectives staked out the Taft Hotel. Wary of a trap, Rumrich called Western Union to have them deliver his package from the hotel to a telegraph office at Grand Central Station. When it arrived at Grand Central he called Western Union again, telling them to take the package down to its Varick Street office. Still cautious, Rumrich called to have it taken to another location. Finally, with detectives trailing along, a messenger dropped it off in a tavern at Hudson and King Streets. Even then Rumrich hesitated to enter the place. Instead, he offered a boy on the street some money to pick up the package. The boy did so, and as he handed it to Rumrich the detectives moved in.

Though Rumrich was a prisoner, the detectives proceeded with a caution unusual in New York policing of that era—probably because stealing blank application forms did not seem particularly serious, and they were not sure exactly what they were dealing with. Instead of being thrown into a cell, Rumrich was put up for two nights in a hotel room. The situation almost became a repeat of the Lonkowski affair. Police were about to book Rumrich on a minor charge, in which case he would have posted bail and fled the country. However, when a garbled version of the arrest appeared in a New York newspaper, Leon Turrou inserted himself into the investigation. He confronted Rumrich with information from the letters seized in Scotland, and when he accused him of being Crown, the suspect quickly broke down and confessed. In his statements he implicated Dr. Griebl and other members of the ring, including Karl Schlüeter and Johanna Hoffman, as well as his superiors in Germany. The FBI learned that Schlüeter and Hoffman were due to arrive in New York on the *Europa* two days later, so they staked out Pier 84. When the ship docked, Schlüeter was not on board. Over a week had passed since the arrest of Rumrich, giving the Abwehr time to get Schlüeter off the vessel before it departed. Hoffman was on board. She stepped off the *Europa*, still wearing her hairdresser uniform, and stood around without a coat, freezing in the winter weather. It appeared obvious that she was waiting to meet

------

(continued)

LaGuardia to conduct undercover operations, leaving other investigations to the Alien Squad. After the war began, the two were merged. In 1946 the name of the unit was changed to Bureau of Special Service Investigations (BOSSI). In 1970 its duties were transferred to the newly created Intelligence Division. Today the Intelligence Division remains but shares some of its responsibilities with the Counterterrorism Division.

someone, probably to receive a package from another courier. The watching agents guessed that if he didn't show up, Hoffman might become alarmed and go back on the vessel and stay there. In that event the FBI would have had to go through a complicated diplomatic procedure to arrest her. By then the shipping line would have arranged for her to be furnished a lawyer, who would advise her not to talk. The pier was on U.S. soil, so the agents snatched her and hauled her to the FBI office.

When questioned, Hoffman claimed she knew nothing about Rumrich. In the movies, German spies were usually portrayed as icy Prussian officers and haughty aristocrats like Maria de Victorica, who had been arrested in New York in 1918. But when Rumrich was brought into the room where Hoffman was being interrogated, instead of pretending he did not know her, he exclaimed, "Hi, Jenni." The naive hairdresser, realizing she was in serious trouble, began to cry. She agreed to write a note allowing FBI agents to retrieve her bag from the *Europa*, which contained some letters she was supposed to deliver. When they did, they found that the letters were written in code. Hoffman claimed she had no key to decipher it, but a further search of the bag turned one up. One of the letters was addressed to Rumrich. In it Schlüeter urged him to get the plans for the aircraft carriers *Yorktown* and *Enterprise* and directed him to turn over the stolen passports to Hoffman. Confronted with the evidence, Jenni dictated a full statement in German.

Moving quickly, Turrou and other agents dropped in on Dr. Griebl at his Yorkville practice and invited him to accompany them to the FBI office. There, Jenni Hoffman identified him as a man she had received material from to take back to Germany. Griebl first denied knowing her. Then he admitted that he might have given her a few propaganda pamphlets. To prove his innocence, he agreed to let the FBI search his office. While Griebl watched, the agents turned his suite upside down but did not discover anything incriminating. Finally their attention was drawn to an empty pack of matches. Inside the cover, written in red ink, were some symbols. It was the same code found in Jenni Hoffman's bag. As Griebl sparred with the agents, Kate Moog, wearing an expensive fur coat, burst into the office and began kissing the doctor and screaming at the G-men, calling them imbeciles. Both were ordered to appear at the FBI office the next morning at nine. To prevent a repeat of the Lonkowski fiasco, agents were posted outside the homes of Griebl and Moog to ensure that they did not leave. The next day, at the FBI office, Griebl broke down and confessed. He was debriefed for six days, during which time he gave information about everyone from the long-gone Lonkowski to Rumrich and Gestapo agent Herrmann.

The case had the necessary ingredients to become a tabloid sensation: a respected physician and U.S. Army Reserve officer betraying his country, and photogenic young women serving as aides to the spy ring. Indictments were handed down against eighteen individuals, including Commander Pheiffer, Mrs. Jordan, and Willie Lonkowski—all of whom were beyond U.S. jurisdiction. Prodded by Herrmann's Gestapo bullies, during the period between their arrest and the start of their trial, Griebl (who had been released on bail) and others managed to flee to Germany.* Back home, the doctor convinced his superiors that he had not given away any significant information. There was no chance of having anyone extradited from Germany, so only four defendants were left to appear in an American courtroom: Rumrich, Hoffman, and two bit players who had worked in aviation on Long Island. Defense lawyers sought to impugn Turrou by alleging he was a Communist and a Jew. In fact, he had spent much of his career hunting Soviet agents and was a Christian. They also cooked up a charge that he had been given a $5,000 bribe by Dr. Griebl to allow him to escape. Federal investigators traveled to Austria (which Germany had annexed) to take a statement from Griebl, by then installed in a lucrative Vienna medical practice that the Nazis had seized from a Jewish physician. He denied the bribery charge.

At her New York trial, Jenni Hoffman, who supposedly spoke no English, answered questions through an interpreter from Columbia University. When her lawyer disputed the accuracy of his English translations, Hoffman was recalled to the stand. Somehow, during the course of the trial, she had acquired a good command of English. She not only answered questions in that language but was able to analyze the difference in meaning between some German expressions and their English translation. Though she had been only a courier, to deter others the judge sentenced her to four years in

---

* Karl Schlüeter continued to work as a ship's steward. In 1940, after the German liner *Columbus* was scuttled to avoid capture by the British, U.S. authorities placed the crew in detention on Ellis Island. During their processing, Schlüeter was identified and culled from the group to answer the previous charges against him.

prison. Rumrich, the spy, was given only two years because he had turned government witness.

Turrou was invited to sign a contract with the *New York Post* to write a series of articles on German espionage in America. When his superiors, fearing the Nazi government would protest, refused to permit him to do so, he resigned from the FBI and spent the next four years lecturing and writing. His book, *Nazi Spies in America*, was made into a film, *Confessions of a Nazi Spy*, with Edward G. Robinson playing a character modeled on Turrou. In some instances, Turrou's understanding of Nazi spies was incomplete. He seemed to think the Abwehr and the Gestapo were the same organization, and he named a Colonel Busch as head of the service.* Canaris must have smiled at that. While J. Edgar Hoover was reported to be furious with Turrou for going public, it may have been an act. Turrou, the highest-paid agent in the New York office, had long been a Hoover favorite. By publishing and speaking out, he forced Congress and the president to appropriate more money for FBI security investigations, incidentally positioning the bureau as the country's chief spy catchers, although the case would have never been broken except for MI5's tip, the passport officials' suspicions, and the NYPD officers who nabbed Rumrich.

━━━━━

In addition to spies, there were a number of pro-Nazi groups operating in New York. The most prominent one was the German American Bund, led by its "führer," Fritz Kuhn, a World War I German soldier who had immigrated to the United States in the 1920s. For a time he worked as an engineer at the Ford Motor Company in Michigan. Later he moved to Jackson Heights in the New York City borough of Queens. In 1936 he became leader of the Bund, which he claimed had a quarter of a million members in forty-two states. The squat, bandy-legged Kuhn surrounded himself with brown-shirted storm troopers. Twice he visited Germany to obtain the personal blessing of Hitler.

Kuhn attracted national publicity when he scheduled a mass meeting at Madison Square Garden for February 20, 1939 (ostensibly to celebrate

---

* A Major Busch was a lower-ranking Abwehr officer.

Washington's Birthday).* Many New York Jewish leaders demanded that Mayor Fiorello LaGuardia ban the meeting. LaGuardia refused, saying, "I would then be doing exactly as Adolf Hitler is doing in carrying out his abhorrent form of government." Once, when a German official had demanded police protection, LaGuardia furnished him with a security detail made up entirely of Jewish cops. On February 20 a large force of police was stationed outside the Garden to hold back protesters. Inside, eighteen thousand people listened for six hours as Kuhn and his supporters railed about how "the Joos iss responsible" for the various problems of the world. A Jewish man who had managed to gain entrance to the Garden charged the stage and was beaten senseless by Kuhn's storm troopers. Afterward there were clashes outside, and some cops were assaulted or knocked off their horses. A few days after the meeting, LaGuardia sent city investigators to the Bund offices on East Eighty-Fifth Street, in Yorkville, to check the financial records of the organization. Their findings led New York County district attorney Tom Dewey to charge Kuhn with forgery and grand larceny over a missing $14,548.†

Kuhn, with his pronounced German accent and his Nazi-uniformed, goose-stepping bully boys shouting, "Heil Hitler," was too foreign to draw any mass following in the United States. Fascist-minded Americans gravitated toward homegrown movements. Surprisingly, liberal New York was a center of extremism. In 1938 Arthur Derounian, a young freelancer (who wrote under the pen name John Roy Carlson), began researching the American fascist movement. Posing as an Italian American named George Pagnanelli, he gained entry to the world of "Christian patriots." On a summer night in 1939, at a meeting in the basement of St. Paul the Apostle Church at Fifty-Ninth Street and Columbus Avenue on the west side of Manhattan, he observed men wearing small metal crosses in their coat lapels enter the room and greet their comrades with the Nazi raised-arm salute. When everyone had assembled, a leader stepped to the front of the room, rendered the

---

* In 1939 Madison Square Garden, the most famous indoor arena in the United States, was not located anywhere near Madison Square, which is in the East 20's. Early in the century it had moved two miles north to the West 50's. Today its fourth incarnation is located in the West 30s.

† The following year, while out on bail, Kuhn was arrested as he attempted to flee the United States. Brought to trial, he was convicted and sentenced to prison. When he was released in 1943, the United States was at war and Kuhn was interned as an enemy alien.

same salute, and called out, "Pro Patria et Christo!" ("For country and Christ!").
To which the assemblage rose, saluted, and replied "Pro Patria et Christo!"

"Members of the Christian Front . . . ," the speaker began.

The men in the room were among the first recruits to a movement that
aspired to turn America into a fascist state under the leadership of a radio
preacher. Even though he has been totally forgotten by today, in the 1930s
a Catholic priest, Father Charles Coughlin, was one of the most influential
men in the nation. An obscure parish priest in Royal Oak, Michigan, early
in the decade he mastered the techniques of the newly invented radio to
assemble a nationwide flock of millions. But it was not conventional religious sermons that drew people to Coughlin; rather, it was his unconven-
tional political lectures. His vigorous denunciations of eastern financial
interests—"moneychangers," he called them—was a message that resonated
with many Americans overwhelmed by the Depression. Coughlin's newspaper, *Social Justice*, was read by a million people every week. As a representative of the conservative Catholic Church, he was listened to by
Americans who would have rejected similar pronouncements from others
as Communist propaganda. In 1932 Coughlin's vigorous support of
Franklin Roosevelt's campaign for the presidency was a significant contribution to FDR's landslide victory.

Eventually Coughlin broke with the Roosevelt administration because
he claimed it was too accommodating to Jews and liberals. By the late 1930s,
the good Father's hero was the Spanish nationalist leader Gen. Francisco
Franco, and his new bogeymen were godless Bolsheviks who, he believed,
were using the New Deal to destroy Christian values. Coughlin threw down
the gauntlet to them, saying: "We will fight you, Franco's way if necessary.
Call this inflammatory, if you will. It is inflammatory. But rest assured we
will fight you and we will win."[3]

In 1936 a "popular front" of Communists and Socialists had won the
French elections. In 1938 Coughlin organized a Christian Front. By the fall
of 1939, the movement had spread from New York to other big cities. While
the Coughlinites were not Nazis, as fellow fascists they shared many of
Hitler's views and maintained working relationships with such groups as
Kuhn's German American Bund. Nazi propaganda frequently appeared in
the columns of *Social Justice*.

A key leader among the New York fascists was Joe McWilliams, who formed his own band of storm troopers known as the Christian Mobilizers. A dynamic speaker, the handsome, dark-haired McWilliams was a magnetic figure. His orations carried the standard denunciation of democracy, combined with attacks on the Jews. McWilliams had only recently become a fascist. Born in Oklahoma in 1904, he had arrived in New York in 1925 to work as a self-taught mechanical engineer. He did fairly well, managing to patent several minor inventions such as an improved razor blade. In the early 1930s, according to people who knew him then, McWilliams was a passionate Marxist of the Trotskyite variety and strongly anti-fascist. In 1935 his health broke down from rheumatic fever, and only help from his friends, most of whom were Jewish, pulled him through the crisis. Afterward, McWilliams made a sudden about-face, becoming an arch-fascist and anti-Semite. In his new incarnation, Joe became very affluent. Some of his funding came from outwardly respectable people, including Wall Streeters. Other money was traced to Nazi sources. Though not German, McWilliams transferred his base to Yorkville. A Protestant, he forged a close bond with Father Coughlin. The unmarried McWilliams attracted ladies from dowagers to teenagers and was frequently accompanied by a group of young women who were generally regarded as his "harem."

The Mobilizers contained a number of antisocial characters, including some hardcore criminals. It was such men who spearheaded the strong-arm squads that roamed the streets of New York and beat up Jews. Many New Yorkers were aware that McWilliams's thugs were acting as though they were in Berlin, but bystanders chose to avert their eyes. Even officials treated McWilliams's hooligans as though they were just high-spirited boys. One Mobilizer arrested for hitting a Jew was released by a judge with the warning that next time he should count to ten. In the climate of tolerance for their activities, the Mobilizers became even bolder. On the night of August 13, 1939, McWilliams's sluggers stood guard as one of their speakers addressed a crowd on a Bronx street corner. Among his statements were, "We'll fix the Jews the way Hitler fixed them." After listening to the speech, Capt. John Collins of the Alexander Avenue precinct mounted the platform, declared the meeting unlawful, and ordered the crowd to disperse. Immediately a group of Mobilizers, shouting, "Shut up, you Jew," dragged Collins down and pummeled him. Sgt. Robert McAllister, who ran to assist the captain, was struck over the head with a lead pipe. When the assailants, a pair of ex-convicts, were wrestled down by other officers, the crowd raced to the police station and surrounded it to prevent the cops from taking their prisoners inside. For a time they held the precinct under siege until reinforcements could be summoned to clear the streets.

At about the same time, the NYPD received a shock. In response to an official questionnaire, four hundred officers admitted to being Christian Front members. Leaders of the city's Jewish community wondered if some cops were deliberately ignoring the storm troopers' assaults on Jews. To reassure them, Mayor LaGuardia appointed a tough Jewish career cop, Louis Costuma, as chief inspector, the number-two position in the department.

When it dawned on the priests at St. Paul's what type of organization they were hosting, the Front was refused permission to continue using the church as a meeting place. So the members moved over to Donovan's Hall, off nearby Columbus Circle, where they gathered regularly to engage in military drills. Offshoots of the Christian Front, calling themselves the Iron Guard, the Phalanx, or the Sportsmen's Club of Brooklyn, assembled at other locations to prepare for the day when they could launch a putsch.

In 1940 McWilliams formed the American Destiny Party and announced his candidacy for Congress. His goal was not to win but to draw attention and solidify his position as a top fascist leader, while also attracting new contributors. Anti-fascists played into his hands by attacking him. Walter Winchell, then the most widely read columnist in America and with a Sunday night radio show that half the country tuned in to, led the pack. He regularly denounced McWilliams and his "Ratzis." One of Winchell's best lines was, "Every time Joe opens his mouth, some good New Yorker puts his foot in it." Of course, as Winchell should have known, the publicity raised McWilliams from an obscure agitator to a national figure.[*]

---

[*] Today, if Winchell is remembered at all, it is as some kind of lightweight buffoon. Onscreen, a character based on him was played by comedian Jack Benny. In his time, though, a mention by him could make a book a bestseller, or a star out of an unknown, and could turn an ordinary musical into a smash hit. Love him or hate him—and with most people it was the latter—he was a force. A master showman from his own vaudeville days, he knew how to hold his audience in thrall. His radio show always opened with Winchell intoning, in his staccato voice, "Good evening, Mr. and Mrs. North America, and all the ships at sea, let's go to press." Then, to a background of a clicking telegraph key, he would rattle off a series of stories ranging from predictions of Hitler's next move to the latest Hollywood divorce, often preceding them with "Flash!"

In the 1930s, many Americans believed that going to war with Germany in 1917 had been a mistake. Between 1934 and 1936, Senate investigations, led by Gerald Nye of North Dakota, introduced the term "merchants of death" to describe the men who had bankrolled Allied munitions purchases in the United States. Their claim that the war was fought "to pull J. P. Morgan's chestnuts out of the fire" resonated with many people. Nye and "isolationist" colleagues like Burton Wheeler of Montana and William Borah of Idaho were able to secure the passage of legislation forbidding the United States to sell munitions to belligerents in any future war.

In 1937 President Roosevelt made a controversial speech in Chicago calling for dictators to be quarantined. In September 1939 when a new war broke out in Europe, he believed that the United States would eventually have to intervene to stop the Nazis. But he was way ahead of public opinion. Polls found that an overwhelming majority wanted the United States to remain neutral. Like most of their countrymen, New Yorkers did not feel particularly menaced by Nazism. Instead, they went to the movies three times a week to watch stars like Cary Grant, Clark Gable, and Judy Garland in box office smashes like *The Philadelphia Story*, *Gone with the Wind*, and *The Wizard of Oz*. Huge crowds flocked to Yankee Stadium in the Bronx; the Polo Grounds in Manhattan, home of the Giants; and Brooklyn's Ebbets Field, where the Dodgers played. In the dog days of summer, hundreds of thousands rode the subway to Brooklyn's Coney Island amusement park. A Christmas ritual for New Yorkers was to journey to Midtown to gaze into the shop windows on Fifth Avenue, or Macy's and Gimbels in Herald Square. There was no way Roosevelt could persuade a war-hating, pleasure-loving population to mobilize against the Nazi threat.

Even when fascist activities were exposed, the public tended to be apathetic. In January 1940, on information supplied by an informer, the FBI charged thirteen members of the Christian Front groups with conspiracy to overthrow the government of the United States. The case was weak. Under cross-examination, the young informer admitted that the FBI had arranged for him to obtain guns and ammunition stolen from a National Guard armory. None of the defendants were convicted. Afterward, instead of decrying the activities of American Nazis, the press was generally critical of the Justice Department.

After the 1939 Hitler-Stalin non-aggression pact was signed, the Department of Justice proceeded to bring charges against Americans who, contrary to a law against joining foreign armies, had served in the Soviet-controlled Abraham Lincoln Brigade in the Spanish Civil War. In predawn raids, FBI agents in Detroit arrested eighteen individuals named in indictments. The case aroused a storm of protest. Because U.S. marshals led the defendants into the courtroom in chains, J. Edgar Hoover was denounced for his "chain gang methods."* For a time Hoover appeared to be in jeopardy, and many of the best-informed journalists in Washington predicted he would be fired. While President Roosevelt allowed the attorney general to dismiss the charges against the defendants, at a black-tie dinner of the Washington Press Club, Roosevelt called out to Hoover, "Edgar, what are they trying to do to you?" When Hoover replied, "I don't know, Mr. President," Roosevelt, in full view of the reporters, turned his thumb down and exclaimed, "This for them."[4]

The fall of France in June 1940 finally awakened many people to the Nazi threat, enabling Roosevelt to persuade Congress to enact peacetime conscription and to provide aid to Britain. In response, the Nazis prepared a two-pronged counterattack. They would step up espionage and preparations for sabotage in the United States while financing propaganda to keep America neutral. In 1940 President Roosevelt sought an unprecedented third term. And while he would not admit it, back in office, he intended to bring America into the war. Many Americans opposed U.S. intervention, and there arose a vigorous movement to "defend America first," which became the America First Committee. Unlike the western isolationists, like Nye and Wheeler, the leaders of America First were drawn from the ranks of big business and distinguished academic institutions such as Harvard and Yale. The movement had been originally founded on the campus of Yale, and one of its leading lights was young Kingman Brewster, later president of the university. Its principal spokesman would become the flyer Charles Lindbergh. A mass movement that combined divergent factions, fronted by a man like Lindbergh, would not be as easy to combat as the cartoonish Führer Kuhn or the Christian Front thugs.

---

* The raids could not have been carried out without the approval of the highest levels of government. Around the same time, in Minneapolis, members of a Trotskyite faction of the Teamsters union were indicted, convicted, and imprisoned under the Sedition Law. Studies of the case are in agreement that the impetus for the government's action came from the White House at the request of the president's ally Dan Tobin, president of the Teamsters International.

Lindbergh's antiwar views had been handed down to him by his father, Minnesota congressman Charles Lindbergh, a Republican Populist who served ten years in the House of Representatives. In 1917–1918, Charles Sr.'s public statements were so strongly antiwar that he was investigated by federal security agencies. When he sought a Senate seat, he was decisively defeated. In 1921, at age nineteen, young Charles flunked out of the University of Wisconsin and took up flying. In 1925 he graduated from an Army pilot training program and was commissioned a second lieutenant in the Reserve. There were few vacancies in the tiny peacetime Army Air Corps, so Lindbergh became a commercial pilot, doing stunts and flying the mail. In 1927 his solo flight across the Atlantic propelled him to fame and adulation. President Coolidge sent a warship to bring him home and upon his return promoted him to colonel in the Army Reserve. The "Young Eagle" became even more popular than his contemporary Babe Ruth. In 1929 he married Anne Morrow, the daughter of former Morgan partner Dwight Morrow, who had left the bank to become U.S. ambassador to Mexico and later senator from New Jersey. Ironically, Lindbergh's father had frequently denounced Wall Street and the House of Morgan.

In 1932 the whole country sympathized with Colonel and Mrs. Lindbergh over the kidnapping and murder of their baby. During the investigation, the family's privacy was constantly invaded by the press. In the mid-1930s, Lindbergh announced that he was moving his family to England to try to obtain a surcease of publicity. During his European stay he made five visits to Germany, which was then in the process of building the world's most formidable air force. Each time he was given the red-carpet treatment, and on one occasion he received a Nazi decoration from Marshal Göring. Impressed by the Luftwaffe, he began telling people that no country in the world could defend itself against it. So enamored was he of Germany as a nation that he planned to build a home there. President Roosevelt became incensed with some of the America Firsters and asked J. Edgar Hoover to investigate Lindbergh, Nye, and Wheeler.

━━━━━━

The New York World's Fair of 1939 was meant to celebrate the 150th anniversary of the founding of the United States, present achievements of the host nation (television debuted there), and promote international peace and friendship. Unfortunately, 1939 was not exactly the right time to celebrate peace among nations. Before the fair closed that year, a new European war had broken out. Nevertheless, the event drew huge crowds and helped to cheer a city still in the throes of the Depression. One indication of economic conditions was the fact that the NYPD recruit class of 1940 was filled with lawyers and accountants—not the sort of people traditionally attracted to police work. In 1940, despite the war, the fair reopened. On Thursday, July 4, holiday crowds flocked to its site in Flushing Meadow, Queens. At the British Pavilion, a short distance from the imposing Court of Peace Building, the mood was anxious. A few weeks earlier, France had collapsed, and the British Expeditionary Force had evacuated the Continent from Dunkirk, leaving most of its equipment scattered on the beach. Britain lay practically defenseless. On June 10 Mussolini had declared war on the Allies. The Italian Building at the fair was directly across the street from the British, making for a somewhat strained relationship.

On July 2 an anonymous phone call had been received at the British Pavilion warning that the occupants "better get out because the place is going to be blown up." Security at the fair was provided by private guards and an NYPD detail that operated out of a substation on the grounds. After the warning, the number of police officers assigned to keep an eye on the British Pavilion was increased, and detectives were told to mingle with crowds in the area.

At 3:30 p.m. the service staff at the British Pavilion was preparing for the rush of visitors who would soon be arriving to partake of the English ritual of teatime. Because it was a holiday, the place would be packed. On the second floor an electrician, working in a room that controlled the air conditioning, noticed a small (12x18x6 inches), buff-colored canvas overnight bag sitting unattended. When he leaned down to examine it, he thought he heard ticking from within. Thinking it was a radio that had been left behind, he carried it down the public stairway through a crowd of about fifteen hundred people to the office of his supervisor. Together they took it back through the crowded building to the Magna Carta room, where they gave it to the security staff. Security notified the commissioner general of the exposition, who came over and listened to the ticking in the bag. With Britain fighting a war for its survival, it should have occurred to someone that the package might contain a bomb. Finally, instead of everybody sitting down to discuss the situation over a nice cup of tea, somebody thought to notify the NYPD. Two detectives who had been assigned to mingle with the crowd were the first to respond. Fair security staff suggested that the bag be doused with water, but Det. Fred Morlock explained that if it was an electric bomb the water might cause it to explode. (Two weeks earlier, a device of that type had been left at a German commercial agency in downtown Manhattan.) He proposed that the bag be removed from the packed pavilion. Once again it was carried through the crowds, this time to an area fifty yards from the nearest building, where it was placed alongside a cyclone fence that enclosed the grounds. At 4:45 p.m., Bomb Squad detectives Joseph Lynch and Ferdinand Socha reached the scene.

Since its founding in 1903, the Bomb Squad had gone through a number of permutations. It was variously part of Lieutenant Petrosino's Italian Squad and Captain Tunney's Neutrality Squad. In the 1920s it was incorporated in the Radical Bureau, and in 1935 it was combined with the Forgery Squad. It also continued to conduct some security investigations. In the late 1930s, the squad met twice a month to study cryptography and how terrorists might use inks, codes, and other methods to get secret messages to their cohorts.

In 1940 Bomb Squad detectives lacked protective gear or special equipment, so they proceeded as best they could. After examining the package, they decided to stand it on end and cut a small hole in it so they could look inside. When the detectives peered in, they saw sticks of dynamite. Detective Morlock started to walk over to a group of pavilion officials, who were standing about thirty-five feet away, to tell them that what they had found was "the (real) business." Suddenly there was an explosion. Detective Socha lost both feet, and Detective Lynch was completely mangled. Both died from their wounds. Two other severely wounded detectives attempted to crawl away from the scene on their hands and knees. A patrolman and another detective were also injured, though less seriously. Some of the pavilion officials were knocked backward or had their hats blown off.

Many people at the fair who heard the noise thought it was just part of the Fourth of July fireworks that had been going off all day. Not until emergency units came pouring into the grounds did they grasp that something terrible had happened. Police commissioner Lewis Valentine arrived to personally supervise his officers. Mayor Fiorello LaGuardia also showed up. At headquarters, Chief Inspector Costuma assembled a meeting of detectives and top brass. With two officers dead and two critically injured, the cops were furious. Costuma dispatched a strong force of detectives to round up any known "Bundists, Fascists or members of the Christian Front" who showed up for the nightly open-air meetings at Columbus Circle. That night the police descended on the Circle, seizing twenty-one suspects and hauling them off to headquarters for the kind of "vigorous" third-degree interrogation common in those days.*

The number of casualties at the fair could have been much greater. Investigators concluded that had the bomb exploded where it had originally been placed, it would have destroyed the roof supports, bringing the whole structure down—in which case more than a thousand people would have been killed or severely injured.

The NYPD never did solve the World's Fair bombing. It was unlikely that German intelligence had set the device. At that time, Berlin was looking to keep the United States out of the war, not give President Roosevelt a reason to bring it in by killing a thousand Americans. However, some German agents were reckless. About the time of the bombing, one of them asked his superiors for permission to blow up President Roosevelt while he was attending church services in Hyde Park, New York. Another possibility is that the bomb was retaliation for the one set at the German commercial office in downtown Manhattan. An intriguing theory, which some detectives pushed, was that it had been the work of the Irish Republican Army. At the time, the IRA was in the midst of conducting a terror bombing campaign in England in an attempt to force the British out of Northern Ireland. In New York, the relationship between Irish revolutionaries and the Nazis was very close. Sean Russell, chief of staff of the IRA, had been living in the city while he attempted to recover from a serious illness. In 1940, with the aid of the Nazis, he managed

---

* Commissioner Valentine was an old-school cop. On one occasion, when a well-dressed gangster appeared in a police lineup, Valentine demanded to know why the man's clothing was not covered with blood. Mayor LaGuardia, though a labor lawyer and fighter against injustice, drew the line with hoodlums. When civil liberties lawyers protested to him because some jewel thieves had been brought into court with their faces battered, LaGuardia's response was, "Well, that's just too bad."[5]

to reach Berlin, but he died on a German U-boat while being transported to Ireland. Arguing against the involvement of the IRA was the fact that much of its funding and other support came from the United States. It would have shrunk from killing American families out for a holiday in Queens. However, the IRA in New York was not tightly controlled, and it is possible that some individual or faction acted alone.* The bomber could also have been some crazy repeating what Eric Muenter had done at the U.S. Capitol in 1915. Following the bombing, a number of NYPD officers cut their ties with the Christian Front, and Mayor LaGuardia and the police brass began operating as though the United States were at war.

---

* Sean Russell left the United States two months before the World's Fair bombing. Some researchers who have studied the case reject the notion that he died at sea from a burst gastric ulcer. They believe Russell was poisoned by an Irishman named Frank Ryan who accompanied him. Ryan himself died in Germany in 1944. Shortly after Russell's death, the commander of the U-boat that transported him supposedly died in an automobile accident in Berlin. Other accounts claim British agents caught up with Russell on the continent.

6

ALL THE PRESIDENT'S MEN

June 1940–December 1941

In 1941 the Abwehr assigned Maj. Ulrich von der Osten to be resident director of its American operations. An aristocrat from an old military family, he had served in German intelligence for twenty years. Osten entered the United States at Los Angeles after a brief stopover in Hawaii, where he spied on the area for the Japanese. On March 16, using the name Julio Lopez, he checked into the Abwehr's favorite New York hotel, the Taft.* His stay was short. That night, accompanied by an agent named Kurt Ludwig, he was struck by a taxicab while crossing Broadway in Times Square, then was run over by a second car. Ludwig managed to recover the briefcase that "Lopez" was carrying and quickly left the scene. Taken by ambulance to St. Vincent's Hospital, Osten died the next day. Ludwig tried to retrieve some of Osten's belongings at the Taft, but the management refused to give them to him and notified the NYPD. When detectives showed up, Ludwig fled, leaving the dead man's luggage behind. A police search of the contents revealed Osten's mission. Some researchers who have studied that case do not believe his death was an accident. According to them, the hit-and-run cars were driven by British intelligence agents. Arguing against this theory is that the victim and Ludwig had been debating about how to cross the confusing intersection when Osten suddenly darted forward and was struck.

---

* The Taft had no connection with German intelligence. Its attraction was that it was reasonably priced, conveniently located in the heart of Midtown, and respectable (i.e., the vice squad would not be running in and out all night long).

A mass influx of British agents began after Winston Churchill had taken over as prime minister on May 10, 1940, the day Germany launched a blitzkrieg on the western front. In the next six weeks, Belgium, the Netherlands, and France fell. Faced with an imminent German invasion, Britain was in a desperate situation. Its army, shattered in France, was short of everything from rifles to tanks. A hastily formed home guard, made up of older men who had fought in the previous war—and in some instances as far back as the Boer War (1899–1902)—drilled with broomsticks. The Royal Air Force did not have enough pilots or planes. The Royal Navy lacked sufficient destroyers to guard the convoys that brought the island nation the materials it required to live. If Britain was to survive and continue the war, it urgently needed massive help from the United States.

While the fall of France had enabled President Roosevelt to persuade Congress to authorize aid to Britain and to pass a draft law, he had to assure the public that American boys "will never be sent into a foreign war." Since Roosevelt knew that the Nazis could not be defeated without American intervention, he was being somewhat disingenuous. Winston Churchill, better than most Englishmen, understood the constraints on Roosevelt. His mother, Jennie Jerome, was the daughter of a sharp-dealing New York City millionaire with close ties to Tammany Hall. As a boy, Churchill had acquired his speaking style from Tammany congressman Bourke Cochran, who acted as a mentor to him. Churchill regularly received stock market advice from New York tycoon Bernard Baruch. In 1931, after leaving Baruch's apartment, he was struck by a car while crossing Fifth Avenue and so seriously injured that it took him a year to recover.

Shortly after taking office, Churchill made several changes in the British intelligence services. He fired the director of MI5, Maj. Gen. Sir Vernon Kell, who had held the job since the agency was formed in 1909. He replaced him with David Petrie, a former director of the Indian Police Service's Intelligence Bureau.[*] In 1939, while still First Lord of the Admiralty, after the admiral who headed MI6 died, Churchill sought to secure the post for his own naval intelligence chief, Adm. John Godfrey. A rival candidate was the deputy chief of MI6, Sir

---

[*] Churchill's dissatisfaction with Kell was triggered when the MI5 files were destroyed during a German air raid. At first it was believed that the information within them had been totally lost. Later it was found that copies were available.

Stewart Menzies, a Scottish aristocrat, officer in the Household Cavalry, member of the best London clubs, and a leading figure in the foxhunting world. It was also widely believed (probably correctly) that he was an illegitimate son of King Edward VII. Given Menzies's social connections and the support of the foreign secretary, E. F. L. Wood, First Earl of Halifax, another fox-hunting aristocrat (and arch-appeaser of Hitler and Mussolini), Menzies got the job.

In 1940 Menzies's head was also on the chopping block. Through various blunders, MI6 had lost its continental spy networks. Churchill initially had so little confidence in MI6 that he created the Special Operations Executive (SOE) to carry on sabotage and guerrilla warfare. Luckily for Menzies, civilian code breakers, operating a sort of super version of the World War I Room 40 out of a country house known as Bletchley, broke the German codes. The politically astute Menzies began personally delivering summaries of the intercepts to Churchill, thereby managing to hang onto his job. Day-to-day management of the agency began to pass more and more to Menzies's deputy, the ruthless Col. Claude Dansey, the man who had been so helpful to Colonel Van Deman in World War I.

Churchill appointed a forty-four-year-old Canadian businessman, William Stephenson, to head British Security Coordination (BSC) in the United States. Stephenson's mission as head of BSC was (1) to investigate (spy on) Axis activities in America, (2) to protect British shipping, and (3) to carry on British propaganda activities, possibly bringing America into the war. Menzies objected to Stephenson's appointment because he was not a career MI6 officer. Another person who was not happy was Lord Halifax, who feared that the BSC would usurp the authority of the British ambassador to the United States, Philip Kerr, Eleventh Marquess of Lothian. Churchill reasoned that, as a Canadian and a businessman, Stephenson was much more likely to get along with the Americans than an aristocrat would. Before the war, the MI6 representative in New York, Sir James Paget, had managed to call attention to himself in American newspaper stories by engaging in public disputes with the IRS over unpaid taxes. After Lothian suddenly died at the end of 1940, Churchill, wishing to be rid of Halifax, shipped him out as ambassador to the United States.*

---

* In 1940 Halifax had been Churchill's only rival for prime minister. Some historians believe that even after Churchill's appointment, Halifax and the appeasers were scheming to cut a deal with Hitler. It is one of those

Stephenson was no aristocratic lord. A product of the Canadian prairies, he had been a World War I flyer and lightweight boxing champion. Later he became a millionaire in communications and manufacturing. Between wars, as part of Colonel Dansey's hidden intelligence network, known as "The Z Organization," he gathered information on German military technology. In 1939 he personally attempted to blow up ships carrying iron ore from Sweden to Germany. When his plot was uncovered, Stephenson barely managed to get out of the country one jump ahead of the Stockholm police. Physically and mentally tough, he knew how to maneuver among the Yanks. In order to establish a relationship with FBI director Hoover, no fan of the British, Stephenson arranged to be introduced to him by a mutual friend, former heavyweight boxing champion Gene Tunney.

Whatever his affinity with Yanks, Stephenson would find it very difficult to lure them into the war. Americans still remembered the exaggerations and outright falsehoods that British propagandists had put forth in 1914–1917. Between the wars, the American public manifested ambivalent attitudes toward Englishmen. Such screen actors as Basil Rathbone and Ronald Colman, with their cultured accents, were popular. Other Englishmen with the same accents were considered hoity-toity. In the summer of 1939, King George VI and Queen Elizabeth visited the United States to gain support for Britain. Though they tried to act like regular folks, pretending to enjoy the hot dogs President Roosevelt served them for lunch at Hyde Park, behind the scenes it was a different story. When American officials asked for guidance on how the king wished to be treated, they were informed that his bed must not be along a wall, his blankets must have a silk cover, and he required an eiderdown quilt. (All were unnecessary in Washington's summer heat.) When the memo was circulated, Secretary of the Interior Harold

---

(Continued)

continuing mysteries, like the belief that the Duke of Windsor, formerly King Edward VIII, sought to return to the throne with Hitler's support. In 1940 Churchill ordered the duke to leave his comfortable lodgings in Portugal to assume the governorship of the distant Bahamas. Another mystery of the time is why, in May 1941, the number-three Nazi, Rudolf Hess, flew to Scotland and parachuted near the estate of the Duke of Hamilton. Apparently, Hess meant to make contact with Hamilton, an intimate of the royal family, to arrange peace between Britain and Germany so that Hitler would not have to worry about his western front when he launched his planned invasion of Russia. What is not clear is whether Hess's actions were his own idea or if he was invited to Britain. All of these alleged contacts with the Nazis involved either royals or the high nobility. Perhaps in the twenty-first century, the truth about them will finally emerge.

Ickes wrote in his diary that if the king and queen "thought they were going slumming . . . they ought to stay home."[1]

In New York, former police commissioner Grover Whalen, who was in charge of arrangements for the royal visit, proposed to have the king and queen driven slowly up Broadway in an open car. The U.S. Secret Service was aghast, because New York was full of Bund members, fascist sympathizers, and Irish revolutionary types. Police Commissioner Valentine stepped in and scotched the plan.

As ambassador, Lord Halifax did not disappoint. With Nazi bombs falling nightly on London, a photograph appeared in U.S. newspapers of him foxhunting with some rich American friends. When he tried to put on an ordinary-guy act by attending a major league baseball game in Chicago—probably the most anti-British city in America*—he ended up looking like a fool. He posed for photographers sitting in a box with a hot dog in his hand, but alert reporters noted that he left early, and the papers ran a picture of the uneaten hot dog discarded next to his chair.

Stephenson took charge of the existent New York MI6 organization (assuming the regular title of passport control officer) and augmented his staff with agents from MI5, the Royal Canadian Mounted Police, and a number of civilian professionals. Instead of using the British consulate facilities downtown, Stephenson opened offices on the thirty-sixth floor of the 630 Fifth Avenue building in Rockefeller Center, taking room 3603 for himself. The choice was not random. To accomplish his mission, Stephenson had to operate at the highest levels of business and government. The center was a complex of buildings erected by the Rockefellers during the Depression to express optimism in New York's future. It also symbolized America's international position, with flags of all nations flying over its plaza. Known in his ring days as Captain Machine Gun because of the rapid succession of blows he could land on an opponent, Stephenson employed the same tactics in America. BSC went on the offensive against the Nazis, sending strong-arm squads to protect British shipping and agents to keep watch on suspected spies and saboteurs. It divided the harbor into three zones and maintained regular waterborne patrols over them.

---

* The publisher of the *Chicago Tribune*, Col. Robert McCormick, epitomized the word Anglophobe. In the 1920s, Chicago mayor William Hale Thompson had won votes by threatening to "punch King George V in the snout" if he came to Chicago.

According to its semi-official history, all this was done with the approval of the NYPD because Stephenson opened up back channels to Mayor LaGuardia.

BSC did not limit its efforts to spies and saboteurs. It also targeted powerful Americans who opposed British interests. One was William Rhodes Davis, a wealthy independent oilman who had been able to ship fuel to Germany by evading the British blockade. In 1939, shortly after the fall of Poland, at the request of Marshal Göring, Davis sought to enlist FDR to broker a peace settlement favorable to the Nazis. On the urging of an important supporter, John L. Lewis, head of the United Mine Workers of America union and president of the Congress of Industrial Organizations (CIO), Roosevelt agreed to meet with Davis. But the conversation was a cool one. In the 1940 election campaign, Davis and Lewis (who by then had broken with FDR) worked together in an effort to defeat the president's (successful) bid for a third term. Between them they were able to raise about $1.5 million (including some from Nazi sources) for anti-Roosevelt propaganda and to purchase delegates to the Democratic Convention. BSC agents spied on Davis at his home in suburban Scarsdale and his office in Rockefeller Center. In both places he was observed meeting with a German official. In 1941 William Rhodes Davis, only fifty-two, died unexpectedly. According to one BSC history, the cause of death was given as "a sudden seizure of the heart," and further police inquiries were discouraged by the FBI at "BSC's request," implying that Davis's death was caused by its agents.*

An even more prominent American who had ties to the Germans was Capt. Torkild Rieber, the chief executive officer of Texaco Oil Corp., who had begun his career as a sea captain. While William Davis was regarded in the business world as a slippery operator, Rieber was seen as an executive of the first rank. Even Roosevelt, who called him "Cap," liked him. When Rieber told his fellow executives that Germany had won the war and the United States should make the best of it, they listened. Nor was Rieber the only top executive who

---

* In 1976 Stephenson was the subject of a best-selling book, *A Man Called Intrepid.* Later it came under attack for making false claims. In many instances, Stephenson was given credit for events in Europe with which he had no connection. Even his supposed code name, Intrepid, was actually the cable address of the New York MI6 office long before his arrival. The book contained purported pictures of BSC agents in training, which were later identified as stills from a postwar British feature film. Churchill's top confidential aide disputed the claim that Stephenson regularly dropped in to 10 Downing Street for chats with the prime minister. Thus, many of the book's assertions must be viewed with considerable skepticism, though its accounts of BSC's work in New York generally tally with official records and historical studies.

believed that America should reach an accommodation with Hitler. The German conquest of the European continent had shut off markets for a large number of U.S. companies. From their standpoint, cozying up to the Nazis was smart business. The BSC decided American tycoons needed to be taught that it was dangerous to be pro-German. Rieber was involved in a scheme for shipping oil and petroleum products to Germany through neutral ports in South America. BSC agents assembled a dossier on his activities and leaked it to the *New York Herald Tribune*, organ of the eastern establishment. When the story broke, Cap was forced out of his post at Texaco. He then volunteered to work in the national defense effort. Other business executives took note of Rieber's fate and adjusted their activities accordingly.

In 1940–1941, several spy rings and a sabotage crew were operating in New York. The latter group was a bit too much for German foreign minister Joachim von Ribbentrop's diplomats. In February 1940, when two Germans came to Dr. Hans Thomson, chargé d'affaires at the German embassy in Washington, and announced that they were Abwehr saboteurs in need of funds, he panicked. Thomson sent off a message to Abwehr headquarters in Berlin, which denied knowing anything about the men. When Thomson confronted the would-be saboteurs with the denial, they provided details about their training and the names of their superior officers. After more exchanges of information, the Abwehr remembered that it had sent these men to New York, but only as "observers." Translated, it meant they were scouting targets, such as New York Harbor, bridges, and transportation facilities. After protests by Ribbentrop, the Abwehr ordered its crew to stand down.

Another Abwehr ring, controlled by Major Ritter, who had stolen the Norden bombsight, was spearheaded by Col. Frederick Joubert "Fritz" Duquesne. A distinguished-looking man in his late fifties, known as the Old Boer, Duquesne claimed that as a boy living in South Africa during the Boer War he had witnessed his mother tortured and killed by the British. Supposedly, this caused him to devote his life to working against them. During World War I he was a German spy in both Britain and the United States. Duquesne was a productive agent, but like Guenther Gustave Rumrich, he was given to wild schemes. Duquesne was the man who had asked to be allowed to kill President Roosevelt by planting a bomb inside a church the president attended near his home in Hyde Park, New York.

Duquesne moved among a higher class of people than the Gestapo thugs or Abwehr saboteurs. He took up with a non-German businesswoman, who helped him in contacting U.S. corporations to obtain information on products of interest to the Germans. In 1941 she moved into his apartment on West Seventy-Fourth Street, off Central Park. Other members of Ritter's organization included a courtesan, Lilly Stein. The former Viennese model, who operated out of an Upper East Side apartment, was not the blonde beauty of spy fiction. Her figure had sagged and her face had become haggard since her Viennese days. Stein's services to Duquesne were basically as a courier. Another member of the ring was Herman Lang, not yet suspected of having stolen the Norden bombsight.

Ohio-born Kurt Ludwig, the agent who had tried to retrieve Osten's luggage at the Taft, had been brought up in Germany. When the war started, he was trained as an Abwehr spy. A nondescript little man, he arrived in the United States in 1940 and quickly acquired a seventeen-year-old assistant named Lucy Boehmler. Lucy had come to the United States with her German parents when she was five, was raised on Long Island, and attended high school in Queens. Though her parents were anti-Nazis, she was attracted to mystery men.

As America began to raise an army, Ludwig was ordered to make a survey of U.S. bases in the eastern states, so he and Boehmler went off on a four-thousand-mile auto journey. Lucy's winning ways and wide-eyed innocence allowed the pair to wander around Army posts without being challenged. At one base, when she expressed disappointment at not seeing soldiers, a sentry explained that most of the troops were away on maneuvers and provided a detailed account of which units had gone where.

To some German agents, so easy did their work seem, and so contemptuous were they of the Americans, that they made elementary mistakes. The German enclave in Yorkville, often called "Little Berlin," was an obvious place for the FBI or the NYPD to troll for spies. Fritz Duquesne frequently met with his contacts at a place known as the Little Casino on East Eighty-Fifth Street.

The work of the various spy rings was facilitated by an illegal Abwehr radio transmitter operating out of Long Island. In 1939 William Sebold (né Debrowski), who had immigrated to the United States in the 1920s, went back to the Fatherland to visit his family. There he was contacted by Gestapo officers, who asked him to spy in the United States. When he balked, they threatened to tell the Americans about his police record as a smuggler—in which case, instead of being allowed back into the United States, he would have to stay in Germany, most likely in a concentration camp. So Sebold agreed to go through an Abwehr training course. On his return to New York in February 1940, he opened a radio station at Sayville, Long Island, code-named "Tramp," which broadcast information from Nazi agents back to the Fatherland. Though Sebold's educational background was limited, his operation was a model of efficiency. Not only did Fritz Duquesne, Kurt Ludwig, and other New York spies give him information, but spy rings from outside New York began bringing him their material for transmission.

Given the size of the challenge from the Nazis and their sympathizers, American security forces were unprepared. The United States still had no equivalent of Britain's MI5 or MI6. The FBI and some big-city police departments performed duties similar to those of Scotland Yard's Special Branch, but they did not have the unity of command that existed in the United Kingdom or the skill of British counterintelligence. The follow-up investigation of the World's Fair bombing illustrated some of the shortcomings. In a pep talk to detectives, urging them to solve the case, Commissioner Valentine mentioned that some bombs found in Philadelphia had been meant for the Republican National Convention, which was being held in that city. When Valentine's remarks were reported, the Philadelphia Police Department denied the accuracy of the story. The Pennsylvania State Police would only confirm that there was a plot to assassinate their governor, and the FBI issued confusing statements. Clearly, U.S. security forces were not on the same page. Under the direction of President Roosevelt, in the period from the summer of 1940 into the beginning of 1942, the United States developed a state security apparatus that would remain basically unchanged throughout the century and even today is still largely intact. As in World War I, the principal security battleground would be New York City, and New Yorkers would play major roles in fighting the battle.

Though Roosevelt had been involved in intelligence matters since World War I, he was not an expert on the subject. In addition, as scholars have frequently pointed out, he was not a textbook manager. His administrative style was to assign a particular task to several individuals and agencies, often without telling one about the other. Nor did he hesitate to bypass the organizational chain of command and deal directly with subordinate officials. In 1938 the president appointed Assistant Secretary of State George Messersmith to coordinate U.S. intelligence operations. In Washington the appointment was taken so lightly that FBI director Hoover refused to attend coordinating meetings until he was finally given a direct order to do so by the president. Messersmith was replaced by Assistant Secretary of State Adolph Berle, a Columbia law professor who had been an original member of then governor Roosevelt's New York advisory group, known as "the brain trust." The president's reasons for appointing Berle were similar to Wilson's choice of Frank Polk in World War I: a top lawyer was deemed better equipped to handle the complexities of intelligence work than a law enforcement or military officer, and the State Department was more sophisticated than the Justice or War Department. The downside was also the same as in World War I. State Department types were not aggressive enough to run clandestine operations in time of war. Berle tended to spend so much time contemplating possible problems that he hesitated to act. He also spooked easily. When a Hearst executive informed him that a fifth column had secretly taken over New York City and was about to seize control of the whole country, Berle bought the story. Not until the FBI proved that the information was totally false did Berle breathe a sigh of relief. He also continued to keep his hand in New York City politics, distracting him from his security duties.

In 1940 Roosevelt began looking at other possible candidates for intelligence director. An obvious one was FBI director Hoover, with whom the president had a mutually beneficial relationship. It was the New Deal government that had expanded the bureau from a small, relatively unimportant backwater to the nation's premier law enforcement agency. The publicity generated by Hoover's war against "public enemies" reflected favorably on the Roosevelt administration. By 1940 the FBI had essentially shoved aside the rival Secret Service and was pressing hard for exclusive control of domestic security investigations.

Another prominent figure who was available for security and intelligence duties was New York City mayor Fiorello LaGuardia, who was bored with his municipal job. Though a Republican, he supported Roosevelt and the New Deal. A flamboyant figure, he had critics on both the Right and the Left. During a long stint in Congress, he had been further left than most liberal Democrats. At the same time, he was a tough-minded patriot. After his World War I heroics, he always preferred intimates to address him by his military title of major. Adolph Berle, who had worked for LaGuardia at City Hall, thought so highly of the mayor that in 1940 he touted him to be Roosevelt's successor as president.*

In 1940 the mayor secretly ordered the NYPD to establish a special squad to investigate Nazi and Communist activity in New York City and announced publicly that the department would form a 150-man antisabotage unit. Hoover did not want a repeat of the World War I situation, where big-city cops like Tunney's unit played a major role in combating foreign agents. On learning of the mayor's plan, Hoover sprang to defend his turf. In a memo to the attorney general, he complained that other agencies were trying to "chisel in" on FBI territory, and he pressed the president to issue a proclamation giving the FBI exclusive jurisdiction in cases of suspected espionage and sabotage.

The relationship between the NYPD and the FBI had never been smooth. In 1933–1934, New York City was the center of the hunt for the kidnapper of the Lindbergh baby. With both agencies working on the case, there was often friction. In 1936, after bureau agents, attempting to arrest a fugitive, shot up a Manhattan neighborhood, Commissioner Valentine charged that Hoover's men had broken an agreement to work cooperatively with the NYPD. LaGuardia, as intractable a man as Hoover, carried his case to the White House. In typical fashion, Roosevelt agreed to a compromise. Hoover would be given the premier role in domestic security cases; however, LaGuardia would allow the NYPD to investigate security matters and to cooperate closely with military counterintelligence agencies and the British secret services. As in World War I, some New York detectives held dual civilian

---

* FDR, who by then was already planning to run for an unprecedented third term, dismissed Berle's notion out of hand. He explained that, in addition to LaGuardia's plebeian manner, the American people were not yet ready to elevate the son of Italian and Jewish immigrant parents to the White House.

and military titles. Roosevelt later appointed LaGuardia to head civil defense for the entire nation, retaining his New York City post. Naming LaGuardia was meant to emphasize that the principal civil defense problem was the prospect of German air raids on U.S. cities, particularly New York. The position was largely symbolic, and even in his own bailiwick, the routine work was turned over to a high-ranking NYPD chief, Arthur Wallander, who was elevated to the rank of deputy mayor.

Hoover continued to display some of his shortcomings. He distrusted foreigners, never traveled to Europe, and sought to defend and expand his power, often throwing tantrums and resorting to end runs to gain his way. After tangling with the Army intelligence chief, Gen. Sherman Miles, Hoover had immediately gone to the White House to demand that Miles be fired. In doing so he bypassed his presumed boss, the attorney general, and acted as though he were on the same level as the secretary of war. Army chief of staff George C. Marshall said of Hoover, "He behaved more like a spoiled child than a responsible officer."[2] Despite Hoover's shortcomings, he not only sought absolute control over domestic security but also wanted to expand his operations to foreign intelligence. He stationed FBI agents as legal attachés (legats) at U.S. embassies abroad as a ploy to head off the creation of an American version of MI6. Once again FDR compromised: he gave Hoover control of all nonmilitary U.S. intelligence in Latin America.

Some contemporary writers have sought to psychoanalyze Hoover, a man long dead whom most of them never met, placing great weight on the fact that he lived with his mother until her death and never married. As the great Hollywood director John Huston once said of books about Marilyn Monroe, "They tell you more about the author than they do about the subject."* Rather than explain Hoover's behavior in terms of his personal life, it makes more sense to examine his official one. In 1919, when he became head of intelligence at the Justice Department, the twenty-four-year-old Hoover, an outsider to the world of law enforcement and counterintelligence, was in the difficult position of having to exert authority over men much older and more experienced than himself. When he became director of the Bureau of Inves-

---

* Those written by conspiracy theorists link her to the Kennedys and point to the CIA as her murderers. Feminist authors blame her death on the mistreatment she received from men. Entertainment writers see Hollywood as the cause of Marilyn's death.

tigation at the age of twenty-nine, he assumed control of a struggling agency. To survive and thrive in the bureaucratic wars of Washington, he had to be assertive. In the 1930s, even after the FBI became an important agency, he was always hypersensitive to what he regarded as threats to his power. The real question in Hoover's career is why his various bosses, especially Franklin Roosevelt, allowed him to ride roughshod over other officials.

Some have argued that the dossiers Hoover was known to maintain on officials, and his demonstrated willingness to leak their contents when someone displeased him, permitted him to blackmail the president. Though such tactics may have worked with members of Congress at budget time, the president had more important reasons for placating the FBI director. While Hoover constantly decried political influence in law enforcement, he was always willing to use FBI agents to investigate Roosevelt's political enemies, including members of Congress. Having a powerful weapon like the FBI at his disposal was a source of great strength for a president, whereas a hostile bureau could pose a real problem.

Following his practice of not putting all his eggs in one basket, FDR did not fully rely on Berle and Hoover. He also set up three personal spy services. He ordered ONI to appoint a civilian, Wallace Banta Phillips, as head of a secret unit operating out of the New York Naval District. Phillips claimed that, based on a business career in London, he had very close contacts with leaders there, including Churchill. Some American intelligence officers suspected that Phillips was himself a British agent. Then in his early fifties, he had served in intelligence during World War I. Phillips's presence upset the Navy brass. His position was mysterious and undefined. Nevertheless, armed with the president's authority, he had the freedom to look through secret reports from other agencies (including the FBI) and was provided with substantial funds to disburse as he saw fit. Phillips himself worked for a dollar a year, but some of his agents were paid higher salaries than FBI men. Every Annapolis grad put a premium on looking like an officer on a recruiting poster. FDR's man Louis Howe had flunked the Navy's appearance test in World War I. Phillips, who was hunchbacked and hairless, didn't pass it in World War II.

Another Roosevelt appointee was John Franklin Carter, a syndicated newspaper columnist whose ties to the National Broadcasting Company permitted him access to the corporation's shortwave radio network and the information filed by its foreign correspondents. Roosevelt differed from Churchill in his approach to intelligence. The British prime minister, though a traditionalist, preferred to receive modern "SIGINT" (signal or communications intelligence) of the type supplied by Bletchley. Roosevelt, though he was at home in the modern world, preferred old-fashioned "HUMINT" (human intelligence) provided by spies and informants. He also did not like to read long reports written in bureaucratic style, preferring short summaries spiced with interesting gossip. Carter was the man to deliver such information. Between 1940 and 1945, he prepared 660 reports for the president. Sometimes his information was off the wall. He once sent a memorandum to Roosevelt advising him that three Americans served on Stalin's secret strategy board and that one of them was helping the Soviets plan an air strike of 8,300 planes (hidden underground in Vladivostok) that would burn Japan "from one end to the other." In another report he declared that Free French leader Charles de Gaulle and the American labor leader John L. Lewis were plotting to seize control of the U.S. government.

Seemingly anyone could pass on to the president information that would be taken seriously. Even FDR's old sweetheart, Lucy Mercer, got into the act.* She wrote to the president about a possible spy ring being run by John Perona, owner of café society's New York hangout El Morocco (known to the in crowd as "Elmos"). When authorities investigated, they found that her suspicions were aroused because the Italian gardener had been unfriendly after she suddenly barged onto the grounds of Perona's New Jersey estate. The State Department presented a report that identified pianist José Iturbi as the chief Axis agent in Latin America. In fact, Iturbi spent most of the war working for MGM in Hollywood, which attempted to turn the portly, middle-aged, plain-looking man into a romantic star.

For a time it appeared that Roosevelt would make his close friend Vincent Astor overall head of intelligence and security. Of all the possible candidates for intelligence head (Berle, Hoover, LaGuardia, Philips, Carter), Astor was the most formidable. His longtime friendship with the president, their mutual

---

* Twenty-five years earlier, Mercer had been driven from Roosevelt's life after Eleanor learned of her husband's affair. When she resurfaced, it was as the Widow Rutherfurd. Not surprisingly, J. Edgar Hoover was among the first to find out about it.

interest in espionage from the days of the Room, and his great wealth and social standing gave him the inside track.* In 1938, accompanied by Theodore Roosevelt's son Kermit, Astor had sailed his yacht into the Pacific on a mission to spy out the Japanese-mandated islands.† At the time, FDR was so concerned for Astor's safety that he had a radio with a special frequency installed on the vessel and instructed the Navy to stand by to mount a rescue mission if Astor sounded the alarm. The intrepid yachtsmen never landed on the Japanese islands and obtained little information. According to Astor, one of the principal benefits of the trip was that it kept the heavy-drinking Kermit away from hard liquor. Astor was more useful in taking advantage of his position as a director of Western Union to obtain the confidential communications of foreign governments, and in using his contacts with the Rockefeller-controlled Chase Bank to gather information on Axis financial dealings.

In 1941 Roosevelt ordered Astor commissioned a commander in the U.S. Navy and appointed him coordinator of all intelligence operations of the FBI, the military, and the State Department in the New York area. Observers saw this as a dress rehearsal for Astor assuming the same title on a national basis. In practice, Astor's concept of intelligence gathering did not extend much beyond picking up gossip in Manhattan's posh watering holes or social gatherings on Long Island. He conducted an investigation of reports that the Norden bombsight had been stolen by questioning his society friends. His conclusion was that the Germans had not been successful in obtaining America's top-secret device. By that time the Luftwaffe was already using Norden features on its bombers sent against Britain. When Kermit Roosevelt went off with a girlfriend on a prolonged bender, his wife appealed to Astor to find him. Flaunting his position as coordinator of intelligence, Astor immediately

---

* At the time of his death in 1848, John Jacob Astor, founder of the family fortune, was the richest man in America. Vincent's grandmother was the leader of New York society in the Gilded Age. Not to be one of the four hundred people invited to her annual ball was social death. In 1912, when the *Titanic* struck an iceberg, Vincent's father, John Jacob IV, escorted his pregnant young second wife to a lifeboat. Then, instead of emulating some other wealthy men, who pushed women and children aside or donned a dress to clamber into a lifeboat, he remained on board and went down with the ship.

† Germany's former Pacific colonies given in trusteeship to Japan by the Paris Peace Conference. Because foreigners were never permitted to visit them, naval intelligence suspected (wrongly) that they were being illegally fortified.

bypassed Director Hoover and instructed an FBI supervisor to locate the wayward Roosevelt. When Hoover learned of Astor's action, he ordered the investigation halted. Astor upbraided the head of the New York FBI and threatened that the FBI director himself might be removed. When the conversation was reported to Hoover, he became enraged. To assuage the director, Astor had to grovel like an errant schoolboy and beg forgiveness. It was a defining moment in American history. A security policeman proved he was more powerful than an individual of great wealth and the highest social standing who was an intimate of the president of the United States.

To his shock, Astor also learned that he was not FDR's only secret intelligence source. When he found out that Phillips was running a rival service, he set out to undermine him with the president. Phillips returned the compliment, and John Franklin Carter produced reports criticizing both of them. It began to dawn on Roosevelt that Astor and any of his other supposed intelligence chiefs were not the men to defeat the Nazi war machine.

In 1941 a strong candidate for U.S. intelligence chief emerged in the person of a prominent New York lawyer, William "Wild Bill" Donovan, a rugged self-made man in the mold of Bill Stephenson. In World War I, as colonel of New York's own "Fighting 69th" Regiment, he had been awarded the Medal of Honor. Later he served as assistant attorney general of the United States. In 1928, when Herbert Hoover was elected president, the Republican Donovan expected to be named attorney general but was passed over. During his service in the Department of Justice, Donovan had supervised J. Edgar Hoover, and the two did not hit it off. Hoover later boasted that he was the one who had blocked Donovan's appointment. In fact it was Wild Bill's Catholic faith and disapproval of Prohibition that caused his rejection. Though the president offered to name him secretary of war, Donovan resigned and went off to build a large Wall Street law firm. In 1940 his practice was bringing him $250,000 a year (or more than $3 million in today's dollars). For a poor boy from Buffalo, New York, he had come a long way. Married to the daughter of a prominent Buffalo society family, he lived on Manhattan's exclusive Beekman Place and moved in high international circles.

When FDR's ambassador to the United Kingdom, the Irish Catholic Joe Kennedy, began sending back reports that Britain had no chance to survive a German onslaught, the president was not happy. So Roosevelt twice sent

Donovan to assess the situation. Bill Stephenson arranged for him to get the red-carpet treatment by British officials, from Churchill on down. One key figure he consulted was Claude Dansey. The old World War I MI5 officer had not only become the de facto operating head of MI6 (while the official chief, Menzies, handled the protocols, often from a table at White's, London's most exclusive private club), but he also kept a close watch over both MI5 and SOE. Donovan's report that Britain could survive with U.S. help delighted Roosevelt.

Astor had latched onto Stephenson, too, putting him up at one of the family-owned hotels and flaunting his social position. Stephenson allowed Astor to inspect the British mail-opening operation at the Bermuda clipper station. BSC even provided him with copies of some of the information that it had gathered there. Astor was delighted and could not wait to run and tell the president what he had learned. Had one of Britain's aristocratic representatives been able to make the call, he would probably have picked Astor to head intelligence. But Stephenson recognized that to fight Nazism successfully, and thereby advance the interests of Britain, America needed an MI6-type agency, with a man at the head who was tough enough to get things done and flexible enough to take guidance from his British cousins. He decided that Astor was not strong enough for the post. Adolph Berle would not cooperate with the British; indeed, he loathed them and did not hesitate to tell them so.* Hoover would never take advice from anyone. The obvious man for the job was Bill Donovan. Though he was a Columbia Law School classmate of Roosevelt's, the two men were not close. Donovan had been critical of the New Deal and had run (unsuccessfully) for governor of New York on the GOP ticket. In 1940, in order to present a bipartisan national defense team, Roosevelt had appointed Republicans as secretary of war and secretary of the navy. Another man impressed by Donovan was Secretary of the Treasury Henry Morgenthau, a longtime friend of Roosevelt's and an ardent advocate of aid to Britain. As head of

---

* While attending a dinner at the British Embassy in Washington, presided over by a British naval officer's wife, Berle became upset because she kept using the expression "out here" as though she were in a British colony. Berle responded with sentences that began, "When I was out in London." Completely clueless, the lady did not take his meaning. Finally, he called her to account by saying, "You should not say 'out here' when you are in the capital of the United States."

the Treasury, Morgenthau had responsibility for the U.S. Secret Service, which was a rival to the FBI.

Stephenson, acting on behalf of Churchill's government, pushed openly for Donovan's appointment as head of what eventually became the Office of Strategic Services (OSS), the forerunner of the CIA. He reached out to Sir William Wiseman, who had headed British intelligence in America during World War I. Wiseman contacted his friend Arthur Hays Sulzberger, publisher of the *New York Times*, who arranged for Adm. John Godfrey, the director of British Naval Intelligence, to meet personally with President Roosevelt. FDR was a great admirer of British intelligence from his Navy days on through the Room. He frequently told the story about the time when he had visited Room 40. On that occasion, Admiral Hall had pointed to a young man and told Roosevelt to ask him where he had been twenty-four hours earlier. In answer to Roosevelt's question, the man replied that he had been alongside the Kiel Canal (the German navy's route of passage from the Baltic to the North Sea). It was a lie meant to impress the gullible Yanks with British expertise. When Donovan visited Britain, he had observed large numbers of well-armed British troops standing guard against invasion. Had he looked closely at them, he would have noticed that the troops he saw at location B were the same ones he had seen earlier at location A. Such ploys were an old trick in the great game. Always make others think that you are stronger than you really are.

Roosevelt had his own tricks. He knew how to keep favor seekers at bay with small talk in order to prevent them from bringing up the topic they really wanted to discuss. Godfrey was accompanied to the United States and briefed for the meeting by his brilliant administrative assistant, Cdr. Ian Fleming (later the creator of James Bond). Helped by Fleming's coaching, he managed to get his point across. Afterward Godfrey told Fleming that it was obvious from Roosevelt's conversation that he had swallowed many of Hall's tales.

Hoover was strongly opposed to Donovan's getting the job, but Stephenson held a trump card. He could provide access to British tradecraft and intelligence information, which the United States badly needed. The president named Donovan coordinator of information, which eventually morphed into director of the OSS. "Big Bill" Donovan and "Little Bill" Stephenson became close allies. Given his sponsorship and need to learn the tricks of the trade, Donovan's OSS was for a time practically a British agency.

Donovan's appointment was a great victory for Churchill. However, the British were not infallible, nor could they always count on the support of the American elite. Menzies had insisted that Stephenson's number-two man in New York be an old MI6 hand, an Australian named Richard Ellis. In recent years, charges have been made that over a long period Ellis sold secret information to both the Soviet and Nazi intelligence services.*

Eventually Stephenson went too far. In one instance, he supplied the Americans with a map—which BSC had supposedly stolen from a German agent—that showed how Hitler intended to carve up South America after he had conquered the Western Hemisphere. In October 1941, at a Navy Day dinner, FDR revealed the map's contents in a radio address. Later, he was chagrined to find out that he had been taken in by a forgery. The BSC also began to regard the United States as a virtual colony. In Baltimore Stephenson's agents (many of them Canadian Mounties) swept through local bars, rounding up seamen who had deserted British merchant vessels in the harbor. Then they forcibly loaded them into trucks and delivered them back to their ships. When the State Department learned of this flagrant breach of American sovereignty, Berle lodged a strong protest with the British government.

After Berle pushed for a law that would require BSC operatives to register as foreign agents, one of Stephenson's officers, Dennis Paine, began collecting negative information about him. As with Cap Rieber, the intention was to leak it to the papers, thereby embarrassing the assistant secretary into resigning. The most serious charge Paine could muster was that Berle and

---

* In a postwar interview, Ellis supposedly confessed his treachery. However, nothing is ever totally clear in the world of intelligence. During his BSC service in New York, one of Ellis's assistants was Maj. Ronald Sinclair of MI5. Years earlier, both men had played the original great game in Central Asia. Sinclair, whose real name was Reginald Teague-Jones, served in the Indian Police and Secret Service. In the 1920s the Soviet government publicly charged Teague-Jones with responsibility for executing twenty-six Bolshevik commissars in Baku. Though the British government denied it to prevent Teague-Jones from being killed by a Soviet hit squad, it ordered him to change his name and disappear into the fold of MI5. If Ellis had been working for the Soviets, it would seem likely that he would have led them to Teague-Jones/Sinclair. Then again, that would have meant betraying an old comrade, something that just wasn't done by a proper gentleman—at least, not until the Cambridge spy ring came along. Teague-Jones/Sinclair died in 1988 at the age of ninety-nine.

his wife had twin bathtubs. J. Edgar Hoover had also become disenchanted with Bill Stephenson because of the role he had played in making Donovan intelligence chief. He spread the word that "Stephenson had 3,000 spies in the United States." When Hoover found out about the plot against Berle, FBI men called on Stephenson and gave him an ultimatum: either Paine would leave the United States by 6 p.m. that day or the bureau would arrest him. Like Captain Renault in *Casablanca*, Stephenson professed total shock and ignorance about the affair. The bluff did not work with the G-men, and Paine was put on the first plane to Montreal.

─────

As tension grew between the United States and the Axis powers, American authorities launched a preemptive strike. Unknown to the Germans, after the Gestapo threatened William Sebold, he had immediately gone to a U.S. consul who told him to play along with the scheme, assuring him that upon his return to New York he would be contacted by government agents. The FBI set him up in an office at Forty-Second Street and Broadway with facilities to photograph and record spies bringing him information. Two FBI agents, who had learned to replicate Sebold's radio sending style, ran the transmission station on Long Island. Using information developed by Sebold's operation, on a single day in June 1941, the FBI rounded up twenty-nine Nazi spies in New York City, including Fritz Duquesne, Lilly Stein, and Herman Lang. Other spies were hauled in across the United States. The wave of arrests surprised the Abwehr, which several days later was still querying its American contacts as to the whereabouts of "Tramp." After Sebold's real identity was publicly disclosed, there were mutual recriminations among top German spy chiefs in an attempt to avoid Hitler's wrath. The arrests gave the U.S. government a reason to order all German and Italian consulates closed.

Brought to trial in federal district court, Fritz Duquesne and Herman Lang were sentenced to eighteen years' imprisonment; Lilly Stein got ten years. When Kurt Ludwig heard of the roundup, he left town and drove west, hoping to board a liner bound for Japan. When he stopped in Nebraska to call Lucy Boehmler for money, she sent him a whole twenty dollars. The FBI trailed him all the way and finally took him off a Greyhound bus in the state of Washington. Boehmler and other members of the group were arrested in New York. Tried in federal court, Ludwig was sentenced to twenty years. Lucy Boehmler cooperated and got five years.

The Abwehr was not ready to admit defeat on the American front. During World War II, the quickest and safest form of travel between Europe and the United States was the Pan Am Clipper flights from neutral Lisbon to New York City. In August 1941 a wealthy Yugoslavian playboy, Dusan "Dusko" Popov, arrived in New York via that route. With his comic name and flamboyant behavior, he appeared to have stepped out of the cast of *The Merry Widow*. Actually he was a spy, in fact a double agent. In Belgrade he had made contact with MI6, which set him up to be recruited by the Abwehr. After training, he was sent to operate in Britain, arriving in the midst of the German blitz. MI6 turned him over to MI5, which put him under the control of its XX Committee—the Roman numerals standing for double-cross. It used him to send reports to the Germans. The information he furnished was mostly false, but to give him credibility, the XX Committee allowed him to include some true facts they were certain the Germans were already aware of.

The Abwehr was pleased with Popov's work, and in the summer of 1941, in despair over the demise of its American spy networks, it ordered Popov to go to the United States and help shore up its operations. MI5 approved, and with $60,000 in Nazi funds, Popov headed across the Atlantic. Before he arrived, the British notified the FBI that he was coming. When he got off the clipper on Long Island, bureau agents were waiting. He was debriefed by Assistant Director Percy "Sam" Foxworth, the head of the New York division.* Popov expected to be immediately taken to see J. Edgar Hoover. However, the New York office was not going to arrange that until they were sure what Popov's game was. Foxworth kept Dusko cooling his heels for several weeks while agents trailed him, searched and bugged his room, and tapped his phones. The wily double agent was not unaware that he was being spied upon. He complained to British intelligence agents, "If I bend over to smell a bowl of flowers, I scratch my nose on a microphone." Most of his time was spent throwing wild parties in the rented penthouse of a building at

---

* While other FBI offices were headed by a special agent in charge (SAC), because the New York office was the largest and most important, it had an assistant director of the bureau in charge, with SACs working under him.

Sixty-First Street and Park Avenue. When his handlers questioned him about his lavish expenses, Popov shrugged, saying, "It's only Hitler's money." The bureau men also looked askance at his practice of bedding two women at the same time. In Britain this had caused his more worldly MI5 contacts to give him the code name "Tricycle." Among his sex partners were French movie star Simone Simon, then living in New York, and her mother, though not at the same time.

Popov showed Foxworth a detailed questionnaire on U.S. military installations in Hawaii. He drew even more interest when he explained how German technicians could photograph a regular-sized sheet of paper and reduce it to the dimensions of a postage stamp. Then, by using a new type of microscope, they could photograph it again and shrink it to the size of a dot. Afterward it could be blown up to its previous size. In that way, the periods at the ends of sentences could contain pages of secret information. When Hoover was informed of this discovery, he included it in a report he sent to the president describing the good work the FBI was accomplishing.

Sam Foxworth knew J. Edgar Hoover's likes and dislikes very well; he could hardly have reached so high a position in the bureau if he had not. So he warned Popov that the director was a straitlaced man. This did not impress the continental playboy. He had come out of a milieu where the quality of a spy's information was more important than the tone of his moral life. When Popov finally did meet Hoover, the head G-man was unimpressed. He brushed off the Hawaii questionnaire. Like most cops, he disliked double agents, who, by definition, could never be trusted. Often such characters ended up embarrassing lawmen who worked with them, though sometimes they provided valuable information. The puritanical director tongue-lashed Popov and sent him on his way. After the bureau threatened to arrest him for violating the Mann Act, his British handlers shipped him off to Rio de Janeiro.

Historians have differed on the importance of Popov's information. Some have argued that the FBI should have launched a full investigation and notified other agencies that the Abwehr, acting as a surrogate for the Japanese, was gathering information about U.S. defenses in Hawaii. Other accounts claim that the information was not specific and did not point to Pearl Harbor as a target.* The explanation for Pearl Harbor that has won the most favor among historians is Roberta Wohlstetter's thesis. According to her, there were so many warnings about attacks that the "noise" in the intelligence system overwhelmed its capacity to properly evaluate information. Still, had Hoover gone on record warning of a possible attack against Hawaii, he would have looked very good a few weeks later when it actually happened.

Franklin Roosevelt was a sloppy administrator and a devious man. In organizing U.S. security, he appointed incompetents to important posts, set up agencies with no clear demarcations between them, and deliberately played one man or group against another.† Yet, in the end, he pretty much got things right. Trying out several potential intelligence chiefs, without actually giving any of them the top job, allowed him to assess their performance, with the advantage that if a candidate flopped, the president did not have to publicly fire him. He set up overlapping spy agencies because he knew that the only way he would get straight information on any of them was from a rival service. Finally, he realized that it was the British who had the knowledge and professional skills that the Americans needed to learn. So he put their candidate, Donovan, in charge of the foreign end of the business, but without giving him any control over military intelligence. He allowed J. Edgar Hoover, who he knew would never be a tool of the Brits, wide latitude over domestic security. Roosevelt kept the FBI at bay by sometimes backing men like LaGuardia and Donovan against Hoover.

Although Roosevelt managed to create a security system that could keep Nazi spies in check and provide the United States with foreign intelligence, the one problem he could not overcome was the strength of the domestic antiwar movement. In September 1941 Charles Lindbergh, speaking on a

---

* The questionnaire is reproduced in Masterman, *The Double Cross System*, pp. 196–98, and West, *Thread of Deceit*, pp. 72–75. Masterman, an Oxford don and prewar mystery novelist who chaired the XX Committee during World War II, takes the position that it did point to an attack on Pearl Harbor. West (né Rupert Allason), a young researcher who wrote several books on British intelligence (which benefited greatly from the cooperation of the secret services), has argued that the questionnaire was too vague to be seen as suggesting an attack on Pearl Harbor. My interpretation of the document would tend to agree with West's.

† One of the Republicans Roosevelt had appointed to key posts was Henry Stimson, who was named secretary of war. Stimson was the man who, as secretary of state, had shut down the American Black Chamber in 1929. His appointment in 1940 caused the chief of the Army Signal Corps to query the president's military aide whether his staff should stop intercepting and decrypting messages sent by potential enemy powers. When the president was informed, he ordered the Army to continue its work but not to tell Stimson about it.

national radio hookup, declared: "The leaders of both the British and Jewish races, for reasons which are understandable from their viewpoint as they are inadvisable from ours, for reasons which are not American, wish to involve us in the war. . . . We cannot allow the natural passions and prejudices of other people to lead our country to destruction."[3]

A storm of protest followed, particularly over Lindbergh's characterization of American Jews as "other people." Still, the America First movement continued to flourish.

By late 1941 U.S. naval and air units were in action against German submarines in the North Atlantic, and two American destroyers had been torpedoed, resulting in the deaths of 126 U.S. sailors. As the situation escalated, an incident could have provided a plausible justification for Congress to declare war. However, the United States would have entered the conflict against the will of a substantial segment of its population.

In 1917 the Zimmerman telegram, urging Mexico to declare war on the United States, had enabled President Wilson to cast the U.S. declaration of war as a response to a planned attack against American soil. In 1941 the torpedoing of U.S. vessels was not seen as an equivalent justification. To the isolationists, American ships did not belong in the fight against Germans in the North Atlantic. In 1917 Americans had been more willing to accept the idea of "a war to end wars." The postwar disillusionment made them skeptical of such claims. If the United States had gone to war, America Firsters would not have rioted or set off bombs. Well ensconced in the establishment, they would have used more insidious methods of resistance. In that event Roosevelt might have ordered Hoover to arrest men like Nye, Wheeler, Lindbergh, and other Americans who shared their views. When Churchill became prime minister in 1940, he had approved the detention of a number of prominent Englishmen considered to be security risks, including dukes, earls, former generals and admirals, and even a member of Parliament.

━━━━━

In 1941 the National Football League was not the colossus it would later become, though its popularity was growing. On the cold and windy Sunday afternoon of December 7, 1941, a crowd of fifty-five thousand turned out at the Polo Grounds in Upper Manhattan to watch the New York Giants play the Brooklyn Dodgers.* A little after 2:30, the public address system began blaring out announcements. A typical one was, "Attention, please! Attention! Here is an urgent message. Will Colonel William Donovan call operator 19 in Washington, D.C." When he called in, the president's son, Marine captain James Roosevelt, informed him that Japanese planes were bombing Pearl Harbor. Typical of the manner in which the Washington bureaucracy operated, after FDR named Donovan coordinator of information, he ordered all government agencies to supply him with intelligence information. Naturally, they dragged their feet, so Donovan assigned Captain Roosevelt the duty of collecting the data. Not surprisingly, the flow of information improved. Donovan also shrewdly observed that with young Roosevelt on board, it would be the same as his agency's having a seat at the White House breakfast table.

Shortly after Donovan spoke to Captain Roosevelt, some of the crowd at the Polo Grounds, who were listening to the game on their portable radios, heard an announcer's voice report, "The Japanese have attacked Pearl Harbor, Hawaii, by air, President Roosevelt has just announced." As the news spread through the stands, people began to shift uneasily; some, especially military personnel, started to leave the stadium. The game went on, with the Dodgers winning 21 to 7.

At Carnegie Hall the orchestra was returning to the stage, where, accompanied by pianist Arthur Rubinstein, it was about to play a selection from Brahms on a national radio hookup. Suddenly, stagehands in the wings (who had been listening to radios) began shouting. Then the orchestra conductor, Artur Rodzinski, announced to the audience that Pearl Harbor had been attacked. After a quick huddle, Rubinstein and Rodzinski agreed that the performance should go on. The national anthem had already been played at the start of the concert, but they decided it should be played again. So with Rubinstein at the piano, Rodzinski led the orchestra in "The Star-Spangled Banner." Unlike the Metropolitan in 1917, Carnegie Hall in 1941 was not neutral.

---

* The historic Polo Grounds was the site of two legendary baseball games. In 1908 first baseman Fred Merkle's failure to touch second base ultimately cost the New York Giants the pennant. In 1951 third baseman Bobby Thomson hit a dramatic home run that won the pennant for the Giants. Despite its name, polo was never played at the Polo Grounds. It retained the title of an earlier Giants baseball field, at another Manhattan site, which had once been a polo field.

Later that day Donovan was flown to Washington in an official plane. When he arrived at his office, a platoon of infantry in battle dress was guarding it. He was pleased at how quickly they had moved into position. He was less cheered by their World War I uniforms and equipment. It was a reflection of America's lack of readiness for war. A few months earlier, Congress had come near to disbanding the U.S. Army. In the summer of 1941, with the first batch of draftees scheduled to be released in October, President Roosevelt had asked Congress to extend their one-year term of service to eighteen months. In Army camps across the country, the word "Ohio" was scrawled on walls. It stood for "over the hill in October"—indicating mass desertion by draftees if their service was extended. The vote on it in the House of Representatives was sure to be very close because of the impact it might have on the careers of individual members of Congress. A young New York lawyer named Arthur Klein, who had won a special election to fill a vacancy, was advised by knowledgeable politicians not to take the oath of office until after Congress had voted on the draft extension. He ignored them and was sworn in. In August Congress had voted 203 to 202 in favor of extension. Before any waverer could change his vote, House Speaker Sam Rayburn slammed down his gavel. Had Klein not been present to vote yes, the bill might not have passed.

At midnight Donovan was ushered into the Oval Office, in company with the broadcaster Edward R. Murrow, for a thirty-five-minute discussion with the president. Back in New York, Mayor LaGuardia had gone on the radio that afternoon to announce that he "wouldn't be surprised if the city were attacked at any minute." As the mayor spoke, detectives entered the Nippon Club on West Ninety-Third Street. The few staff members they found there were taken to the local precinct. Cops and federal agents surrounded the Japanese consulate in Rockefeller Center. From outside the building they could smell paper burning within. Because the United States was not officially at war, they hesitated to break in for fear of breaching diplomatic protocol and triggering retaliation against U.S. diplomats in Japan.

LaGuardia, in his capacity as director of civil defense for the nation, had seen to it that New York City was well staffed with emergency workers. By late Sunday night, 110,000 volunteer air-raid wardens had reported for duty. During the night, the Army set up antiaircraft guns around the city. The next morning, there were long lines of men waiting outside the recruiting stations. In Washington President Roosevelt addressed a joint session of Congress and asked them to declare war. This time there was no debate or delay. Even Senators Nye and Wheeler voted aye. In the House, despite entreaties from fellow isolationists that the vote be made unanimous, Congresswoman Jeannette Rankin of Montana (who had voted against entry into World War I) cast a nay vote. When she rose to explain it, an angry colleague yelled, "Sit down, Sister."* With war declared, the State Department authorized federal officers to take possession of Japanese consulates.

In West Coast cities such as Los Angeles and San Francisco, there were immediate reports of Japanese ships and planes in the vicinity. In New York on Tuesday morning just before noon, civil defense officials were notified that hostile aircraft over the Atlantic were headed toward the city. Air-raid sirens were sounded, and fighter planes took off from Mitchel Field to intercept the raiders. Police cars equipped with loudspeakers cruised the streets, announcing, "Information received that a squadron of airplanes is headed toward Long Island; identity unknown at this time." A million schoolchildren were dismissed for the day. By 1:30, the police were warning that the raiders were expected over the city in ten minutes. Finally it was determined that the approaching aircraft were Navy planes, and the all clear was sounded.

The Pearl Harbor attack solved U.S. domestic security problems. Thanks to the Japanese (and Hitler and Mussolini, who declared war against the United States on December 11), America entered the struggle a united nation. Though a handful of fascists were arrested, the only large-scale incarceration was of Japanese rounded up in the western states, most of whom were totally loyal. If there had not been an attack, instead of Japanese occupying the prison camps, they might have been filled with America Firsters opposed to the war.

---

* As with Nye, Wheeler, and most other isolationists, her career was over. They would not be reelected.

7

ENEMIES REAL AND IMAGINED

1942–1945

When France went to war in September 1939, the French luxury liner *Normandie*, the largest vessel in the world, was in New York Harbor. Fearing German raiders might intercept it at sea, the French government ordered it to remain there. Since then it had been berthed alongside Pier 88 at Forty-Ninth Street and the Hudson River. After Pearl Harbor, it was taken over by the U.S. Navy and, as a bow to Gallic sensibilities, renamed the *Lafayette* for the French nobleman who had aided the American revolutionaries, although most people still called it the *Normandie*. At the end of 1941, fifteen hundred workmen began laboring to convert it to a troop ship capable of carrying more than ten thousand soldiers. The vessel's U.S. Navy captain was told to be ready to hoist anchor by February 28.

The refitting of the *Normandie* was no secret. Pier 88 was adjacent to busy commercial areas, and thousands of motorists passed it every day. The Broadway theater district was less than a fifteen-minute walk away. Security on the vessel was in the hands of a private agency hired by the U.S. Maritime Agency. The standards for rent-a-cops had not changed since the days when Black Tom was blown up or at the 1940 World's Fair, where security officers had carried a bomb back and forth through crowded rooms while no one thought to notify the police. Along the waterfront, it was whispered that the *Normandie* was a sitting duck for sabotage.

The gossip came to the attention of a small New York tabloid called *PM*. Its owner was Marshall Field III, of the Chicago department store family, but its voice was the furthest left of all New York papers except the Communist *Daily Worker*. PM reporter Ed Scott, assigned to investigate the situation on the *Normandie*, had no trouble getting on board; anyone willing to pay a $50 union initiation fee could obtain a stevedore's card. In the guise of a longshoreman, Scott wandered around the vessel unchallenged. In casual conversation he learned about the ship's sailing orders and the armament it would carry. He noted how easy it would be to plant incendiary devices or other explosives in out-of-the-way places on the giant vessel. It was a terrific story, but his editors hesitated to use it. It was wartime, and they might be accused of aiding the enemy. Instead, they notified the Coast Guard captain who headed the Maritime Commission's antisabotage section. According to *PM*, he disputed their findings and warned them, "Get your reporter off there before he gets shot."[1]

At 2:30 on the afternoon of February 9, a welder working in the main salon of the *Normandie* accidentally dropped some sparks on a bale of burlap bags filled with highly flammable life preservers. As the flames spread, workmen and the vessel's fire brigade attempted to extinguish them. It was a losing struggle. Their hoses lacked water pressure, and the fire extinguishers didn't work. The ship's lights failed, plunging the below-deck areas into darkness. As smoke began to fill, corridors, the *Normandie's* loudspeaker blared out, "Get off the ship, get off the ship." At the World's Fair, security men had not called the police because they did not realize that they were holding a bomb. On the *Normandie*, it was obvious that the ship was on fire, but not until ten minutes after the blaze had started was the city fire department notified. Then scores of pumpers, ladder trucks, and fireboats raced to the scene. As the workers and crewmembers abandoning the ship scrambled down gangplanks and rope ladders, they blocked firemen trying to come on board. Fire units poured tons of water on the vessel, but because the watertight doors had been shut to keep the flames from spreading, the water was trapped on the upper decks, making the ship top heavy.

Huge clouds of smoke from the fire drifted over Manhattan. Thousands of New Yorkers gathered along the waterfront to watch. Mayor LaGuardia, as he always did with big fires, raced to the scene, donned his chief's helmet, and began directing operations. Thousands of LaGuardia's civil defense volunteers, wearing their new helmets, swarmed to the area, adding to the confusion.

Vincent Astor reached the *Normandie* shortly after the outbreak of the fire. It would be his last bid for a starring role in U.S. intelligence. Amidst the turmoil, Navy officers and fire chiefs squabbled. The sailors did not think the fire department should keep pouring water on the top-heavy vessel. The fire commissioner disagreed. Sailors suggested it be scuttled, making for a relatively easy salvage job. The firefighters argued that they could put the blaze out. The NYFD considered itself the best in the world. Since the department's founding in 1865, New York had not experienced the kind of conflagration that had destroyed Chicago in 1871 and San Francisco in 1906. Its towering skyscrapers presented daunting problems for firefighters, but the department always mastered them.* The firefighters were his own people, and LaGuardia waited too long before ordering them to stop.

Even before Pearl Harbor, LaGuardia had become bored with the mayoralty. Had FDR not endorsed the Republican mayor over fellow Democrat and Brooklyn district attorney Bill O'Dwyer in the 1941 mayoral contest, LaGuardia would not have been reelected. After Pearl Harbor he repeatedly requested to be given a general's commission in the Army so he could take a more active role in the war. Roosevelt always gave him a soft refusal, telling him he was more valuable as mayor. From the president's perspective, that was true. As in the Civil War and World War I, it was important for the national interest that the New York police not be in the hands of an antiwar municipal administration. But the mayor's appointment as civil defense director had been made for symbolic reasons. LaGuardia was an inspirational leader, not a skilled administrator.

There were other foul-ups at the scene. A man approached police who were holding back the crowds and informed them that he was the naval architect who had designed the ship. He requested to be let on board, but hearing his heavy foreign accent, the cops did not believe him, so he got the usual "move along" response. Had they taken him to a supervisor, his claim could have been verified. While he might not have been able to do much, it would have been helpful to officials to have the advice of the man who knew the most about the vessel. Twelve hours after the fire broke out,

---

* Three years after the *Normandie* fire, when an Army bomber, lost in the fog, plowed into the seventy-ninth floor of the Empire State Building, incinerating fourteen office workers, the fire department had to deal with the highest blaze in city history. Yet they brought it under control in nineteen minutes and completely extinguished it in forty.

the *Normandie* capsized. Heavily damaged, it lay on its side for eighteen months until workmen finally chopped it up for scrap.

One man had been killed while evacuating the vessel; two hundred more had to be treated for injuries. The final casualty was Vincent Astor. He was exposed as an intelligence chief by Hearst's *New York Journal American.* It was believed that the story had been leaked by Astor's rival for FDR's affection, John Franklin Carter. Astor, now regarded as a lightweight dilettante, was shunted off for the duration of the war to a minor job chartering fishing trawlers for the Navy.

At first, everyone believed that the Germans had pulled off a mini Pearl Harbor in New York. Several agencies rushed to conduct investigations to determine who was responsible. All concluded that the fire had been caused by sparks from the workman's torch. With the Pearl Harbor attack fresh in everyone's memory and German U-boats sinking ships up and down the East Coast, often within sight of the American shore, many people thought the findings were rigged to cover up official incompetence or to prevent further depression of U.S. morale.

═══════

Following Pearl Harbor, the actions of U.S. domestic security agencies varied from smooth and professional to blundering and amateurish. Within a few days of the attack, FBI men and other federal agents rounded up more than three thousand German, Japanese, and Italian nationals who had been previously identified as potential spies. Some of them were reserve officers in Axis forces. Within the first few months, the Department of Justice filed charges against a few American fascists. Laura Ingalls, a noted flyer who received $300 a month from the German Embassy for writing favorable articles about the Nazis, was given a two-year sentence for failure to register as a foreign agent. George Sylvester Viereck, who during World War I had worked as a propagandist for Dr. Albert, was still at it. In 1940–1941, he was paid large sums by the German embassy. Viereck traveled between New York and Capitol Hill carrying articles that isolationist congressmen could mail out in bulk, with the government paying for them. Before Pearl Harbor he had been indicted for failing to disclose payments from Nazi sources when he registered as a foreign agent. Afterward he was convicted and sentenced to two to six years in prison. A phony Russian count, Anastase Andreivich Vonsiatsky, who was married to a wealthy American woman and living on a vast estate in Connecticut, sought to organize an action group for sabotage within the United States. FBI agents trailed him around the country until they had gathered enough evidence to charge him under the Espionage Act. Vonsiatsky pleaded guilty and was given five years in prison. The relatively light sentence suggests he squealed on his accomplices.

False rumors about sabotage by Japanese civilians in Hawaii led to a demand that Japanese Americans on the West Coast be transported inland. J. Edgar Hoover went on record as saying that, other than the small group of subversives who had already been incarcerated after the roundup immediately following Pearl Harbor, the Japanese population was not a threat to security. Gen. Ralph Van Deman, America's greatest military intelligence expert, who had retired to the San Diego area, declared that "a roundup of the Japanese was crazy."[2] Their words made no difference. The general commanding the West Coast area and California attorney general Earl Warren, then running for governor, demanded removal of the Japanese. Under pressure from California officials, President Roosevelt authorized the detention of 117,000 Japanese (many of them U.S. citizens) in concentration camps. In some instances, military police, with guns drawn, burst into the homes of the hapless Japanese Americans and hauled them away.

On the East Coast, the wholesale torpedoing of ships was attributed to information supplied by German spies. While loose lips may have sunk a few ships, there were more basic reasons for the German success. One was that the U.S. Navy was slow to develop effective antisubmarine tactics. The other was that cities and resorts along the Atlantic continued to operate with lights blazing as though it were still peacetime. The illumination made coastal vessels highly visible to German subs. It took months for the government to institute a blackout along the coast, and it was only accomplished over protests that it would harm business.

In the wake of the *Normandie* fiasco, a new rumor swept New York. It was alleged that the fire was not the result of German sabotage; rather, it was a signal to authorities from Mafia bosses, who controlled the waterfront, not to bother their rackets. The individual responsible for determining the validity of the rumor was a Naval Reserve commander named Charles Haffenden. Not an old salt, an experienced attorney, or a detective, he was put in charge of the investigative section (B3) of the New York branch of ONI, where he directed fifty officers and eighty civilians. Since serving in the Navy during World War I, Haffenden had held a succession of minor jobs in the private sector. He also coordinated a business group that maintained offices in the fashionable Astor Hotel at Forty-Fourth and Broadway. On the side he dabbled in politics on behalf of the Democratic boss of his home county, Queens. Before World War II, Haffenden, a police buff, had maintained contacts with law enforcement officials throughout the New York area. Opinions about him varied. Some saw him as a hardworking, patriotic individual. His many detractors described him as a political "glad-hander" and "blowhard."

Haffenden, fifty-two at the time of the *Normandie* fire, conceived the idea of opening up a liaison with the Mafia to enlist their support for the protection of the harbor against spies and saboteurs. Among those ONI contacted was Joseph "Socks" Lanza, mob overseer of the Fulton Fish Market. At the time, Lucky Luciano, the top figure in the New York Mafia, was serving a thirty-to-fifty-year sentence in Dannemora prison for running a prostitution ring. Known as the Siberia of New York's penal institutions, Dannemora was a bleak, depressing place situated along the Canadian border, far from New York City. Since Lucky's 1936 conviction, the mob had been moving heaven and earth to get him out. The greatest barrier to doing so was fear of the man who had prosecuted him, New York County district attorney Tom Dewey, who in November 1942 was elected governor of New York.

When two of Dewey's former assistant district attorneys, then serving in the ONI, made an approach to some gangsters, the mob saw an opportunity to obtain Lucky's release. They told the ONI men that Luciano's name was still law along the waterfront, and that if he could personally pass on word to the boys, they would do his bidding. The Navy acquiesced and made arrangements for Luciano to be transferred from Dannemora to a much more relaxed facility on Long Island, not far from New York City. There he was able to meet regularly with such mob big shots as Meyer Lansky, supposedly to instruct them on how to win the war.

Haffenden enjoyed the perks of his job. He spent little time at the ONI offices on Church Street. Instead, he made his headquarters in an expensive suite at the Astor Hotel (paid for by Uncle Sam), where he entertained VIPs and politicians. In 1944, after an investigation by the Navy Department brass, which, among other things, found he had accepted gifts from Lanza, he was removed from his post and sent to the Pacific. When Luciano sought parole based on his wartime services, Haffenden furnished, without official permission, a written testimonial claiming not only that Lucky had helped protect the harbor but also that, through him, the government had received information useful to U.S. forces during the 1943 invasion of Sicily.

At the end of the war, Governor Dewey released Luciano and ordered him deported. Dewey's justification was that Luciano "may" have rendered the services described by Haffenden. Walter Winchell, a Naval Reservist himself and a friend of Frank Costello, the prime minister of the New York underworld, wrote in his column that Lucky was in line to receive the Medal of Honor. Even Hollywood seemed to favor the mob. In the 1944 movie *Mr. Lucky*, Cary Grant played a gangster on the New York waterfront who aids in the war effort.

In 1946, when Haffenden was demobilized, the new mayor, William O'Dwyer, appointed him to be commissioner of marine and aviation. According to City Hall rumor, the appointment was owing to the influence of Frank Costello. After Pearl Harbor O'Dwyer had gone into the Army and had risen to brigadier general, but his military duties were not so demanding that they kept him from visiting Costello's Central Park West apartment to garner support for his postwar run for mayor. In 1945 with Costello's backing, O'Dwyer was elected.* Haffenden was not a success in his new job. After just six months, O'Dwyer removed him. In 1951 he was summoned to appear before the U.S. Senate committee chaired by Estes Kefauver that was investigating organized crime in America. On the stand, Haffenden withdrew his claims about Luciano's wartime assistance. The committee report concluded that there was no reason to believe that the gangster had furnished any wartime service worthy of gubernatorial commutation. O'Dwyer himself received a rough going-over from the committee about his contacts with Costello and other organized crime figures.

Some writers have claimed that Luciano obtained his parole by bribing

---

* In 1949 Costello supported O'Dwyer for reelection. In 1950 a huge police corruption scandal forced O'Dwyer to resign the mayoralty and pull strings to be named ambassador to Mexico, where he remained for some years, safe from New York law enforcement.

Dewey. A more likely explanation is that Dewey, who was the Republican nominee for president in 1944 and again in 1948, saw the Luciano case as a potential embarrassment. For example, there were allegations of perjury by prosecution witnesses and pro-Dewey bias on the part of the judge. Luciano had the resources to carry on extensive appeals. Thus, some court might have issued a critical finding against Dewey. From the perspective of a presidential candidate, it was better that the Luciano case go away—far away.

———————

J. Edgar Hoover and his agents had done a professional job in rounding up suspected spies and Axis stooges. His opposition to removing the Japanese from the West Coast put him on the side of the angels.* However, he could not shake his propensity for engaging in turf wars and puffing his image. Bill Donovan's OSS† and Hoover's FBI would constantly be at loggerheads. It did not help the relationship between the two agencies that they were miles apart culturally. The OSS was full of men from the eastern elite who had attended such schools as Exeter, Yale, and the Sorbonne. Critics claimed that OSS stood for "Oh So Social." In contrast, the typical FBI agent was of middle-class origins and more likely to have grown up in some place like Mississippi or Nebraska. His college degree was usually from a state school or a Catholic one, such as Notre Dame. OSS men drank fine wines and lunched at chic French restaurants, where they spoke to the headwaiter in his native tongue. G-men liked straight bourbon (before the war, Middle Americans didn't drink scotch); for lunch they slipped into a diner, where they told the waitress to bring them a burger and Coke. Hoover imposed strict rules on his men, even to prescribing their attire and grooming: white shirts, conservative ties, and short hair were required. An FBI man who took a drink at lunch risked dismissal. An OSS man who didn't was likely to be marked down by his colleagues as a provincial, not fit for the company of sophisticated gentlemen.‡

———————

* The good-guy role of Hoover and the political opportunism of Warren in the Japanese exclusion affair are invariably ignored by those who like to pillory Hoover and put Warren on a pedestal.

† Not until June 1942 did his organization receive the designation Office of Strategic Services. To avoid confusion, I will refer to it by that title.

‡ The FBI rule about drinking on duty was standard in all law enforcement agencies because officers were armed and gunpowder and alcohol did not mix—although in some organizations that rule was more honored in the breach than in the observance.

FBI men invariably went "by the book." Donovan, a lax administrator and at heart a commando, was a swashbuckler, not a bureaucrat. His recruits were individualists, always ready to try something new and daring. Because of Donovan's interests, the OSS operated more like Britain's SOE than like MI6. In the postwar era, SOE was disbanded, whereas the American CIA continued its commando operations. As a result, it later suffered heavy blows to its reputation in such affairs as the Bay of Pigs.

One of Donovan's acquisitions was FDR's spy chief, Wally Phillips, who left ONI to head the Latin American section of OSS. Donovan, always open and warm hearted, selected his lieutenants on the basis of their ability to do a job, not because they looked like all-American boys.* Phillips's appointment infuriated Hoover because he believed that Latin America was his exclusive turf.† When queried by the director, Donovan dissembled. Rivalry between the two agencies sometimes led to Keystone Kops moments. In 1942 the OSS began making surreptitious entries into the Spanish Embassy in Washington, D.C., looking for codebooks. With American troops scheduled to land in Morocco, adjacent to Spanish territory, it was important to be able to read messages sent by fascist dictator Franco, whom Hitler was then courting. Hoover assigned G-men to trail Donovan's break-in team. One night, when the OSS men were prowling the embassy, FBI cars, with sirens blaring, pulled up outside, awakening the neighborhood and sending the OSS men fleeing into the night.

Donovan was a man who attracted fervent admirers and harsh critics. Early in 1942, Attorney General Francis Biddle, Undersecretary of State Sumner Welles, Assistant Secretary Adolph Berle, and Coordinator of Latin American Affairs Nelson Rockefeller joined with FBI director Hoover in demanding Donovan's removal. The heads of the Army and Navy made it known that they, too, wanted him out. General MacArthur forbade the OSS to operate in the Southwest Pacific theater. Despite the opposition of the

---

* In the FBI, each academy graduating class was taken into the director's office to shake hands with Hoover. Some agents never made it any further. Men were known to have been fired for having a sweaty palm or weak handshake. Others made the mistake of wearing a red tie (which Hoover regarded as a mark of insincerity).

† President Roosevelt's decision to let the FBI control Latin American counterintelligence was meant to assuage Hoover, though the OSS might have been a better choice because it had access to a wide range of specialized talent with knowledge of the area. However, the FBI's South American contingent, headed by Sam Foxworth, did a credible job. While carrying out his duties, Foxworth was killed in a plane crash.

Departments of Justice, State, War, and Navy and such heavyweight figures as Biddle, Rockefeller, Hoover, and MacArthur, Donovan managed to not only retain his post but eventually to be promoted to the rank of major general by President Roosevelt.

———

Even before Pearl Harbor, the Sebold fiasco and the arrest of Nazi agents prompted the Abwehr to develop a plan, designated Operation Pastorius (for an early German visitor to America), to send sabotage teams to the United States. After Pearl Harbor, the roundup of potential spies, the departure of German diplomats, and the imprisonment of Axis sympathizers had left the Germans with virtually no resources to carry on sabotage, so they activated Pastorius. It was intended to be more than a quick in-and-out commando raid behind enemy lines. The German army had plenty of crack units that could do that sort of thing. The team sent to America would be expected to operate over wide areas for an extended period of time. For that they would have to be able to speak American English and blend in with the local population. So the recruits were chosen from men who had lived in the States. The officer in charge of selecting the teams, Lt. Walter Kappe, age thirty-seven, had joined the Nazi Party early. After Hitler's 1923 coup failed, Kappe went to America, settling in Chicago. There he worked for five years as a reporter for a popular German daily. In 1930 he was fired for writing a crude, anti-Semitic article about a local businessman. He moved to Cincinnati and, after Hitler's rise to power, became involved with American pro-Nazi groups. In 1936 he attempted to oust Fritz Kuhn as führer of the German-American Bund in order to grab the top job for himself. When his own coup failed, he returned to Germany and took a job broadcasting propaganda to the Western Hemisphere.

Operation Pastorius was to commence with two four-man teams landing by submarine, one in New York and the other in Florida. After they were established, Kappe himself would come over and take charge of the operation. When the men he recruited had lived in the United States, they had held jobs such as machinist, mechanic, waiter, and cook. None fit the profile of a dashing young officer like Witzke or Jahnke, who had blown up Black Tom. To command the New York team, Kappe selected thirty-nine-year-old

George Dasch, the oldest member of the group. Its assignment was to attack war plants throughout the East, Midwest, and upper South. The Florida team was to concentrate on transportation facilities such as railroads, bridges, and canals.

At the end of May 1942, the teams boarded submarines at a base in Lorient, France. Each team leader was given $50,000 and an additional $20,000 to be divided among the men as needed. Individual members received $4,000 apiece in a money belt and $400 in small bills. Included among their equipment were TNT, dynamite bombs disguised as lumps of coal, and the old reliable incendiary bombs that looked like pencils. On the night of June 12, the Dasch team landed from U-Boat 202 off Amagansett, Long Island, one hundred miles east of New York City. Immediately they ran into trouble. They were spotted by a U.S. Coast Guardsman, twenty-one-year-old John Cullen, who was patrolling the shoreline alone, on foot, unarmed, and without a radio. With America at war and the East Coast the front line of naval action, Cullen should have been accompanied by a partner, both of them armed and equipped with a walkie-talkie. A motorized backup team should have been cruising in the vicinity, ready to respond to a radio call for assistance. A decade earlier, during Prohibition, the Coast Guard had fought pitched battles on land and sea with armed gangs smuggling booze into the United States, so it had experience in that line of business. It might have dusted off its old battle plan, and where it said "rum ship," substituted "submarine," and for "bootlegger," inserted "saboteur." The explanation for not doing so lies in the nature of bureaucracy. Commanding officers did not want to place loaded weapons in the hands of young Coast Guardsmen for fear that they might shoot innocent civilians. Such concerns were not entirely unwarranted. In the first decade of Prohibition, federal enforcement officers killed 137 civilians. However, the answer to that was to see that the men were properly trained and supervised.

When Cullen asked the men who they were, Dasch replied that they were fishermen who had run aground in the fog. Cullen was immediately suspicious. They did not look like fishermen, and their whole manner was furtive. He insisted that they accompany him back to his Coast Guard station; Dasch refused. During their training, the German teams had been instructed that if they ran into this type of situation they were to kill their challenger, and then turn over the body to the U-boat sailors who had rowed the team ashore, who would take it back on board for disposal at sea. Instead, Dasch handed Cullen $260 and told him to forget about what he had seen. The Coast Guardsman realized he had stumbled into a dangerous situation, so he took the money and quickly disappeared into the fog. By the time he returned with reinforcements, the invaders were gone. The Coast Guard party found German uniforms and equipment buried in the sand and flashed the alarm. While Dasch and his team walked to a railroad station and proceeded to New York City by train, the FBI and ONI launched a search for them.

The four Germans did not appear eager to start their mission. Instead, they used the funds they had been provided to enjoy New York City's nightlife. After a while, team leader Dasch confided to one of his colleagues that their best course would be to turn themselves in and claim that they had accepted the mission as a means of getting back to the United States. He even imagined that they might be treated as heroes by the Americans. When he called the New York FBI office to tell them who he was and that he was going to Washington to personally surrender to Mr. Hoover, the agent who took the call logged it. But because he assumed it was from a crank, there was no follow-up investigation.

Six days after landing on Long Island, Dasch checked into the ritzy Mayflower Hotel in Washington, D.C. From there he called FBI headquarters, which transferred him to Special Agent Duane Traynor. While Traynor, too, thought the call was from a crank, he dispatched a team of agents to Dasch's hotel room. After a brief conversation, they took him to FBI headquarters; there he gave them full details of Operation Pastorius. The information Dasch provided enabled the FBI to pick up his comrades in New York City and to track the Florida team to Chicago. In announcing the arrests, Hoover neglected to mention that the men were captured as a result of the leader having turned himself in. Instead, he made it to appear that the group had been caught in the FBI's security net.

In order to avoid a repeat of the World War I bombing fiasco, President Roosevelt wanted to make an example of the saboteurs. He ordered them put on trial by a military court-martial, which sentenced six of them to the electric chair. Dasch and another saboteur were given long prison terms.

Most counterintelligence professionals did not favor a simple deterrence-by-terror strategy in dealing with enemy agents. Rather, they sought to turn them into assets. In Britain, captured spies were given the option of becoming double agents and transmitting false information back to the homeland. If they accepted, they were spared; if not, they were executed. Most chose the former. In the run-up to the 1944 Allied invasion of France, bogus information supplied by double agents was an important factor in tying up masses of German troops far away from the actual landing site in Normandy.

Had a more sophisticated individual than Hoover been heading U.S. counterintelligence, he might have tried to persuade the president to keep the saboteurs' arrest secret. If he had, they could have been used to lead U.S. agents to Nazi sympathizers who posed a security threat. They might also have been able to lure other German spies and saboteurs to the United States. The possibilities were endless. Instead, Hoover went for the quick newspaper headline.

Very few German spies and saboteurs came to the United States during the war. In November 1944 two of them landed in a submarine off the coast of Maine. One was an American seaman named William Colepaugh. After jumping ship in Lisbon, he had volunteered his services to the Abwehr. The other was a German, Erich Gimpel. The two managed to board a train to Boston and then another from there to New York City. Equipped with spy gear and a suitcase containing $60,000 in cash, they checked into a hotel on East Twenty-Third Street. Eventually they rented an apartment on the top floor of a townhouse on Beekman Place in an upscale Midtown neighborhood. They then repeated the behavior of the Dasch team by spending their time eating and drinking in fancy restaurants, attending Broadway shows, and picking up girls. When Gimpel urged that they get on with their mission, Colepaugh decided to desert. He went to visit a friend in the Richmond Hill section of Queens and told him his story. The friend advised him that it was best to call the FBI. During his interrogation by G-men, Colepaugh gave away Gimpel, but when agents went to arrest him, he had fled. A thousand FBI agents and other law enforcement officers were mobilized to search for Gimpel. As Christmas crowds made their way through New York streets, men in trench coats flashing badges stopped them to ask if they had seen a thin, good-looking, 5-foot-10-inch-tall man in his mid- to late thirties who spoke English with a noticeable German accent. Other agents staked out a newsstand in the Times Square subway station where, according to Colepaugh, Gimpel went to buy foreign-language newspapers. After a few days the stakeout team snagged him. The two men were tried for espionage by a military court on Governors Island. Colepaugh was sentenced to life imprisonment, and Gimpel was condemned to execution. Two months after the verdict was handed down, President Roosevelt died. His successor, Harry Truman, commuted Gimpel's sentence to life and released him after the war.

━━━━━━

While still the center of New York nightlife, wartime Manhattan shone less brilliantly than it had before Pearl Harbor. Streetlights were kept dim so as not to illuminate the waterfront for German submarines. Gas rationing reduced automobile traffic. Many New Yorkers either reserved their cars for essential tasks or laid them up for the duration. Bustling crowds, including men in uniform, thronged Midtown, but in other parts of Manhattan, people who might have been found on the streets were away in the service or working the night shift in war plants.

On Monday night, January 11, 1943, lower Fifth Avenue was practically deserted. At 9:30 the famed anarchist Carlo Tresca and a companion emerged from an office building and crossed to the northwest corner of Fifteenth Street and Fifth Avenue, where they stood talking under a street lamp. Suddenly a figure appeared out of the darkness and fired three shots at Tresca, hitting him twice. The gunman then ran to a waiting dark sedan, which raced away. An ambulance removed Tresca to St. Vincent's Hospital, where he was pronounced dead. When cops asked the usual "whodunit" questions of Tresca's companion, a man named Calabi, he told them that it was too dark and the attack too swift for him to have had a good look at the assailant. One of the officers found a .38-caliber Police Special revolver behind a trash barrel. As the report of Tresca's murder made its way from the Tenth Precinct up through the police chain of command and then on to pressrooms, everyone immediately realized that this was what the NYPD called a major case—a very major case. The mayor, police commissioner, district attorney, and FBI would all have to be notified. High-ranking detective commanders took personal charge of the investigation, and editors ordered their top reporters to get busy. So varied were the possible motives for the murder that suspicion fell on Italian fascists, Soviet agents, and the New York Mafia.

At the time of his death, Tresca was a few weeks short of his sixty-fourth birthday. Since he had arrived in the United States in 1904, he had been in the middle of conflict almost nonstop. In Italy Tresca had been a Socialist, as was Benito Mussolini back then, although the two men detested each other. In the United States, he became an anarchist. Because he was tall, bearded, and unkempt, with a pronounced Italian accent, he fit the cartoon image of a bomb thrower. As far as is known, he never threw a real one in America, but he hurled plenty of verbal and literary explosives. He used his newspaper, *Il Martello*, or "The Hammer," to pound everybody. In addition to the usual denunciations of capitalism, he attacked corrupt labor leaders and their mob allies. His favorite enemy was Mussolini, who in 1931 put Tresca on the official fascist death list. Like Berkman and Goldman, who were deported in 1919, Tresca believed the Bolshevik government in Russia was a monstrous tyranny, thereby earning a place on the Communists' enemy list. Since World War I, he had been under attack constantly by factions of anarchism that labeled him a police spy. By 1943 Tresca's enemies were legion. Balancing the scale, he also had many friends among the non-Communist Left who found him inspiring, warm, and charming, a man who loved life and people (particularly females). By the afternoon of the next day, the case appeared to break wide open. On the night of the 11th, a minor hoodlum named Carmine "Lilo" ("little cigar") Galante had reported to his parole officer at 80 Centre Street in downtown Foley Square, the center of Manhattan's criminal justice world. Because of information the officers had received that Galante was violating his parole by associating with known criminals, a parole officer was assigned to trail him when he left the building. However, as soon as Galante got to the street, he jumped into a dark, four-door 1938 Ford, New York license IC 9272, and was whisked off. Because of wartime shortages, the parole officers did not have cars.

A few hours after midnight, a patrolling police officer found the Ford sitting empty near Eighteenth Street and Seventh Avenue, half a mile from the Tresca murder scene. The doors of the vehicle were open, suggesting the occupants had made a quick exit. When the parole report was forwarded to the NYPD, detectives were dispatched to bring in Galante. That night they collared him as he left a gambling club on the Lower East Side. His alibi for the time of the murder was that he and a girlfriend, whose name he refused to reveal—"to protect her reputation"—had been in a Broadway movie theater watching *Casablanca*. When asked to describe the film's plot, Carmine could not recall anything about one of the most memorable movies ever made, even though he claimed to have seen it twenty-four hours earlier.

Over the years, there has been a consensus that Galante killed Tresca, though there is no agreement as to why. One explanation relates to Italian politics. In January 1943 it was clear that Italy itself would soon be a target of invasion. The U.S. government hoped that Mussolini would be removed from office by the Italian government—after which, Allied troops could land unopposed, and the Italians would switch sides and fight alongside the British and Americans. To facilitate this goal, U.S. propaganda focused on Mussolini's villainy, while ignoring other fascist leaders and the complicity of the king and some of his officials in allowing Il Duce to align his country with the Axis. Italians in America—whether exiles, resident aliens, or citizens—were split over what course the United States should follow. Some, who had been friendly toward Mussolini until shortly before Pearl Harbor, favored a policy of letting bygones be bygones. Carlo Tresca and many of his liberal friends denounced the notion of excusing the past, whether in Italy or the United States, arguing that fascism needed to be rooted out.

A second possibility was that Tresca was murdered because he had offended the Mafia by criticizing its leaders and exposing some of its rackets. The individual boss most commonly mentioned in this respect was Frank Garofalo, a man who posed as a civic leader but was mixed up in strong-arm work and drug smuggling. At the time, Garofolo was Galante's capo, or crew chief, in the Bonanno Family. Another hypothesis linked Mafia involvement with Mussolini. In 1936 Vito Genovese, second in command to Lucky Luciano, had fled to Italy because prosecutor Tom Dewey was on the verge of indicting him for murder. Genovese's flight and Luciano's conviction by Dewey opened the way for Frank Costello to become the most important mob figure in New York. In Italy, Genovese maintained a lavish lifestyle but was totally dependent on the favor of Mussolini's government. In the 1920s the dictator had carried on a war against the Mafia, jailing hundreds of them, killing some, and pushing more into exile. At any time he might decide to throw Genovese into prison—or worse. According to some accounts, Genovese arranged to have Tresca murdered in order to curry favor with the dictator. As Luciano later told a biographer: "God dammit if Vito doesn't put out a contract from Italy on Tresca."[3] The final theory was that Soviet agents had Tresca killed because he continued to denounce them and posed an obstacle to their plans for gaining increased influence in Italy. A few years before his own death, Tresca had accused the Soviets of murdering a prominent New York Communist. A socialite and former Columbia professor named Juliet Stuart Poyntz was a founding member of the American Communist Party who always adhered to Moscow's line. In 1934 she went to the Soviet Union, where, according to informed sources, she was trained for espionage duty by the GRU, the Soviet military intelligence agency.[*] About that time, Stalin and had begun a massive purge of his own followers. Leading Bolsheviks from the revolutionary days were arraigned at show trials, where they confessed to treason against the USSR. Neutral observers noted that the accused appeared to have been drugged or beaten. Many veteran Communists were dismayed by the spectacle. In 1936 Poyntz returned to New York and began telling her friends that she could no longer support Stalin's regime because she was shocked by what she had seen at the Moscow trials. In June 1937 Poyntz dropped out of sight. Not until six months later did her lawyer inform the police that she was missing from her apartment at the American Women's Association on West Fifty-Seventh Street. When an NYPD detective went there, he found her clothes hanging in the closet, her lingerie in the drawers, her passport in a desk drawer, and food left on the kitchen table.

In 1938 Tresca told the *New York Times* that he believed Poyntz had been "lured or kidnapped" to the Soviet Union. According to Tresca a prominent Communist, formerly a resident in New York and subsequently connected with the secret police in Moscow, was sent specially to this country for the purpose of delivering her to Moscow. The Poyntz disappearance was never

---

[*] The political intelligence service (then known as the OGPU and later the KGB) was a combined spy organization and Gestapo-style secret police.

solved. One theory is that she was murdered in New York City and buried behind the wall of a house in Greenwich Village.[*]

A man named Frederick "Blackie" Myers was a vice president of the National Maritime Union, as well as a member of the Communist Party's national committee. The night that Carmine Galante went to see his parole officer at 80 Centre Street, Myers accompanied a parolee named Ramsey to 80 Centre. Ramsey's parole had recently been transferred to New York from San Francisco, where, in January 1937, he had been given a five-years-to-life sentence for ordering the murder of a man who was an anti-Communist.

Galante was kept in custody for a year. During that time, a police informer was placed in a cell with him.[†] According to him, Galante admitted the murder. But because he had been used as a witness so many times by the district attorney, New York courts had ruled his testimony could no longer be introduced in criminal proceedings. A committee of Tresca's friends was organized to press the authorities to solve the murder. It included such men as Norman Thomas and Roger Baldwin. On several occasions they inquired of the district attorney whether some aspect of politics, foreign or domestic, was preventing an arrest in the case.

In retrospect, the most likely explanation for Tresca's murder is that it was Mafia connected. Some prominent Italian Americans, who before the war had praised Mussolini, wanted to silence Tresca. Although not regarded as gangsters, they had organized crime connections that would have enabled them to put out a contract on someone. Galante was eventually released and, by the 1970s, rose to be the boss of the Bonanno crime family. In 1979 he was murdered during a power struggle within the New York mob world. If he ever revealed who was behind the hit on Tresca (and given his low rank at the time, he might not have known), the information has never been made public by law enforcement.

---

[*] Poyntz was not the only person Soviet agents were suspected of murdering in America. In 1938 Gen. Walter Krivitsky, head of the GRU in Europe, defected. After a debriefing by British intelligence, he came to the United States. In 1941 Krivitsky was found shot to death, with a gun beside him, in his Washington, D.C., hotel room. Though officially ruled a suicide, it is generally believed he was killed by a Soviet assassination squad.

[†] The informer Emilio "Nick" Funicello was the model for the character played by Victor Mature in the 1947 movie *Kiss of Death*.

The American intelligence community of 1945 was largely the creation of FDR. From 1939 on, he had considered a number of people for intelligence director. All had deficiencies: Astor was a dilettante, Donovan was more suited to lead troops than spies and counterspies, and Hoover was a prima donna. When the FBI director ended up with the largest share of responsibility for U.S. domestic security, his strengths and weaknesses were again revealed. On the plus side, he did not allow amateurs of the APL type to operate on his turf.* He was able to apply the FBI's investigative talents against German spies. Luckily, Pearl Harbor united the country, so the FBI did not have to deal with any significant antiwar movement. If it had, there might have been a repeat of the Red Raid tactics. On the debit side, Hoover's constant feuding with Donovan's OSS was as unnecessary as it was petty. The war was big enough to accommodate both men and their agencies. Hoover's insatiable desire for publicity led him to present the capture of the submarine saboteurs as a triumph, when it actually illustrated weaknesses in American security. His unwillingness to learn from the British meant that the United States would not have a double-cross group that could turn spies into assets.

Throughout his search for a top intelligence leader, the president had an excellent choice working under his nose, an American version of Admiral Hall, the British officer who had impressed Roosevelt during World War I. It was naval captain Ellis M. Zacharias. Like General Van Deman, he had dedicated his career to the field. In the opinion of many officers, such as Marine general William Worton (later chief of police of Los Angeles), Zacharias "was probably the foremost intelligence officer the United States had." If the Navy had pushed him forward—for example, made him director of ONI in 1940—he might well have impressed Roosevelt enough to be considered for the job that went to Donovan in 1941.

The Florida-born Zacharias had graduated from Annapolis, class of 1912. In 1920, after active service at sea in World War I, Lieutenant Zacharias, who had learned Japanese, was posted as an assistant naval attaché in Tokyo. When he returned to the ONI in Washington, he established a blanket surveillance of the Japanese naval attachés and suspected agents within the

---

* Though in a later period, Hoover did utilize the services of American Legionnaires to provide information, although they were not allowed to exercise any law enforcement authority.

United States. Like Van Deman, Zacharias was forceful in expressing his views. Sometimes this rankled his superiors, particularly those who had no experience in intelligence work. As a district intelligence chief on the West Coast, he had taken it upon himself to set up a meeting with J. Edgar Hoover to arrange a joint Navy/FBI counterintelligence operation. As noted, Hoover resented advice from anyone; his character was such that he could never concede that he might learn something from a more knowledgeable person. He took an immediate dislike to Zacharias and had him ushered out of his office. After that, he was on the head G-man's enemies list. Where Van Deman had been essentially colorless, Zacharias resembled a James Bond character. His naval colleagues were always amused at his practice of attending diplomatic receptions and remaining until the end of the evening, nursing a single martini, in the hope that some of the other guests who imbibed too much would reveal secrets. He also liked high-skill card games and frequented glamorous settings, keeping his eyes and ears open. Even when serving as a ship's officer, he would personally carry out intelligence missions.

In the 1930s, based upon his knowledge of Japan and extensive acquaintance with its civilian and military leaders, Zacharias believed that if a crisis arose, its armed forces would strike a blow at the U.S. fleet immediately before a declaration of war. Since Japan had done that against China in 1894 and Russia in 1904, he was not the only one to hold that view. In 1933 the U.S. Navy Fleet Problem for the year had been the defense of Pearl Harbor against a surprise air attack. During the exercise, a task force managed to move within striking distance of the target, without being detected, and launch planes. Umpires ruled that the attack was successful, sinking a large number of ships in the harbor. The exercise, Fleet Problem 14 in the annual series, was noted by Zacharias and other observers. In 1941, when the U.S. fleet was transferred from California to Hawaii, he became convinced that Pearl Harbor would be the Japanese target. He conveyed his apprehension to the commander of the Pacific Fleet, Adm. Husband R. Kimmel, who was not impressed. After Pearl Harbor, Kimmel was relieved of his command and given no further duties.

In the early months of the war, ONI did not perform well. Its failures in the New York area were typical. The enlistment of the Mafia to help safeguard the harbor was, at best, ill conceived. ONI agents were no more successful than the FBI in locating the German saboteurs who had landed on Long Island. In January 1942, although U.S. intelligence was fully aware that Germany did not possess either aircraft carriers or long-range bombers capable of an air strike against the Atlantic Coast, the New York ONI warned that the Luftwaffe was going to blitz New York City. The ridiculous report was simply a panicky response in the aftershock of Pearl Harbor. Having been criticized for not having anticipated what happened there, the agency was crying wolf in every possible situation.* President Roosevelt became so dissatisfied with the situation that he ordered his personal spy chief, John Franklin Carter, to investigate naval and military intelligence in the New York area. Carter's report was highly critical.

In June 1942, with the Navy in the Pacific crippled from the Pearl Harbor attack, German submarines having a field day on the East Coast, and the New York ONI office making a number of mistakes, Zacharias was recalled from sea duty to take charge of ONI worldwide. In the previous twenty-six months, five separate officers had held the post. Wartime ONI was a large operation, with more than eight thousand members, including fifteen hundred in Washington. Zacharias, then fifty-two, was the obvious man to revitalize its operations. Immediately upon his arrival, though, bureaucratic politics kicked into gear. He was informed that he would only be the assistant director. Another officer (with zero intelligence experience), who had just been passed over for rear admiral, was given the director's post as a consolation prize. Despite his disappointment, Zacharias threw himself into his work. He urged that instead of sitting back and receiving information passively, ONI should become proactive, emphasizing psychological warfare, special operations, counterespionage, propaganda, and operational intelligence. He opened up a relationship with the civilian Office of War Information (OWI) and brought in social scientists to advise him.

In his zeal Zacharias clashed with hidebound bureaucrats, including his old enemy J. Edgar Hoover. In 1943 Secretary of the Navy Frank Knox, publisher of the *Chicago Daily News* and 1936 Republican nominee for vice president, passed Zacharias over for promotion to rear admiral and ordered

---

* The New York ONI office also forwarded a seriously inaccurate charge to the president. It reported that the chairman of the U.S. Senate Naval Affairs Committee was a patron of a Brooklyn male brothel frequented by Nazi spies. A later investigation determined that the information was false.

him sent to a minor post in California. Behind the scenes there were inti-
mations that Zacharias was the victim of anti-Semitism (which was by no
means uncommon in official circles at the time). As his consolation prize,
he was given command of an old battleship.

When Harry Truman succeeded to the presidency upon the death of
Franklin Roosevelt in April 1945, he was largely unprepared for the job. During his brief tenure as vice president, he had not been a member of Roosevelt's
inner circle. Not until he was sworn in as president was he even told about
the atomic bomb project. Roosevelt and Truman were as unlike as two American high officials could be. On matters of intelligence and domestic security,
they might have come from different planets. All his life, Roosevelt had lived
in a world of rich and influential easterners who were attuned to international
politics. For over thirty years, as a public official or private citizen, he had
maintained a relationship with intelligence agencies—both British and American. He enjoyed receiving briefings and reading secret reports. Truman, the
plain midwesterner, had no such experience or inclinations. As a private citizen or a senator, he was not one to sit around with influential friends listening to a British intelligence officer provide a briefing on some international
problem. He tended to instinctively distrust such agencies as the FBI and
OSS. The man who made Truman's political career, Kansas City political boss
Tom Pendergast, had been sent to prison by Treasury agents.

When Truman became president, Germany was nearly finished, but
American leaders believed that Japan would continue the war until it had
been invaded and conquered (at a cost of upward of one million casualties).
An alternative was that Japan might be compelled to surrender if the United
States dropped the atomic bomb on its cities. It was a discussion that had
been commenced under Roosevelt. Shortly before the president died, James
Roosevelt, by then a colonel, dropped by the White House to say goodbye to
his father before returning to his unit in the Pacific. In parting, he remarked
that it might be the last time they saw each other. When his father asked him
why, the younger Roosevelt reminded him that because he would be leading
a Marine assault force in the invasion of Japan, the odds on his survival were
not very good. The president then made a cryptic remark that maybe he
would not have to land on the beaches after all. James, who knew nothing of
the atomic project, was puzzled but did not pursue the conversation.

Most of the U.S. intelligence community was as much in the dark about the atomic project as Colonel Roosevelt. General Donovan's OSS agents had been contacting Japanese diplomats and military men in Europe in an attempt to arrange a surrender. But the OSS no longer enjoyed the ear of the president. Truman only met with Donovan once, and then just for fifteen minutes. It had not gone well. The president recorded in his appointment book, "At 9:45 Major General William Donovan came in to tell how important the Secret Service [sic] is and how much he could do to run the government. . . ."[4] The lack of good intelligence about Japan might have been the cause of what came to be regarded in some quarters as a ghastly American mistake.

The principal source of presidential advice on whether to employ the atomic bomb was a special high-level task force known as the Interim Committee. Its recommendations were stark: (1) the bomb should be used against Japan as soon as possible; (2) it should be used on a dual target (industrial and civilian buildings) so as to demonstrate its power; and (3) it should be used without prior warning about the nature of the weapon. While everyone recognized the willingness of Japanese servicemen to fight to the death, not all Americans subscribed to the notion that the Japanese people were sub-humans who could not see reason and therefore had to be exterminated. Among them was Captain Zacharias. In 1945 OWI asked that he be assigned to them to carry out psychological warfare. Based on monitoring of Japanese radio transmissions and news stories, Zacharias formed the opinion that Japan was willing to surrender, provided the United States agreed to certain conditions, such as the retention of the emperor. With official permission, he made a number of radio broadcasts to the Japanese people. Through his mastery of the subtle complexities of their language and his knowledge of key personnel in civilian and military circles, especially the emperor's close advisers, he helped to convince the Japanese peace advocates that the United States would not impose a harsh regime on an occupied Japan. Some American officials objected, claiming that Zacharias was undercutting the Allied demand for unconditional surrender. In August the bombs were dropped. In later years Zacharias, along with many historians, argued that Japan would have surrendered without America having to use the atomic bomb. In 1945, if U.S. intelligence had been led by a man like

Zacharias, the onset of the atomic age might have been postponed and America would not bear the legacy of Hiroshima and Nagasaki.

＝＝＝＝＝

As in 1918, World War II ended with people celebrating in the streets. Photos of servicemen kissing girls in Times Square became the symbol of VJ Day. In 1941 many military experts had forecast an Axis victory. German and Japanese diplomats and officers had written off the United States as a militarily inconsequential nation—one where the political system and national psyche would always prevent it from making the sacrifices necessary to win a major war. On the surface, it was hard to disagree with that assessment. The separation of powers between state and federal government and the division of powers among legislative, executive, and judicial branches posed obstacles to quick decisions and united action. American culture seemed to revolve around making money and enjoying life. Military forces were small and recruits often hard to obtain. It was never possible to impose peacetime conscription. In 1941 the United States was so unprepared for war that people questioned whether it could defend against an invasion of California. By 1945 American armed forces occupied Berlin and Tokyo, and the enemy generals, admirals, and officials who had denigrated the United States were dead or prisoners.[*]

Despite achieving victory in two wars, American security forces experienced a number of failures. From 1914 to 1917, they were unable to penetrate the German sabotage rings or solve the Black Tom explosion. In 1920 they failed to capture the Wall Street bombers. In the pre–World War II years, they did not uncover Nazi spy rings until MI5 supplied vital clues. They remained in the dark about the theft of the Norden bombsight until long after it had been stolen. However, these could be written off as akin to similar investigative failures in conventional criminal cases. As late as 2005, the NYPD was running down tips on the disappearance of New York State

---

[*] The low opinion of American potential was not shared by all foreign observers. Admiral Yamamoto, who as a Harvard student and later naval attaché in Washington acquired firsthand knowledge of the United States, constantly warned his country's leaders that, if aroused, the Americans would throw themselves wholeheartedly into war. So vigorously did he oppose Japanese militarists that the Navy transferred him out of Tokyo to the command of the fleet, partly to keep him from being assassinated. As a loyal officer, though, he accepted the government's decision for war and planned the Pearl Harbor attack.

Supreme Court justice Joseph Crater in 1930. The FBI is still searching for the mysterious Dan "D. B." Cooper, who parachuted out of a hijacked jetliner in 1971 after receiving $200,000 in ransom money.[*]

The most serious failure of American security was that it underestimated the strength of the American system of government and the loyalty of its people. In World War I, it assumed that anyone not totally supportive of the war effort favored a German victory. This view lay behind the practice of shipping people suspected of disloyalty to Fort Oglethorpe, the "slacker drives," and the prosecution of war critics. In 1919–1920, some American leaders actually believed that a country as powerful as the United States could be overthrown by a few dissidents. This led to mass roundups of suspected subversives during the Red Scare era.

After the war, Captain Rintelen, who had considerable knowledge of the United States, described the patriotism of the American people: "In France . . . we had no difficulty in recruiting native operatives among dissident elements always opposed to the regime in power. In the United States even the lunatic fringe is reluctant to place its services at the disposal of an alien espionage organization."[5]

In World War II, some security actions rose to new heights of absurdity: the New York ONI's flirtation with the Mafia was a case in point. On the West Coast, the idea that Japanese Americans were innately disloyal was demonstrated to be false. When the U.S. Army called for Japanese Americans to volunteer for military service, thousands (including many held in camps) responded. They were formed into the 442nd Regimental Combat Team, which sustained the highest casualty rate and received the most decorations for bravery of any comparable unit in the Army.

The failures of U.S. security in the World War I era could be excused on the grounds that America was new to the status of world power and could not be expected to understand how the great game was played. In some respects, the same argument could be used to explain World War II failures, although the World War I era should have provided a blueprint for FDR, J. Edgar Hoover, and others who had been in positions of power then. By

---

[*] In 2008, after an old parachute was found in an area of Washington State where Cooper was thought to have bailed out, the FBI conducted a search of the area for Cooper's remains. Experts later concluded the parachute was not the one used by Cooper. In 2011 a new claim in the case was under investigation.

1945 the security experiences of the previous thirty years were sufficiently documented to provide guidance to the decision makers of the future. Yet few bothered to study the past.

8

THE JOURNEY TO 9/11

New York Security in the Second Half of the Twentieth Century

America after World War II was a very different country than it had been at the beginning of the twentieth century. New York City typified the changes. In 1900, despite the consolidation of Manhattan with Brooklyn and other outlying communities two years earlier, the city retained the flavor of "Little Old New York." On New Year's Day it resembled a Currier & Ives picture.[*] Skaters whirled around the ice in Van Cortlandt Park, happy crowds filled the trolleys, and fathers took their families out for a carriage ride. In the whole United States there were only fourteen thousand cars, most of them rich men's toys. There were no subways. The tallest building in the country was the Ivins Syndicate Building on Park Row, near City Hall, which stood twenty-nine stories high.

Although the industrial age was in full bloom, the United States was still predominantly a nation of farms and small towns. The center of American life was Main Street, whether it ran through a prim New England village, bustling midwestern county seat, sleepy Southern town, or raucous western cattle railhead. Even though the United States had recently acquired a colonial empire as a result of the 1898 war with Spain, it remained an insular nation. European affairs received little coverage in the newspapers. At the time, the biggest foreign story was the defeats some Boer farmers had inflicted on British imperial troops in South Africa.

---

[*] Whose office was located on Fulton Street in Lower Manhattan.

Behind the Currier & Ives pictures of urban or rural life, there was another reality. The slums of New York were more densely packed than those in Calcutta. In big cities everywhere, life for most people was a constant struggle. Shopgirls and factory hands barely survived on their low wages. Rural poverty was endemic in the South and West; farm life at the best of times required backbreaking labor from dawn to dark for people to simply eke out a modest living.

Still, New Yorkers and Americans in general believed the future was bright. In the thirty-five years since the end of the Civil War, the population had risen from thirty million to seventy-five million. The United States had become an economic giant. Its wealthiest citizens maintained lifestyles that few of Europe's noble families could equal. As 1900 dawned, the papers were full of confident assertions that in the twentieth century life would only get better, and the United States would become the leading country in the world. By 1950, despite the Great Depression and two world wars, the average American was far better off than in 1900, and his country was the most powerful nation on the planet.

America had made great strides, but not without cost. The changes in U.S. security provided a dramatic example of that. At the beginning of the century, government, particularly the federal variety, had little impact on the average person's life. In 1900 an applicant for a job or a loan was not asked for his Social Security number because the system did not exist. Not until a few years later would fingerprints be introduced in the United States, and then they were largely used to catalog criminals, not the citizenry in general. There was no income tax law; one would not be enacted for a decade, and not until long afterward would it affect the majority of the population. Americans of 1900 could travel from one state to another without being required to produce any kind of document. The borders of the United States were open. Immigrants wishing to enter had only to undergo a health check and declare whether they had a criminal record.

The typical young man of 1900 did not have any military obligation. The brief Spanish-American War had been fought by a handful of regulars and volunteers. The Civil War, with all its horror and devastation, had faded from popular memory into a mist of patriotic legend. No one expected that in less than twenty years several million Americans would be drafted to fight, and that government agents would stop men on the street to check their draft papers and arrest those not carrying them. In 1900, other than a handful of specialized big city detectives and the occasional activity of Secret Service operatives, the United States had no security police.

By 1950 employers would not hire anyone who could not furnish a Social Security card. With forty-four million cars on the road, most people had a driver's license. If someone drove a vehicle, whether to the neighborhood grocery or across the country, they were required to display a license plate and to show their operator's permit on the demand of a police officer. Wage earners had to file an annual tax return and submit to an audit if requested by the IRS. Thanks to World War II and the Cold War, the United States had become as much a garrison state as prewar France. Many U.S. citizens' fingerprints were on file in Washington, even if they had never been arrested. There might also be a confidential report on their private doings and opinions. Individuals applying for government jobs or contracts had to sign a loyalty oath and swear, under penalty of law, that they were not members of a long list of "subversive organizations." National security laws forbade citizens to engage in certain political activities, such as belonging to the Communist Party. Secret lists were maintained of American citizens who would be arrested if war became imminent. Persons entering the United States had to obtain permission and in many cases spend years on a waiting list. Those seeking to leave the country might be denied a passport or refused reentry because their loyalty was in question. Every able-bodied male of military age was subject to service. Several million were members of the armed forces, active or reserve. In 1950 some inactive reservists were surprised when they were suddenly called up and shipped to Korea. Even children went through drills at school to teach them what to do in the event of a nuclear attack.

———

In this and the following chapter, we will briefly examine the successes and failures of U.S. domestic security after 1945. Our purpose will be to understand why patterns of organization and operation established during the administration of Franklin Roosevelt have remained until the administration of Barack Obama. As before, our focus will be on New York.

In 1945 U.S. security operations witnessed a changing of the guard. President Roosevelt died. Bill Stephenson's British security operation was closed down. Mayor Fiorello LaGuardia left office and died less than two years later. Vincent Astor and Adolph Berle stepped back into private life. OSS head William Donovan was fired. Of the wartime cast of characters, only J. Edgar Hoover remained.

World War II was barely over when, in September 1945, President Truman gave the OSS ten days' notice to shut down its operations. He did not even bother to send General Donovan the usual flowery letter of farewell or invite him to the White House for the ritual handshake in front of photographers. Instead, he directed an official of the Budget Bureau to draft a curt memo and have it hand-delivered to Donovan.* For a brief time, the United States had no foreign intelligence agency.

The demise of the OSS left an opening for others to propose the creation of a replacement body. John Franklin Carter drafted a plan to establish an intelligence section within the State Department. With FDR dead, the scheme went nowhere. Emboldened by his publicized wartime successes, some real and others illusory, J. Edgar Hoover offered President Truman a plan for the reorganization of U.S. intelligence. He proposed that, in addition to running a large criminal investigation agency that also had prime responsibility for domestic security, he would take over the foreign intelligence activities previously carried on by the OSS. For good measure, he recommended that the U.S. Secret Service be relieved of its presidential protection duties and that task, too, be assigned to the FBI. In effect, Hoover was asking to be made the supreme head of all U.S. intelligence, foreign and domestic, and commander of the presidential guard. Had Truman acceded to the proposal, Hoover would have become the most powerful man in the United States. Any president would have had to rely heavily on the FBI for information and would have been surrounded by bodyguards,

---

* Truman dismissed many of Roosevelt's stalwarts. Treasury Secretary Morgenthau, whose T-men had jailed Truman's patron, Kansas City boss Tom Pendergast, was one of the first to fall. When a Truman intermediary informed Attorney General Francis Biddle that the president no longer wished him to serve, the Philadelphia mainline aristocrat coolly refused to quit. Biddle felt that since he had been personally appointed by a president, he was obligated to leave only when personally dismissed by one. When the embarrassed Truman received the attorney general and fired him to his face, Biddle smilingly put his arms around the president and said, "You see, it's not so hard."[1]

who would report his every move to Hoover (possibly even bug his conversations and film his activities). Truman rejected Hoover's plan.

In March 1946 the president arranged for former British prime minister Winston Churchill to speak at Westminster College in Fulton, Missouri. Instead of delivering the usual Rotary Club address about how delighted the British had been with the American boys who had come to their island in 1942, Churchill declared that "from Stettin on the Baltic to Trieste on the Adriatic, an iron curtain has descended across the continent." The speech, heard on the radio by a national audience and extensively reported by the press, evoked memories of the late 1930s, when Hitler was seizing countries and Churchill was a lonely prophet warning of the coming war.

In 1946 President Truman ordered the creation of a central intelligence group. The following year, it would be designated as the Central Intelligence Agency (CIA),* and veterans of Donovan's OSS would play leading roles in running it. For a while the director's job was rotated among admirals and generals of the three major armed services. With the ascension of Eisenhower to the White House, Allen Dulles, who had headed the wartime OSS in Switzerland, was appointed CIA director. A Wall Street lawyer, he had been involved in U.S. intelligence work on and off since World War I. In the 1920s, along with his brother John Foster Dulles, one of New York's most powerful attorneys, he had been on the fringes of the group known as the Room. With John Foster as secretary of state and Allen as director of the CIA, the agency would wield immense power.

After the creation of the CIA, Truman ordered the FBI to give up its control over intelligence gathering in South America. In some Latin American FBI offices, agents offered full cooperation to their CIA successors and delayed their departure to permit a period of overlap for a gradual and orderly turnover. But in a number of instances the CIA staff arrived in the morning to find the FBI files burned and the G-men booked for departure that afternoon. The excuse given was that some of the CIA people were not sufficiently "security conscious."

The rejection of his reorganization plan and the expulsion of the FBI from South America were defeats for Hoover. The director did manage to head

---

* Unlike the FBI, Central Intelligence Agency employees drop "the," simply referring to their agency as "CIA." To avoid confusion, I will use "the."

off proposals for an American MI5, thereby maintaining for the FBI the primary role in domestic security. He also continued his legal attaché system, which permitted him to run a mini MI6 within his bureau. In the postwar years, Hoover would regard his principal task as combating Communist espionage and subversion.

Before 1945, when U.S. officials received reports about Soviet spying, they were slow to act. In 1939 Whittaker Chambers, a onetime member of a Soviet spy ring, warned Assistant Secretary of State Adolph Berle that Alger Hiss, then Berle's assistant, was a Communist. Around the same time, the U.S. ambassador to France, Bill Bullitt (a close friend of FDR's), notified the State Department that the French intelligence service had information that Alger and his brother were Communists. In 1945 Igor Gouzenko, a defecting GRU code clerk in Canada, reported that an assistant to the secretary of state was a Soviet agent. By a process of elimination, that trail led to Hiss. Nothing was done about any of the accusations.

In England, the so-called Cambridge spies—Donald Maclean, Kim Philby, Guy Burgess, and Anthony Blunt—had been known as Communists at the university; Philby had married an Austrian Communist. In 1938, after GRU general Krivitsky's defection, he was debriefed by British intelligence. At that time he told them about two of their countrymen who were Soviet agents. His descriptions fit Maclean and Philby perfectly. Not only was his information ignored, but during the war some of the Cambridge spies were given jobs in MI5 and MI6 without a background check. Philby did so well that he was sent to Washington as liaison man with the CIA and was being groomed to possibly become chief of MI6. Alger Hiss was made president of the Carnegie Endowment for International Peace, a position that put him in line for a top State Department post.[*]

In 1945 an OSS analyst noticed that an article in the January 26 edition of the magazine *Amerasia* was almost identical to a 1944 report that he had written on Thailand. He reported the matter to the head of the OSS security section, Frank Bielaski, brother of World War I Bureau of Investigation chief A. Bruce, and Ruth Shipley, director of the passport division of the State Department. Led by Bielaski, OSS agents broke into the offices of *Amerasia*,

---

[*] In 1961, President Kennedy chose the president of the endowment, Dean Rusk, to be his secretary of state.

many of whose staff had connections to American Communists and party chief Earl Browder. They found hundreds of classified documents from the departments of State and Navy and the OSS. The Federal Bureau of Investigation was brought into the case. During the course of its investigation, the FBI conducted a number of break-ins, or "black-bag jobs," and installed bugs and phone taps in the *Amerasia* office and the homes of suspects.* In June six people were arrested (including an ONI officer and a State Department employee), and seventeen hundred classified government documents were seized. No evidence was found that any of the documents had been forwarded to a foreign power, so the Justice Department decided not to seek indictment under the Espionage Act. Instead, it charged the six for unauthorized possession of government documents, and a grand jury ultimately indicted three of them. When defense attorneys threatened to introduce evidence of the FBI's unlawful investigative techniques, the Justice Department, fearing the case would be lost at trial, arranged a deal whereby two of the defendants paid fines of twenty-five hundred dollars and five hundred dollars, respectively.

In 1945, twenty-seven-year-old FBI special agent Robert Lamphere was offered a transfer from the general criminal investigation squad of the New York office to Squad SE, Soviet espionage. Lamphere was a more typical G-man than Leon Turrou, the Nazi spy hunter. He came from Idaho and, after graduating from the state university, took a job in Washington, attended law school at night, and in 1941 joined the FBI. Following his rookie year at a field office in Birmingham, Alabama, he was transferred to New York and assigned to criminal work. During the war years, he handled everything from violations of the Selective Service (draft) Law to hunting Nazi spies. Though doubtful that trailing suspected Soviet agents would be very interesting, Lamphere decided to give it a try. About the time that he went to the SE squad, a woman walked into the New York FBI office with information that would have huge repercussions on the American government. Elizabeth

---

* FBI black-bag jobs were carried out with military precision. Each began with a survey of the proposed target. Then two or three agents would conduct the break-in, usually at night. One had the responsibility for photographing documents, another for ensuring that they were correctly replaced. A further eight to ten agents surrounded the area to keep exits and entrances under surveillance. All were equipped with hand radios, and a supervisor coordinated the operation.

Bentley was a Vassar graduate who had joined the Communist Party in the 1930s. According to her, she was assigned to work as a courier and later a spy handler for a Soviet espionage ring. Interestingly, the only person she refused to work with was Juliet Poyntz. After extensive debriefing, Bentley supplied the FBI with the names of more than a hundred people allegedly linked to the ring. Twenty-seven of them were employed by the U.S. government, including Alger Hiss and Assistant Secretary of the Treasury Harry Dexter White, a man touted as a future treasury secretary.

While Hiss and White were supposedly being brought along by the Soviets, another Communist was being groomed to fill a top job in U.S. security—police commissioner of New York City. The first NYPD officer to encounter the Communist cop was Det. Gene Epstein, a member of Special Squad One, the unit Mayor LaGuardia had created in 1940 to investigate Nazi and Communist activities. Like others in the squad, Epstein was also an agent of ONI—which provided him with an additional paycheck, though he had to turn it over to the NYPD. Epstein was assigned to infiltrate the Communist Party, a task a bit more difficult than simply filling out a membership application. The usual procedure was that a party member would spot a likely recruit and persuade him to join. If the candidate passed various checks, he would eventually get in. So Epstein read the *Daily Worker* and other publications in order to become au courant with Communist ideas. He then began hanging around in places where known Communists gathered. Eventually he received a recruiting pitch and, without appearing anxious, responded favorably. While being vetted, Epstein and another man were introduced to an individual identified as Comrade Chester, and together they went to a Brooklyn apartment. There, Epstein noticed that somebody standing behind a drawn curtain was observing him. Nothing happened then, but later Epstein was summoned to another meeting, where Chester told him that he was the head of the Communist Control Commission (the party security organization) and that they had found out that Epstein was a member of the NYPD assigned to infiltrate the party. He was able to tell Epstein, to the exact cent, how much money he had received from ONI and paid back to the department. The fact that someone had such detailed information on him made Epstein and his bosses realize that Special Squad One itself had probably been infiltrated by Communists. An investigation was conducted, and suspicion fell on four civilian employees. Although they denied guilt, they resigned from the department.

In 1944 Lt. Thomas Crane, commanding officer of the combined Special Squad One and Alien Squad, received a report from the FBI about an incident in Las Vegas. Because of the atomic bomb project at nearby Los Alamos, New Mexico, Vegas was blanketed by G-Men. The bureau reported a woman named Sylvia had gone to Nevada in the company of a man named Max, who was seeking a divorce so that the two of them could marry. During her time in Vegas, Sylvia met with several persons already under surveillance for possible involvement in espionage. When the FBI began checking on Sylvia, they learned that she was in contact with Arthur Miller, a New York City police officer living in Brooklyn. A check of the NYPD records revealed that Miller had joined the department in 1937 at the age of twenty-six. At that time his name had been Isidore Cohen. The following year he changed it legally to Arthur Miller. In 1943 he had been promoted to sergeant. Squad One obtained a court order to put a wiretap on Miller's home telephone and assigned six detectives to monitor it. One of them was Gene Epstein. From listening to the conversations, the department became aware that Miller was acquainted with some known Communists. One time, while Epstein monitored the phone, Miller's wife received a phone call and a voice announced, "This is Chester." Epstein immediately recognized it as the man from the Control Commission. The detectives learned that Chester would be coming to dinner at Miller's house. On the night he was scheduled to arrive, Epstein and his partner, Det. Edward Murtagh, staked out the area. At about 8:30, a man walked down the street and rang Miller's doorbell. Epstein turned to Murtagh and said, "I know that guy—that's Chester." Later, when Chester came out, the detectives followed him to a nearby subway station. With the train about to arrive, they had to make a move or risk losing him. So they flashed their badges, shoved him up against a wall, and demanded he show identification. The shaken Chester handed them a draft card made out in the name of Bernard Schuster. Since the detectives had nothing on him, they let him go. The forty-year-old Shuster (né Zuster) was a big shot. Not only did he head internal security for the party in New York, but he was liaison man between the New York KGB and the Communist Party USA (CPUSA). He also recruited for the KGB, was involved in atomic bomb espionage, and supplied party members for courier work.

Under civil service laws, the department did not have enough evidence to bring disciplinary charges against Miller, so they resorted to a classic NYPD ploy: they buried him. Sergeant Miller was transferred to the Prospect Park sub-precinct to keep watch over the squirrels. Chester had gotten word to Miller about the incident with the detectives, and so, after his transfer, Miller realized that the department suspected him of being a Communist. He went to his party superiors and asked them for permission to resign from the NYPD. They refused. Instead, they ordered him to remain on the job and study hard in order to pass the promotional examinations and rise as high as he could. They explained to him that someday the small, but influential, Communist-dominated American Labor Party might be in a position to name the police commissioner.[*]

By 1946 the FBI SE squad had determined that the Soviet consulate on East Sixty-First Street was headquarters for spies and that Consul General Pavel Mikhailov was the chief of the New York office of the GRU. But they had no similar information about the KGB. Bentley's revelations had caused the KGB to order many of its officers in America back to Russia. Among them was the New York station chief, so the post was filled by acting heads. Agents maintained a watch on the consulate and followed employees from their offices to their homes, at that time often apartment hotels on the city's West Side. (Not until the 1970s would the Soviets order all employees and their families to reside in a large compound in Riverdale, up in the Bronx.) Many of the Russians—fresh from the homeland, where rationing was strict and the food unappetizing—favored a smorgasbord restaurant in Midtown that featured heaping plates of delicacies. FBI agents began dining at the same place. By observing close up, they could often infer an individual's standing from the way he was treated by other Russians. If a high-ranking official showed great deference to a low-level member of the staff, it was a sign that the latter was an intelligence officer.

Other clues to the status of Soviet diplomats were their movements and behavior. While most of the Russians were strictly supervised and kept to

---

[*] In 1948, presidential candidate Henry Wallace garnered nearly half a million votes in New York State on the ALP ticket.

their desks, a few seemed to have the freedom to wander around New York. When tailed, these individuals were observed constantly glancing around to see if anyone was following them. As part of their routine, they would peer into a department store window to observe who was behind them, then go inside and up an escalator and switch to the downstairs one to determine whether someone they had seen outside the store was still behind them. Another trick was to go through the front door of a busy hotel and quickly exit through the side door, run down into a subway station, board a train, get off at the next stop, cross the platform, and hop on a train going in the opposite direction.* Like the Nazis, the various Soviet intelligence groups often worked at cross purposes. In addition to the GRU and KGB, the Soviet navy, the Communist International (COMINTERN), and CPUSA had their own intelligence services.

The Soviet explosion of an atomic bomb in 1949, the Communist takeover of China that same year, and the North Korean invasion of South Korea in 1950 convinced the American public that the Communist Bloc, led by the Soviet Union, was out to conquer the world. Most historians today do not accept this thesis, but it looked real enough at the time to many people. As a result, the country began moving into a new, much larger period of Red Scares like those of 1919–1920.

In 1950 Senator Joseph McCarthy first raised charges of Communist subversion within the U.S. government. That year, the Department of Justice indicted eleven Communist leaders under the Smith Act, which made it illegal to organize or belong to a group whose goal was the overthrow of the U.S. government by force. Among the prosecution's key witnesses were mid-level party leaders who were undercover FBI informants. All the defendants were convicted.

Through leads supplied by Elizabeth Bentley, FBI agents determined that a German physicist, Klaus Fuchs, had passed material to Soviet spies while working on the Manhattan (atomic bomb) Project. By that time Fuchs was back at his home in Britain. Under interrogation by MI5, he confessed and

---

* Despite all their shrewd moves, the spies could also make silly mistakes. In 1941 a KGB officer had hidden a cache of weapons in the consulate. In 1947, when the lease expired, no one could remember where they were hidden. A frantic search was undertaken, but nothing was found. Since the new tenants did not report finding weapons, it was assumed that they must have been removed earlier by some officer, but no log entry had been made.

was imprisoned. Questioned in a British jail by FBI agent Lamphere, Fuchs supplied information that led to Harry Gold, who admitted to being Fuchs's contact man with Soviet espionage. Gold, in turn, implicated David Greenglass of New York, an Army sergeant who had worked at the atomic facility in Los Alamos. Greenglass gave up his brother-in-law, an engineer named Julius Rosenberg.

In 1950 Rosenberg and his wife, Ethel, were charged with conspiracy to commit espionage and tried in Manhattan federal court. Found guilty in April 1951, they were sentenced to death by Judge Irving Kaufman, who declared that they had helped the Soviet Union acquire the atomic bomb and therefore were responsible for the outbreak of the Korean War the previous year.[*]

Harry Dexter White died of a heart attack after the accusations against him surfaced at a hearing of the House on Un-American Activities Committee. Alger Hiss was indicted on a charge of perjury before the same committee. His first trial resulted in a hung jury; at the second, in 1950, he was convicted and sentenced to five years' imprisonment.

For years it was an article of faith among many people that the Rosenbergs and Hiss were innocent. However, at the time of their trials, the government had definitive evidence of their guilt that could not be revealed. In 1944 Hoover's archrival, William Donovan of the OSS, had bought a captured Soviet codebook from the Finns. Though Soviet spies within OSS alerted Moscow, which promptly changed its code, U.S. cryptanalysts were able to read messages previously sent and thereby identify Communist agents within the United States.[†]

Historians who have studied the Rosenberg case have concluded that while Julius engaged in espionage, the information he supplied was much less valuable than the data Klaus Fuchs furnished and was not the key to

---

[*] The Rosenbergs were scheduled to be executed at Sing Sing on the night of June 19, 1953. The FBI, hoping to the last that one or both of them would confess and provide further information, set up a command post at the prison and installed a direct phone line to its New York office and Washington headquarters. Both Rosenbergs went to their deaths without confessing.

[†] In 2008 one of the Rosenbergs' codefendants, Morton Sobell, admitted to the *New York Times* that they had been spies. A 2009 book by U.S. scholars John Haynes and Harvey Klehr and former Soviet intelligence officer Alexander Vassiliev, published by the Yale University Press, confirmed that, based on Soviet files, Julius Rosenberg was a KGB spy and Hiss an agent for the GRU.

the Soviets developing an atom bomb. They also believe that Ethel played only a minor role in the operation. Despite Judge Kaufman's overheated rhetoric, they were hardly responsible for starting the Korean War. In a less fevered environment, Julius would probably have received a prison sentence on the order of ten years, and Ethel might not have been charged at all.

The intensive drive against Soviet espionage finally led to the public outing of NYPD cop Arthur Miller. He had followed party directives to study hard and had been promoted to lieutenant. By 1951 he stood high on the list for captain. Then a disgruntled member of the party went to the FBI and named Miller as the leader of a cell of three police officers. With a witness that could be presented at an administrative hearing, the department filed charges against Miller, seeking his dismissal. While they were pending, he quietly slipped into headquarters and resigned, after which he disappeared.

———

President Truman made major errors in his handling of domestic security. When he was informed of Soviet espionage and the fact that some U.S. officials were suspected of being involved, he should have seized control of the investigation. Instead, he took the view that spy scares were "red herrings" designed to distract attention from domestic problems. By doing so, he opened the way for such Republicans as Congressman Richard Nixon, of the House on Un-American Activities Committee, and Senator McCarthy to run with the issue. Ironically, as president, Truman fought the Communists on every conceivable battlefield. The United States conducted espionage against the Soviet Bloc. It provided money, arms, and training for guerrilla bands operating in Poland, the Ukraine, and Albania. In essence, America took the place of Britain in playing the great game against the Russians worldwide. In 1950 Truman sent hundreds of thousands of American troops to battle the North Koreans and Red Chinese on the Asian mainland. But because he did not denounce Soviet spies and their American contacts, he acquired the reputation of being of being "soft on Communism."

Senator McCarthy, like Attorney General Palmer after World War I, sought to ride the "Red menace" to the White House. For a time he dominated the headlines, then he imploded. He was essentially right in his main assertion—that the Soviet government was conducting espionage against the United States and, in some instances, was receiving cooperation from American citizens, including government officials. However, he had no hard evidence, and most of the people he targeted were loyal Americans whose careers were destroyed by his actions. Some of those he drove out of public life were experts on Asia who, if they had remained in government service, might have helped America avoid the disaster of Vietnam. While McCarthy himself appeared motivated by ruthless personal ambition rather than ideology, many conservative Americans used the threat of Communism to discredit liberals. In later years, their actions made it much more difficult to investigate security threats because the targets could always raise the cry of "McCarthyism."

The one man who might have been able to offset McCarthy from the beginning by providing a less exaggerated estimate of the situation was J. Edgar Hoover. Yet he never chose to do so. Even when government informers began to outnumber party members at cell meetings, his view was that it only took a handful of dedicated Communists to make the 1917 revolution in Russia. Therefore, no matter how small the party was, it would always be a major threat. Hoover's argument ignored the fact that conditions in backward Russia, after three years of war, were not the same as those in affluent postwar America. In contrast, Great Britain, which had its share of spy scandals involving government officials, managed to avoid hysteria. There, the security services were always able to present a balanced appraisal of the Communist threat.

In 1945 when Truman dismissed General Donovan, he might also have gotten rid of Hoover. Politically that would have been very difficult, because of the FBI chief's great popularity with the public.* But Truman could have kicked him upstairs. In that year, NYPD commissioner Valentine was sent to Tokyo to reorganize the Japanese police. U.S. Supreme Court justice Robert Jackson was named chief prosecutor at the Nuremberg war crimes

---

* Among Hoover's supporters were Roger Baldwin, head of the ACLU, and the organization's general counsel Morris Ernst, a noted private attorney. On many occasions Ernst defended the FBI. For example, after one unfavorable story appeared, he wrote to Hoover's number-two man, "Can I do anything to help you and Edgar on this stinking series of articles appearing in the *Star?*" On another occasion he wrote to Hoover, "My dear Edgar, you are a grand guy and I am in your army."[2] Baldwin and Ernst also reported information about American Communists to the FBI.

trial. Hoover would have been hard put to refuse an assignment to assist General MacArthur in Japan or to root out Nazism in Germany. *

Soviet espionage continued to be a major problem and New York the primary battleground.† In 1953 a Brooklyn newsboy who had received a nickel in change accidentally dropped it on a stairway; to his surprise it broke open, and microfilm fell out. He thought the contents might interest the police, who turned it over to the FBI. An examination of the coin disclosed that it had been professionally made and the microfilm, containing five-digit number groups (used in coded messages), had been typed on a Russian-model machine. It occurred to bureau supervisor Robert Lamphere that the coin might have come from an "illegal"—a spy who was not affiliated with one of the USSR's diplomatic or trade missions and therefore could operate outside FBI surveillance. Usually such people got into the United States using a forged or stolen American passport and then disappeared into a big city like New York. The bureau began reviewing individuals who had entered the United States on passports issued abroad. However, unlike determining which Soviet diplomat was allowed to go first in the smorgasbord line, locating an illegal in a vast metropolis like New York was like searching for a needle in a haystack.

Not until 1957 was there a break in the case. A hard-drinking KGB officer, Reino Hayhanen, was ordered back from the United States to the Soviet Union. Fearing what might happen to him when he arrived, while passing through Europe he defected to U.S. authorities and informed them about his superior, Col. Rudolf Abel. Born in England in 1903 of Russian immigrant parents, Abel grew up as Vilyam "Willie" Fisher. In the 1920s he went to Russia, where he was trained as a spy. In 1948 he came to the United States as an illegal and for nine years ran a New York art studio. FBI men located Abel in a Manhattan hotel. By that time the United States was using the British double-agent system. Abel was offered the option of continuing to work for the Soviets while actually operating under American control.

---

* The British were much more skilled at getting rid of unwanted officials. On occasion one would be summoned to 10 Downing Street, where the prime minister of the day would tell him, "My language it fails, go out and govern New South Wales," (an Australian state).

† New York was the place for spies to learn U.S. industrial and corporate secrets. In Washington, most of the information received came from cocktail party chitchat. Soviet attachés also had to receive permission from U.S. authorities to travel very far from the capital. This meant that they could be certain that an FBI tail would follow them.

He refused and was given a prison sentence of thirty years. When the news of his arrest became public, a New York couple, Morris and Lona Cohen, disappeared from the United States. The FBI believed that Abel had entered the United States to handle the Rosenbergs and that the Cohens were his liaisons or "cutouts." In 1961 the British broke a spy case at a naval base; among those arrested were a husband and wife named Peter and Helen Kroger, who turned out to be the Cohens. In 1962 the Soviet Union agreed to release American U-2 pilot Francis Gary Powers in return for Abel. The Cohens were eventually traded for a British agent who had been arrested in Moscow. The motive for both repatriations was that Abel and the Cohens were of such importance to the KGB that it feared that if they were allowed to languish in American and British jails, they might be tempted to reveal secrets in order to obtain their release.

Soviet spies were not the only problem security forces dealt with. In 1956 the NYPD was confronted with another Carlo Tresca case. A forty-two-year-old Columbia University scholar, Jesús de Galíndez, disappeared from a Lower Manhattan street. Galíndez, a native of the Basque country of Spain, had supported the Loyalist cause in his country's civil war. In 1937 he fled to the Dominican Republic. In 1946 he came to the United States, where he became involved in the leadership of Spanish Basque groups. Shortly before his disappearance, he was seeking to have his PhD dissertation, critical of the Dominican dictator Rafael Trujillo, published as a book. Galíndez had confided to Norman Thomas that he had been threatened and was fearful that something might happen to him. Four years earlier, a man named Andres Requena had been shot and killed in New York after publishing a pamphlet attacking Trujillo. Galíndez's leftist friends, such as Thomas and Roger Baldwin, claimed he had been spirited out of the country by Trujillo's agents and demanded that the U.S. government conduct an investigation of the case. As with the Tresca murder, the police never solved the case, and the federal authorities essentially dragged their feet.

There were various rumors about Galíndez's disappearance. One was that after being kidnapped, he was taken to the waterfront and put on board a Dominican merchant ship, the *Fundacion*, which promptly departed. It was alleged that while at sea, Galíndez was thrown into the vessel's furnace. Other investigators considered that scenario was a red herring designed to lead them down a false path. They believed that the kidnapped Galíndez was drugged, then put on board an airplane that was flown to Florida and from there to the Dominican Republic, where he was murdered. The plane's pilot, Gerald Murphy, disappeared in the Dominican Republic. His copilot, Octavio de la Maza, confessed to murdering Murphy and then allegedly committed suicide in a Dominican jail. It is believed that both men were murdered by Trujillo's agents to keep them from telling their stories.

One troubling facet of the affair was the role of various individuals with law-enforcement connections. A former FBI agent who later worked for the CIA, then for the Dominican government, was suspected of being behind the Galíndez disappearance and of utilizing his contacts in the NYPD to gather information about Galíndez.

Trujillo hired prominent New York lawyers and public relations figures to assist in presenting his version of the case. In one instance, Galíndez supporters demonstrated outside the office of Trujillo lawyer Franklin D. Roosevelt Jr. The ex-FBI agent was charged with being an unregistered foreign agent and fined $500.

During its investigation, the NYPD called on the services of a young Spanish-speaking officer, Anthony Bouza, who had been born in the Basque country of Spain. Bouza, an intellectual cop who read Sartre, became so fascinated with the case that he wrote a novel about it, though he failed to find a publisher. In 1958, when he was promoted to sergeant, he was assigned to the department's security squad, BOSSI. In the 1960s, as an inspector, he would command the unit.[*]

Not since the World War I era had the U.S. confronted mass antigovernment protests.[†] Given their problematic response in those days and the fact that

---

[*] An outspoken liberal cop, Bouza eventually rose to the position of assistant chief in the NYPD but was denied his ambition to become police commissioner. Instead, he went off to Minneapolis and headed that city's police department for nine years. He also wrote a number of books critical of the police establishment.

[†] The violent strikes by organized labor in the 1930s were aimed at employers, not the government. Fascists and Communists were too small in numbers to constitute a mass movement.

they had not been tested since, it did not take a seer to forecast that should the security agencies face major domestic unrest, they would not be able to deal with it. In the 1960s the organizations designed to fight Nazis, and then the Cold War, were deployed against American dissidents. The civil rights movement, the rebellion of youth, and antiwar protests increasingly occupied the attention of security agencies. Wrong assumptions about the origin and nature of the problems, and attempts to apply World War II and Cold War methods in dealing with them, would bring the security forces into disrepute.

The first spark came three thousand miles from New York. In May 1960 the House Un-American Activities Committee held hearings at the San Francisco City Hall on Communist influence in the International Longshoremen's Union. Some of those under investigation voiced hostility toward the committee. Such behavior was an old story. News films of the time featured shouting back and forth between committee members and unfriendly witnesses. This time the hearings took an unexpected turn. Student protesters from the University of California at Berkeley and San Francisco State arrived en masse to support the witnesses, and a riot erupted. TV viewers all over the country were treated to the spectacle of San Francisco cops dragging protesters down the steps of City Hall. The committee and the police had been caught off guard. J. Edgar Hoover maintained that Communists were behind it.[3] In the 1960s student protests, ranging from sit-ins to campus riots, became almost everyday occurrences. Black civil rights protests spread from the South to the North and turned violent. Militants adopted slogans like, "Burn, baby, burn!" and groups such as the Black Panthers took up the gun. Opposition to the Vietnam War produced large-scale demonstrations that frequently led to clashes with the police and occasional guerrilla warfare, carried on by organizations such as the Weather Underground.

Again New York was an important center of domestic conflict. On Sunday, February 21, 1965, Malcolm X, leader of a significant American Black Muslim movement and almost as well known as Dr. Martin Luther King, addressed an audience at the Audubon Ballroom on upper Broadway in Manhattan. He had been born Malcolm Little; in 1948, while serving time for burglary in a Massachusetts state prison, he had been introduced by a fellow inmate to a group known as the Nation of Islam. When he was released in

1952, he journeyed to Chicago to join the organization, headed by Elijah Muhammad. Bright and charismatic, Malcolm began traveling the country, drawing new recruits to the movement. He abandoned his "slave name" in favor of the initial "X." Eventually he became head of the Harlem Temple of the Nation of Islam. Working in the media capital of the country, he was frequently quoted in newspapers and appeared often on network television. To some Muslims he seemed to be upstaging Elijah Muhammad. In the early 1960s, Malcolm broke with Muhammad, went on a pilgrimage to Mecca, changed his name to El-Hajj Malik El-Shabazz, and formed his own group, the Organization of Afro-American Unity. Afterward he began to receive phone threats, and his home in Queens was firebombed.

As Malcolm rose to speak at the Audubon Ballroom, a man sitting in the middle of the auditorium stood up and screamed, "Get your hand out of my pocket!" to the man sitting next to him. Malcolm observed the commotion and shouted, "Let's cool it, brothers." Suddenly the man who had yelled out produced a shotgun from under his overcoat, two other men stood up and pointed pistols at the stage, and someone else set off a smoke bomb in the rear of the hall. Shots rang out, and Malcolm fell backward. He was pronounced dead at a nearby hospital. Police who were on duty at the ballroom arrested three men for the killing. They were convicted and sentenced to prison.

The murder may actually have been a major blow to domestic security. Malcolm X was a man who could win the confidence of the disadvantaged while in the process of moving from marginal figure to major leader. The mature Malcolm played down "Burn, baby, burn" or "Kill the cops" rhetoric. Had he lived, he might well have discouraged violence and worked within the system.

A few months after Malcolm's murder, a major riot occurred in the Watts section of Los Angeles, leaving thirty-four people dead. Two years later, twenty-six people were killed in Newark and forty-three in Detroit. In April 1968, following the assassination of Dr. King, riots broke out in more than a score of U.S. cities. At the end of the month, after campus anti-establishment militants took over Columbia University in Upper Manhattan, Mayor John V. Lindsay ordered the NYPD to move in. Anyone familiar with the history of New York police actions at protest demonstrations would have taken the time to develop a well-thought-out plan to be carried out under the leadership of specially selected commanders. Instead, the operation was hastily mounted. The campus was cleared, but clashes between police and demonstrators, shown on national TV, brought criticism on Lindsay and the NYPD.

Four months later, at the Democratic national convention in Chicago, a similar scenario was acted out. This time it went on for several weeks and drew a huge international television audience. The stakes were also far higher than whether a dean could reclaim his office. The clashes between police and demonstrators in Chicago destroyed any chance that the party nominee, Vice President Hubert Humphrey, could defeat Richard Nixon for the presidency. Part of the problem was that the initial briefing that the federal government provided to local cops was grossly overstated. They originally estimated the number of demonstrators at one hundred thousand. As late as twenty-four hours before the convention opened, federal officers were estimating that upward of fifty thousand demonstrators would arrive. The actual figure was about half that amount. Scare stories about the student protesters were disseminated among the cops. U.S. college students, heretofore dismissed as passive, drug-using hippies, were portrayed as being as competent at guerrilla warfare as Army Green Berets.

The convergence of black protests, student rebellions, and antiwar activity caused both Presidents Johnson and Nixon to believe that such activities were being directed by Communist Bloc intelligence officers, and they demanded that security agencies document it. FBI director Hoover put his bureau to work to prove the thesis. But if there were two places in America where G-men were less able to blend in, they were 1960s college campuses and the ghetto. In both, white men in well-pressed suits and snap-brim fedoras tended to stand out. Even when agents dressed casually, they were easily spotted. Local police did have some officers who could infiltrate protest groups. However, they usually lacked the knowledge to produce nuanced reports, and the departments that received them did not have analysts who could properly interpret them. President Nixon became so frustrated with the information he was getting from the FBI that he formed his own investigative group, known as the Plumbers. An indirect result was the Watergate scandal.

It should not have been difficult to determine that most of the protest activity was the result of domestic problems, not the work of foreign intelligence services. Blacks had been struggling for almost a hundred years to achieve the equality that the post–Civil War constitutional amendments had bestowed on them. After a world war fought against fascism, it was impossible for most white Americans to defend, or African Americans to accept, legally imposed segregation. Youth protest was to a certain extent simply part of being young. In the first few years after the war, college campuses had been full of veterans, many of them married with children. They were too mature and too busy trying to make up for lost time to engage in any kind of distraction. In the 1950s, a generation of young people, many of them the first in their families to obtain a higher education, saw a college degree as their ticket to a more affluent life than their parents had known. They too kept their noses to the academic grindstone. Not until the 1960s were the student bodies, especially at the elite colleges, filled with individuals from upper-middle-class backgrounds who saw college not as a meal ticket but as a chance to "find themselves." Even at the height of campus protests, though, most institutions were generally quiet. While high-profile schools like Harvard, Yale, UC Berkeley, and Columbia might erupt periodically, it was largely theater. Most people who opposed the Vietnam War were not against all wars. Many were conservatives, even retired generals, who felt that it was the wrong war in the wrong place at the wrong time.

In the 1970s militants turned to assassinations and bombings. In 1971 twenty-one members of the New York Black Panther Party were tried for conspiracy to blow up police stations and department stores. The evidence against them had been compiled by undercover NYPD cops who had managed to infiltrate the party. To the surprise of the authorities, the jury acquitted the defendants of all charges after only ninety minutes of deliberation. During the trial, police guards were assigned to the home of the chief prosecutor, Manhattan district attorney Frank Hogan. One night two officers in a patrol car, checking the DA's house, were riddled with machine gun bullets fired from a vehicle, leaving both of them permanently disabled. A few days later, two officers, one white and one black, were shot to death while walking through an Upper Manhattan housing project after completing a radio run. The following year, a black and a white officer, patrolling together on foot in the East Village, were shot and killed without warning by several men they passed on the street. Some of the assailants who killed the two officers in the housing project were later linked to attacks on police in San Francisco. The gun of one of the dead officers in the East Village was found in the possession of a man who shot it out with the police in St. Louis. Detectives believed there was an organized conspiracy to assassinate cops by a group known as the Black Liberation Army, and they were angry when the city administration, under Mayor Lindsay, was hesitant to support the accusations.

In 1972 two radio car officers in Harlem responded to a false call that an officer needed assistance at the mosque that had been headed by Malcom X and was now being directed by Minister Louis Farrakhan. When they attempted to enter, one officer was fatally shot. To calm tensions, superior officers on the scene released some suspects based on community leaders' pledges that the men would voluntarily appear at the precinct; they did not. When questions arose, Mayor Lindsay was noncommittal and the police commissioner hesitant. The police rank and file blasted both men for failing to back their officers and allowing cop killers to escape.

Black militants came from disadvantaged segments of society. White militants were often from the upper strata. On March 6, 1970, after an explosion tore through an expensive townhouse on West Eleventh Street in Greenwich Village, a neighbor observed two women, one of them nude, run out of the house. She invited them to use her home to shower and gave them clothing, after which both disappeared from the scene. Firemen sorting through the rubble found the bodies of a young man named Theodore Gold, one of the leaders of the Columbia protests, and a twenty-eight-year-old student radical, Diana Oughton. A third body (of a male victim) could not be identified. The Weather Underground would later claim he was a twenty-one-year-old college student from Ohio who had joined their group. The shattered house belonged to a man who was out of town. One of the women who had run out of the house was his daughter, Cathlyn Wilkerson. The other was Kathy Boudin, whose father was a prominent leftist attorney.

Investigators believed that the explosion occurred while the group was preparing bombs that were going to be set off in a social center on the Army base at Fort Dix, New Jersey. A few days later, three bombs exploded in Manhattan skyscrapers. It was seen as a message from the Weather Underground that it was still functioning. For nearly a decade, law enforcement officers searched for Wilkerson and Boudin without success. Finally in 1980, Wilkerson surrendered to the Manhattan district attorney's office and was sentenced to prison for three years. The following year, Boudin was one of a gang armed with automatic weapons that held up an armored car in suburban Rockland County in order to obtain funds for their cause. During the robbery, two police officers and a guard were killed. Captured fleeing the scene of the cop killings, Boudin was sentenced to prison for twenty years.

In the 1970s a group of Puerto Rican nationalists known as Fuerzas Armadas de Liberación Nacional (FALN), or the National Liberation Front, set bombs in New York and other cities. In December 1974 a police officer, responding to a call about a suspicious package in the hall of an East Harlem building, lost an eye when the package blew up. In January 1975 FALN claimed responsibility for the bombing of Fraunces Tavern in the Wall Street area that killed four people and injured fifty. The site was an upscale restaurant and historic landmark (George Washington had bid farewell to his officers there after the American Revolution). It is likely that the bomb was set in order to strike at Wall Street executives, although one of the dead was a Puerto Rican busboy. A few months later, four bombs went off within a forty-minute period in the Manhattan headquarters of such well-known corporations as the New York and Metropolitan Life Insurance Companies and Bankers Trust. Sporadic bombings continued throughout the 1980s. Three NYPD officers were permanently disabled by FALN bombs that exploded on New Year's Eve in 1982.

The most violent militants suffered from the same malady as had German saboteurs. They sought quick results through bombs or other direct action—not, like the Soviets, with the infiltration of the American establishment. Indeed, some of the white radicals belonged to families that were already members of it. If Nixon and Johnson had been right—that the dissidents were controlled by Communist Bloc agents—groups like the Weather Underground might have followed very different strategies.

The decision to assign security forces, designed to combat 1950s-style foreign espionage, to deal with domestic problems of the 1960s reaped the inevitable consequences in the 1970s. After Watergate, Congress began a series of investigations of U.S. intelligence and law enforcement agencies.

The CIA was forced to admit to organizing assassination plots against foreign leaders, including Fidel Castro. It was also revealed that, contrary to its charter, the agency was conducting domestic investigations. The FBI, too, came under fire when it was disclosed that it had mounted an operation to discredit Dr. King and had carried out black-bag jobs against the Weather Underground and other radicals in New York. In 1980 the former operating head of the bureau, Mark Felt, was convicted of authorizing illegal break-ins against the Weather Underground. When Felt argued that the bureau's actions were legal under national security laws, he was supported by the testimony of former President Nixon and several ex-attorneys general. In 1981 Felt was pardoned by President Reagan.[*]

In 1985, after a coalition of groups filed suit against the NYPD, a federal court found that police surveillance of political activity had violated constitutional protections of free speech. *Handschu v. Special Services Division* led to a ruling that the NYPD's intelligence division could only undertake investigations of political groups when it suspected they were engaged in criminal activity—and then only after obtaining the approval of a civilian attorney who served as monitor of the decree.

Toward the end of the twentieth century, the United States would confront terrorist actions carried out by Islamic militants. That would prove to be the most difficult threat for security agencies to comprehend. The terrorists (or, to some, "freedom fighters") were not primarily agents of a hostile state, like the Germans in 1914 and the 1930s, or the product of a world revolutionary ideology such as Communism. Nor did they emerge from the 1960s domestic protests. Their actions were rooted in what they perceive to be threats to their culture.

Jihad, the term for an Islamic holy war, was a word known to many Americans long before a handful of extremists declared one against the United States. From the earliest days of Hollywood, a staple of adventure

---

[*] Nixon's support was ironic. In 2005 it was revealed that Felt had been Deep Throat, the individual who passed on information about the Watergate break-in to the *Washington Post*. The "revelation" did not come as much of a surprise to Nixon's aides or the security community, who long suspected it was him. Felt, who had been Hoover's heir apparent, allegedly had become angry because President Nixon had passed him over for FBI director.

movies was "the rebellious sheikh," who proclaimed a jihad against infidels, usually Western imperialists. Sometimes he was portrayed as a monster, other times a hero like the Red Shadow in *Desert Song*. In all cases, the action took place in some exotic location, not in the heart of an American city. In the 1990s, jihad moved to Manhattan.

Meir Kahane was an outspoken rabbi who formed an organization known as the Jewish Defense League. Made up of young men who trained in the martial arts and the use of firearms, the group was formed to protest against the Soviet Union's denying Jews the right to emigrate. Its members became known for actions like allegedly throwing stink bombs into New York's Lincoln Center for the Performing Arts to disrupt a Russian ballet performance. According to investigators, they were also behind a real bomb that exploded in the office of a theatrical producer who handled the Bolshoi Theatre's ballet company. The blast killed one person and injured thirteen more. After Kahane was dismissed by his New York congregation, he moved to Israel, where he took a hard line against the Arabs, referring to them as "dogs" and demanding they be expelled from the country. He was elected to the *Knesset* (legislature) but was barred by the Israeli government from running for reelection and returned to New York in 1988.

On a November night in 1990, Kahane spoke at the Marriott Hotel on Lexington Avenue in midtown Manhattan. The crowd that gathered in the second-floor ballroom was made up of his supporters, although one person, who appeared to be an Arab, attracted the attention of guards when he entered the room. Because he was wearing a yarmulke, he was allowed to take a seat. The man listened quietly to Kahane's speech and at the end stepped forward to shake the rabbi's hand. He then drew a pistol and allegedly fired into Kahane's neck. As the man, El Sayyid Nosair, a thirty-four-year-old Egyptian, ran from the room, he shot a Kahane supporter who was attempting to stop him. Next he commandeered a taxicab, but the driver slammed on the brakes. When Nosair jumped out of the cab, waving a gun, he was shot by a U.S. Postal Service officer who happened to be nearby. Kahane died of his wounds.

Detectives investigating the case learned that Nosair was a devout Muslim who had immigrated to the United States from Egypt in 1981 and had become a citizen in 1989. In a search of his home, they found fourteen hundred rounds of rifle ammunition, bomb-making manuals, and a memo book in which he had written the names of some Jewish officials, including judges who had extradited an accused Arab terrorist. A jury acquitted Nosair of murder but convicted him of assaulting the postal officer and another man, and criminal possession of a lethal weapon. Some jurors said that they had been persuaded by Nosair's attorney, the noted leftist William Kunstler, that it was actually one of Kahane's followers who had shot the rabbi.

In the aftermath of Kahane's murder, law enforcement officials began to pay attention to Muslim extremists. Despite bombing attacks and assassinations in Europe and the Middle East, including some against American personnel and facilities, the consensus among experts was that no similar events would take place on U.S. soil. The reason offered was that there was not a sufficient domestic support network to sustain terrorists. While this may have been the case in the past, in 1993 the notion of American invulnerability was shattered

On February 26 two men parked a rented Ford van in the public garage beneath the Twin Towers of the World Trade Center complex. The van contained an explosive nitrate compound packed in cardboard boxes, tanks of compressed hydrogen gas, and containers of nitroglycerin. The driver and his passenger then lit 20-foot-long fuses and left the vehicle. At 12:18 p.m. the explosives went off, blowing a 185-foot-wide hole in the basement of the tower, causing damage seven stories up, and knocking out the complex's police emergency command post. There was no comprehensive evacuation plan, and many people were trapped on upper floors.

Scores of police and fire units raced to the scene. Mayor David Dinkins was in Japan, so police commissioner Ray Kelly functioned as de facto head of the city government. Kelly was a man of the two worlds he had inhabited all his adult life: the NYPD and the U.S. Marines (where he rose to colonel). He also held advanced degrees in law and public administration. Of medium height and powerfully built, he had a commanding presence and a no-nonsense manner. Kelly was perfectly cast for the role of emergency chief, and his calm but decisive manner on TV reassured frightened New Yorkers. Though six people died in the initial explosion and a thousand sustained various injuries, over the course of the day and into the evening, police and fire crews got everyone out of the building without any additional loss of life.

In addition to directing the rescue operations, Kelly teamed with Jim Fox, head of the New York division of the FBI, to launch an immediate investigation. Cops and federal agents combed through the ruins, examining the twisted pieces of metal. In a truck they found a vehicle identification number that was traced to a New Jersey car rental agency. The man who had rented it, a twenty-five-year-old Palestinian named Mohammed Salameh, showed up at the office claiming that his vehicle had been stolen and asked for his $400 deposit back. The employees notified the FBI, and he was arrested. Further investigation determined that a group of Muslim extremists in metropolitan New York had planned the attack. Though it took two years to track down the ringleader of the group, Ramzi Yousef, eventually ten people were convicted in the World Trade Center bombing case, including the imprisoned El Sayyid Nosair, the man accused of killing Meir Kahane.

After the February 26, 1993, attack, law enforcement officials abandoned the notion that "it can't happen here." Instead, they believed it was not a question of whether the terrorists would strike again, but when. As in past times, the security forces would have to play catch up.

9/11 AND BEYOND
The Twenty-First Century

Tuesday, September 11, 2001, dawned warm and bright in New York City. It was primary election day, when the parties would nominate candidates to run for mayor in the general election. The winner of that contest would succeed term-limited Mayor Rudy Giuliani at the end of the year. Some New Yorkers who worked downtown would owe their lives to the fact that they were late getting to their jobs because they had stopped to vote.

At 8:45 a.m., John O'Neill, the newly hired security director for the seven buildings of the World Trade Center complex, was starting his second full day of work. The forty-nine-year-old O'Neill had recently retired from the FBI after thirty-one years' service, during which he had risen from a tour guide at headquarters in Washington to chief of the bureau's counterterrorist operations. In that job he displayed the same hard-charging "damn the torpedoes" attitude that had always been his style. In 1995 when his agents collared Ramzi Yousef, mastermind of the 1993 Trade Center bombing, in a Pakistan hotel room, O'Neill requested the U.S. Air Force to furnish a jetliner to transport the prisoner directly to the United States. To get around Pakistan's restriction against foreign military planes landing in their territory, he asked that the Air Force plane be completely repainted to look like a civilian aircraft. The Pentagon complied but sent him a bill for $12 million, which he refused to pay.

Beginning in 1997, O'Neill had become obsessed with a little-known figure named Osama bin Laden, who headed an obscure organization known as al Qaeda. From then on, with messianic zeal, he told everyone who would listen (and some who did not want to) that bin Laden and al Qaeda constituted the greatest terrorist threat the United States faced. Messianic zeal was not the preferred mode of discourse in bureaucracies. When it was accompanied by a flamboyant personality, combative management style, and a somewhat irregular personal life, it could spell disaster for an individual's career.

In 1998 after 224 people were killed by al Qaeda truck bombers who launched almost simultaneous attacks against U.S. embassies in Kenya and Tanzania, the FBI dispatched 500 agents to East Africa. In the days of the British Empire, its overseas security people were military and police officers with long experience in such places as Egypt, India, and China. The FBI had been authorized to engage in international law enforcement only since 1984, the year after an Islamic suicide bomber had driven a truckload of explosives into a Marine barracks in Beirut, Lebanon, killing 241 U.S. servicemen. In 1998 the bureau was still learning, and its inexperience showed. Journalist David Wright, describing the arrival of the FBI contingent in East Africa, would write, "Many of the agents were unfamiliar with the world beyond America; indeed some had not even been given passports until the day of their departure, and here they were 9,000 miles away. They knew little about the laws and customs of the countries they were working in."[1] O'Neill had expected to be put in charge of the investigation, but Washington headquarters ruled that, since it was not clear that al Qaeda was involved, it was not his case.

In 2000 the U.S. destroyer *Cole*, anchored in the harbor at Aden, Yemen, was struck by a nautical version of a truck bomb. Two al Qaeda suicide bombers in a small boat (known as a Boston Whaler) pulled alongside the vessel and detonated explosives that blew a hole in the ship's side, killing seventeen U.S. sailors and wounding thirty-nine more. This time O'Neill was assigned to take charge of the investigation. The U.S. ambassador to Yemen, herself an experienced hand at counterterrorism, did not hit it off with O'Neill. It was the old clash between diplomats and "gumshoes." O'Neill had arrived in the country with a force far larger than she had expected him to bring—"300 heavily armed people," she would say.* The

---

* The actual number, including support personnel, was about 150.

ambassador's job was to deal with the sensitivities of officials in a sovereign country. O'Neill saw his as solving the murder of U.S. servicemen. Given the reluctance of some local officials to pursue the investigation, these were contradictory ends. After the two had continually butted heads, the ambassador pulled rank and had O'Neill removed from Yemen.

It was not O'Neill's only clash with colleagues and superiors. He feuded with the CIA and the higher-ups in his own agency. Again it was an old story: CIA agents, who regarded themselves as sophisticates, viewed G-men as bulls in a china shop. "Brick" (street) agents of the bureau never had a high opinion of the "suits" in headquarters. Of course, it was the top brass who would get the criticism from Congress, the White House, and the media if an operation went bad. One place where O'Neill enjoyed good relations was the NYPD. He was the kind of swashbuckler that cops liked. Always dressed sharply and immaculately groomed, many a night he would lift a glass with NYPD detectives or New York journalists. His favorite watering hole was Elaine's, an in spot on the Upper East Side, which was patronized by Hollywood stars, best-selling authors, and, for a while, a New York police commissioner. It was lucky for O'Neill that J. Edgar Hoover was no longer around. The director would not have approved of his lifestyle. Separated (though not divorced) from his wife, O'Neill formed close relationships with three women, two in Washington and one in New York, all of whom believed that he intended to marry them. Again, it was not an unusual story. Men who behave like Errol Flynn at work are likely to do the same in their personal lives.

O'Neill once seemed headed for big things. For a while it looked as though he would be appointed head of the New York division of the bureau, with the rank of assistant director of the FBI. But he was passed over. When the Bush administration took office at the beginning of 2001, Richard Clarke, President Clinton's coordinator for counterterrorism, had recommended O'Neill as his replacement. If that had happened, a man whose mother and father still drove taxicabs in Atlantic City, New Jersey, would be part of the inner circle of the president. Again he was passed over. Enemies and his own missteps began to take a toll on him. One time he allowed a female friend to enter a secret FBI facility and to ride in a bureau car. Both were violations of agency regulations and led to a reprimand from his superiors. On a trip to Florida, he left his briefcase containing classified documents in a hotel conference room. When local police recovered the case, they found that only a cigar cutter, lighter, and pen were missing; papers in the briefcase were intact, and a forensic examination determined that they had not been touched. The Department of Justice launched a criminal investigation of O'Neill. Although he was exonerated, it was known that the *New York Times* was preparing to print a story about the incident.[2] So in August 2001, he decided it was time to leave.

At 8:46 a.m., when the first plane struck the 92nd through 99th floors of the North Tower (1 WTC), O'Neill made it down from his 34th floor office to the lobby. Already people were jumping from the higher floors. When a second plane plowed into the 77th through 85th floors of the South Tower (2 WTC) at 9:03, O'Neill's fears had come true. Bin Laden had pulled off a major attack on the United States. While directing the evacuation of the buildings, he made a few calls on his cell phone, letting his close associates know that he was safe. After the towers collapsed, O'Neill was not seen or heard from. Many of his friends held onto hope that somehow this larger-than-life Jersey guy would miraculously survive. Ten days later a work crew, digging in the rubble near Liberty and Greenwich streets, brought out a body. When they examined the dead man's wallet, they found it was O'Neill's. A procedure had been instituted among the rescue workers that whenever the body of a police officer or firefighter was recovered, all members of the two services on the scene would stand at attention and salute as the victim, draped in an American flag, was removed. Though O'Neill was now a civilian, he received the same honors.

———

That New York would be hit again was not a surprise. Even the target had been expected. Foreign intelligence sources had warned U.S. authorities that terrorists would likely attack the Trade Center. Other threats caused security forces to stake out locations where it was believed that terror strikes were about to take place. In 1995, during one alert period, the Alfred P. Murrah Federal Building in Oklahoma City was blown up by a truck bomb, killing 168 people. New York investigators assumed that the terrorists had switched their target. However, it was ascertained that the

Oklahoma bombing had been perpetrated by a home-grown, right-wing "militia type" named Timothy McVeigh.*

In 1997 New York City police raided an apartment and recovered pipe bombs that two Palestinians intended to set off in a Brooklyn subway station. During the raid both suspects were shot and wounded. The men were in the United States on visas and had a loose connection with some of the 1993 Trade Center bombers. Both were sentenced to prison.

In December 1999, just before the millennium, a Middle Eastern man attempted to transport a truck from Canada by ferry into the United States at Port Angeles, Washington. A customs officer who questioned him became suspicious and ordered him to drive into a holding area where a more thorough investigation could be conducted. He attempted to flee but was captured. Investigation disclosed that he was transporting explosives, which he intended to detonate at Los Angeles International Airport.

The situation in 2001 resembled the one at Pearl Harbor before December 7, 1941. U.S. officials anticipated that war with Japan was near. They were also aware that the Japanese had a history of attacking the enemy's main base before declaring war. Senior commanders should have remembered the 1933 Fleet Problem, where umpires had ruled that Pearl Harbor had been successfully attacked. Yet they were not psychologically ready to believe that, on a quiet Sunday morning in the "Paradise of the Pacific," Japanese raiders would strike. Consequently, they were not prepared for it. On September 11, 2001, security officials would have conceded that some type of attack was possible, but they, too, were not mentally or organizationally ready for so powerful an onslaught.

In 1993 the response of the police and fire departments had been generally applauded. Commissioner Kelly provided the necessary leadership, and thousands of people in the towers were brought out safely. Police and FBI agents worked closely together, and the bombers were quickly apprehended. It was also reassuring that the plotters appeared to be bumbling incompetents rather than highly trained commandos. Instead of fleeing town or lying low, they tried to get a refund on the $400 deposit they had

---

* McVeigh's action was in retaliation for the FBI's 1993 siege of the Branch Davidian Compound near Waco, Texas, which resulted in the death of seventy-nine people, and an earlier incident where bureau agents had killed the wife and son of an anti-government activist at Ruby Ridge, Idaho. McVeigh was executed in 2001.

put down on the truck they used to haul the explosives. The greatest error they had made was their assumption that the blast would cause the North Tower to topple into the South Tower, causing it to fall. They did not know that it was constructed so that an uncontrolled explosion (as opposed to one set by engineering specialists contracted to demolish a site) would not cause the building to collapse. In fact, some experts were not so sure this was the case. They believed that if the terrorists had used more explosives, the North Tower would possibly have brought down its twin. Even though Ray Kelly was no longer commissioner—at the end of 1993, mayor-elect Rudy Giuliani had decided not to retain him*—it was natural for the public safety services to assume that "we did it before, we can do it again."

From 1994 to 2001, the city continued its counterterrorism efforts. Basically, the possible methods of attack broke down into:

- *CBR Agents*: Chemical, biological, or radiological devices, ranging from the release of gas in the subway, or some other closed space, to the detonation of a "dirty bomb" designed to contaminate an entire city district.
- *Bullets*: This included commando or assassination teams attacking individuals or groups. A terrorist training film, captured in the Middle East, showed an armed team taking over an office building and holding some of the occupants hostage. Security officers were puzzled because the scenario did not present an exit strategy. Finally, they realized that the terrorists' goal was to exploit the situation for maximum publicity, after which they would kill the hostages and fight to the death themselves. The film bore a resemblance to a 1971 incident in Washington, D.C., where members of the Hanafi sect had stormed three buildings, killed two people, seized Jewish hostages, and threatened to decapitate them (though in that instance there was a negotiated surrender).
- *Explosions*: Ranging from bombs in individual backpacks, through cars and trucks loaded with explosives, to missiles fired from a ship in

---

* In doing so, he was following standard practice in New York, where, though commissioners are appointed to five-year terms, in reality they serve at the pleasure of the mayor.

the harbor. Countering a possible air raid was considered the responsibility of the military. However, the North American Aerospace Defense Command (NORAD) was focused on Soviet missiles or other external incursions into U.S. space.*

Some preventive measures were taken. The NYPD made a survey of structures in New York. At those found to be vulnerable to truck bombs, barriers were installed to block vehicles from ramming them. But there was no real sense of urgency, and more might have been done.

Only seventeen NYPD officers were assigned full time to counterterrorism duties, and they were part of an FBI joint terrorist task force created in 1980 in response to FALN bombings. The bureau provided the New York detectives with office facilities, cars, expense accounts, and special credentials, but it was not a true joint venture. When the FBI obtained information on a possible threat, it was closely held, and the NYPD detectives on the task force were forbidden to disclose it to their department superiors.

The city's emergency command post was located on the eighth floor of police headquarters in Lower Manhattan. It was a relatively small and crowded facility, normally used for staff meetings. Its most frequent emergency use was during snowstorms. In 1999 it was decided to open a larger, state-of-the-art center, leaving the one in police headquarters as an alternate. However, city officials made the elementary error of locating the new facility in a building in the World Trade Center complex. It was not only a likely target but also just a few blocks from police headquarters. This created the possibility that one attack would knock out both command centers.

In 1993 some fire department radios had not worked in the towers. Afterward, a new radio system was installed, but it continued to malfunction. The police and fire departments, traditional rivals, did not establish a unified command structure or conduct joint exercises.

The individuals who commanded the security forces in 2001 were not of the caliber of Ray Kelly. Neither the fire nor police commissioner had served as a top officer in his own or another fire or police department. Before

---

* On 9/11, only four U.S. jet fighters were on alert in the Northeast air defense sector, which extended from the Canadian border to Virginia and Kentucky and from the East Coast into Kansas and Nebraska. The nearest fighters to New York City were stationed on Cape Cod in Massachusetts.

his appointment, the fire commissioner, Thomas von Essen, had been head of the firefighters' union. The highest post that Police Commissioner Bernard Kerik had previously held in the NYPD was third-grade detective—the police equivalent of corporal. Under department regulations, his lack of a college degree would have barred him from promotion beyond the rank of sergeant. In the 1993 mayoral campaign, Kerik volunteered to chauffeur Giuliani. Afterward, the mayor named him to top jobs in the city jail system and in 2000 made him police commissioner.

There was also a coordinator of emergency services, who supposedly held equal rank with the police and fire commissioners. In 2001 the position was occupied by former fire dispatcher Richard Sheirer, who had risen to a civilian deputy commissioner post in the fire department. Police commissioner was commonly regarded as the most important job in the city next to the mayor. The fire commissioner also carried great prestige. Both officials were constantly in the newspapers or on television and were well known to the public.* Not many New Yorkers were aware that there was such a position as emergency service coordinator, and even fewer could identify the incumbent. Given the status disparities, the notion that a coordinator could direct police and fire forces at a major disaster was like believing that the facilities manager of the New Jersey Meadowlands Football Stadium could coach the Giants or Jets in a championship game.

On 9/11 the new command center in the 7 World Trade Center building was too close to the towers to be used. It was struck by debris when the towers fell, and later that day it, too, collapsed. Police headquarters lost telephone service. Police and fire departments set up their field command posts at different locations and utilized separate radio systems. Another complicating factor was that the Trade Center was patrolled by the Port Authority of New York and New Jersey Police Department. The Port Authority, comprising more than thirteen hundred officers, also had jurisdiction over several airports, a bus terminal, bridges, and tunnels. Its personnel were trained as both police officers and firefighters. To further confuse responsibility, a few weeks earlier, ownership of the Trade Center had passed from the Port Authority

---

* Though their positions were not fully comparable. The police commissioner was not only the administrative head of his department but the operational boss. The fire commissioner was in charge of administration, but the chief of department ran the operational side.

to a private developer (who had hired John O'Neill to be his security director). The Port Authority had previously formed emergency safety teams (fire wardens, searchers, etc.) that would become activated in an emergency. On 9/11 many of the members faithfully reported to their assigned stations, though the Port Authority was no longer in control of the building.

When the second plane hit, the command personnel realized they were not dealing with an accident but were under attack. Mayor Giuliani and Commissioner Kerik immediately contacted federal authorities to request air cover for the city. In general Kerik remained at the side of the mayor rather than taking active control of police operations. The NYPD was largely directed by First Deputy Commissioner Joe Dunne (who in 2000 had been the favorite to be named commissioner but was passed over in favor of Kerik), assisted by Chief of Department Joe Esposito. The fire department, too, was directed by its first deputy commissioner, William Feehan, and the chief of department, Peter Ganci. All four were veteran cops or firefighters who had risen via the normal career ladder. It was immediately decided by commanders that, given the situation, the primary mission would be one of rescue rather than firefighting. When the North Tower started to fall, Dunne, with his foot in a cast and on crutches because of a recent operation, was saved by a cop who flung him into an armored bomb disposal vehicle where bomb-sniffing dogs were awaiting assignment; the two top fire officials were killed.

In the final analysis, the basic problem was that the collapse of the towers was totally unexpected. If it had not happened, most of the people below the floors where the planes had struck would have been saved. Police and firefighters began sustaining fatalities from the time they arrived on the scene; however, it was the crumbling of the buildings that contributed most to the 403 deaths among public safety officers (343 FDNY, 37 Port Authority, and 23 NYPD).

After 9/11 New York was a sad, frightened city. Many families mourned the loss of a loved one. Thousands of people who witnessed the disaster would never forget the horror of watching victims jump from windows, some holding hands with coworkers, to avoid being engulfed in flames. A young boy, watching the towers from blocks away, asked his father, "Why are the birds on fire?" For weeks, fire stations all over the city were covered with flowers placed there by sympathetic New Yorkers. In Grand Central Station, a large bulletin board was set up containing pictures of people missing from the towers. Often they were accompanied by heartrending pleas from their families such as, "Won't you help us find Mary?" Passersby could only shake their heads, knowing that the lost relatives were undoubtedly gone forever. Stories of heroism on 9/11 were legion. But others would never be known because there were no witnesses left to tell them.*

Some of the more affluent New Yorkers, fearing another attack, switched their domiciles to the distant suburbs or adjoining states. Other people decided to drive to work rather than ride through tunnels on suburban trains or aboard city subways. Whenever people heard a siren, they would stop and watch as emergency vehicles went by and glance nervously at the sky for any sign that a new attack was in progress. In August 2003 New York City experienced a blackout. In the midtown building where this author worked, the emergency command system instructed occupants to remain in their offices. Instead, everyone ran into the streets to avoid being trapped in a collapsing structure.

Some people have argued that the reaction of New Yorkers was excessive and that it added to the fear and depression the terrorists had inflicted. They point out that in Israel, after an attack, the target area is quickly cleaned up, there are brief services for the dead, and then everybody gets back to work. The criticism is not entirely fair. Given the shock and the extent of the losses, the grief of New Yorkers and Americans in general was understandable. Unlike Israel, New York was not a place where the danger from terrorism was always present, every young person was liable for military service, and older reservists were frequently called up for duty.

The real complaint in New York is against those who sought to exploit the carnage. Ideologues of the left and the right reduced the cause of the attack to simple formulations: it had been a justifiable response to America's imperialistic policies; the U.S. government should stop coddling terrorists

---

* Before they died, some victims had managed to phone 911 operators, family, or friends, so that some of their stories could be reconstructed. A great novel along the lines of Dickens' *A Tale of Two Cities* or Wilder's *The Bridge of San Luis Rey* may yet be written.

and start dropping bombs; the Arab-Israeli conflict should be resolved in favor of one side or the other. There was little recognition of deeper issues. In the 1950s many Americans thought their way of life was menaced by "godless" Communism. Many Russians believed that the U.S. capitalists were out to destroy the Soviet Union. Now some Muslims perceive that their culture is under assault by the secular West. Adopting a more balanced view, without excusing the murderous onslaught, would have provided a clearer understanding of the problem. Hundreds of counterterrorism "experts" suddenly emerged out of the woodwork. While some were legitimate, many had only the sketchiest knowledge of the subject. City, state, and quasi-governmental agencies wrangled over who would control the rebuilding. Architects, planners, public relations consultants, lawyers, and even the Mafia rushed to obtain lucrative contracts. Everyone had their own ideas of what would constitute a suitable memorial. New York governor George Pataki named an architect to design a hundred-story "Freedom" tower. Ten years later the architect is long gone, and the structure is just now being built.

════════

At the national level, the public demanded that someone be held accountable for not having prevented the attack. All eyes turned to the CIA and the FBI. Initially President Bush backed the CIA director, George Tenet. FBI director Robert Mueller had been nominated for the job only a few days before 9/11, so he could not be faulted. The first major response by Congress and the administration was predictable: throw money and bodies at the problem. A total of 22 disparate agencies were combined into a cabinet-level Department of Homeland Security, with a total of 180,000 employees. The DHS sought to be, as its title implies, the overall controller of U.S. domestic security. However, both the CIA and the FBI managed to avoid being included within it. That was probably fortunate, because the DHS was troubled from the outset. Its ranks included Secret Service agents who guarded the president, customs and immigration officers patrolling the borders, and airport baggage screeners. To make such a hastily assembled force into an effective body, the DHS required individuals with proven expertise in managing large-scale organizations and experience in handling emergencies. A good place to look for them would have been the military. Instead of General

Schwarzkopf types, however, individuals whose essential qualification was their political standing filled many of the top posts in the department. The practice of appointing notables to head security agencies was not new. FDR had made Mayor LaGuardia director of U.S. civil defense. It was a good symbolic device but a bad practical one. President Bush chose Pennsylvania governor Tom Ridge to become the first secretary of homeland security. As might be expected, in its early days the department was largely noted for its PR work. DHS issued color-coded alerts warning of the likelihood of attack: green for low, blue for guarded, yellow for elevated, orange for high, and red for severe. It was like the children's game Red Light/Green Light, in that it frequently resulted in everyone running around confused. Like the ONI after Pearl Harbor, the DHS identified possible targets of every kind everywhere. In that way, no matter what happened, the department could always say, "We told you so."

In 2004 the DHS issued a yellow alert about possible attacks on certain targets, including the New York Stock Exchange. Some Democrats were suspicious that the alerts coincided with the fall presidential campaign. They noted that every time a terrorism story led the news, President Bush's poll standings improved. The following year, when the NYPD sent out a secret alert about a possible attack on the subway system, an individual in the DHS sent e-mails to his friends in New York warning them not to ride the trains. The media found out and went public with it. The Federal Emergency Management Agency (FEMA), a component of the DHS, drew universal criticism for its performance in the 2005 Katrina disaster in New Orleans. Its head, Michael Brown, a former official of a horse owners' association, was replaced.

Police chiefs complained that the DHS and the FBI did not share information on terrorist threats with America's 600,000-plus state and local police. Within the FBI, agents charged that some superiors ignored pre-9/11 reports about such things as Middle Eastern men learning to fly (but not to land) jetliners. An investigating commission faulted the FBI and the CIA for not sharing information. A revamped intelligence structure was created under a director of national intelligence (DNI) who, in theory, outranked the CIA director. The grouping included a newly created National Counterterrorism Center (NCTC), as well as such established entities as the National Security

Agency (NSA), responsible for communications intelligence; the Defense Intelligence Agency (DIA), which collects intelligence for the military; the National Reconnaissance Office (NRO); and the National Geospatial-Intelligence Agency (NGIA). It is not clear that drawing boxes on an organization chart and ladling out a large helping of alphabet soup enhanced national security. For practical purposes the DNI's office is just one more power center competing with the CIA, the FBI, and the DHS. Since 2005 there have been four directors of the agency. When the most recent one was appointed, the *New York Times* described him as "a director who oversees 16 agencies but does not run any of them."[3] Despite all the various agencies, with their multibillion-dollar budgets, searching for bin Laden the world over, it took ten years to catch up with him. Then he was living in a building near Pakistani military headquarters.

Perhaps the greatest personnel blunder occurred in 2005, when President Bush nominated Bernard Kerik to succeed Ridge as secretary of homeland security. If Kerik's appointment as police commissioner had been greeted with little enthusiasm by many NYC law enforcement experts, then his appointment to head the DHS astounded them.

After Mayor Giuliani left office at the end of 2001, he opened a consulting business in which Kerik became a partner. When the United States occupied Iraq, President Bush appointed Kerik interim minister of the interior in that country. His stay was short and undistinguished, and he quickly returned to Giuliani Partners. In the run-up to the 2004 presidential election, Kerik made a series of political speeches urging support for President Bush. The Senate had not begun to consider his nomination when the president had to withdraw his name, allegedly because of Kerik's failure to pay taxes on the wages of a nanny (though she was never located). At the time of Kerik's nomination, a number of New Yorkers were aware of rumors about his extramarital rendezvous in an apartment made available to workers at the World Trade Center site, associations with unsavory individuals, and irregular financial dealings (which in 2006 required him to plead guilty to a New York State misdemeanor crime). But apparently none of the knowledgeable people were contacted by the White House. In 2007 federal prosecutors charged Kerik with evading taxes on gifts he had received and perjury, the last for lying to investigators conducting a background check on his qualifications for homeland security head. In 2010, after entering a plea of guilty, he was sentenced to four years' imprisonment, the first former New York City police commissioner since the office was established in 1901 to go to prison.

Security still remains a problem, despite the arrival of a new administration in Washington in January 2009. In December of 2009, an al Qaeda operative attempted to detonate a bomb in an airliner over Detroit. Only the action of a fellow passenger prevented him from succeeding. When the Obama administration's secretary of homeland security, former New Mexico governor Janet Napolitano, declared that the system had worked, the storm of criticism and ridicule that followed almost swept her from office. About the same time it was revealed that two Washingtonians, Tareq and Michaele Salahi, had managed to crash a White House dinner and mingle with the president and other VIPs.

———

In 2002 Mayor Giuliani was succeeded by Mike Bloomberg (New York's richest person, with a net worth of $20 billion), who named Ray Kelly police commissioner, the first former commissioner in the history of the department to return to the post. While the federal government floundered, Kelly moved to restore the safety and morale of New Yorkers, and he didn't care whose toes he stepped on. Under Bloomberg, Kelly has been granted more autonomy in running the department than any previous commissioner. In addition to the normal responsibilities of his job, post-9/11 counterterrorism has become a task for the police commissioner to an extent unimagined by his predecessors.

From the start, he was not willing to accept the federal government's policy of refusing to share information with local police. He assigned a hundred detectives to the joint task force on terrorism and boldly demanded that the NYPD be put in command of it. The FBI agreed to joint command.

Before 9/11 the NYPD intelligence division had been used as "coat holders," the cops' name for detectives who escort dignitaries.* Kelly wanted a

---

* For a description of NYPD domestic security operations in the 1950s and 1960s, see the account by longtime squad member Det. Tony Ulasewicz in *The President's Private Eye*. Based on his recollections, most of the squad's members appeared to have spent their time shepherding VIPs. It was through this work that Ulasewicz became acquainted with Richard Nixon. During Nixon's presidency Ulasewicz left the NYPD to work as an investigator for the White House. Some readers will remember him testifying during the Watergate hearings.

true intelligence operation. To head it, he brought in as a deputy commissioner David Cohen, formerly the number-three official in the CIA. In an unprecedented move, Kelly and Cohen stationed detectives abroad in London, Tel Aviv, Singapore, and eight other cities to maintain liaison with the local police. When a terrorist incident occurs overseas, an NYPD detective quickly responds to the scene, gathers information, and flashes it to New York. Working from an out-of-the-way facility in New York City, skilled linguists monitor the al Jazeera TV network and other Arab media, looking for clues to a future attack. Others listen to recorded conversations between terrorist suspects. As in the Pentagon or the CIA headquarters at Langley, Virginia, highly educated specialists, working with streetwise detectives, prepare sophisticated studies analyzing various problems.

As deputy commissioner in charge of counterterrorism operations, Kelly appointed Frank Libutti, a recently retired Marine lieutenant general. When Libutti left, he was replaced by Mike Sheehan, a West Point–educated Army colonel who had served as the U.S. ambassador-at-large on terrorism. It would be an understatement to say that the FBI was not thrilled with the NYPD's foreign intelligence operations. Bureau legats assigned to U.S. embassies did not like the idea of NYPD detectives being stationed at the headquarters of the host country's police. Nor did the FBI look with favor on Cohen, Libutti, and Sheehan opening back channels to their old employers, the CIA and the Pentagon.

Under the leadership of the new deputy commissioners, NYPD security operations began to display a professional touch. Instead of seventeen officers assigned full time to counterterrorism duties as before 9/11, now at least a thousand are, and in periods of high alert the number might be triple that figure. It has become a familiar sight for New Yorkers to see black vans suddenly pull up outside the United Nations complex, Rockefeller Center, or similar places and disgorge teams of officers in helmets and flak jackets cradling automatic weapons. These "Hercules teams" are sent out because of a possible threat, but mostly they are trying to keep potential terrorists off balance. Additionally, on signal, each of the NYPD's seventy-six precincts can dispatch a patrol car on a "surge" to a designated location.

Threats to the city can come from a variety of sources. On the foreign front, there is al Qaeda central and its affiliates. According to intelligence officials, al Qaeda central under bin Laden was still fixated on spectacular operations like the World Trade Center attack or destroying a bridge. "It's in their DNA," one noted.[4] The affiliates concentrate on smaller targets that can be attacked by simpler methods, such as truck bombs. Groups such as Hamas or Hezbollah have their own methods and priorities. Then there are rogue states like Iran, whose leaders have warned that if there is an attack on Iranian nuclear facilities, suicide bombers will be dispatched to America. Within the United States there are "Jihad Joes" and "Jihad Janes" who have become radicalized by watching TV or surfing the Internet. In 2007 six American Muslims were charged with planning to carry out an attack against the Army base in Fort Dix, New Jersey. None of them had received any training or assistance from the usual suspect terrorist groups. On the right there remain a number of hate groups and militia types, of whom Timothy McVeigh was a prime example.

In 2003 an al Qaeda operative, conducting a surveillance of the Brooklyn Bridge, was overheard in an intercepted phone conversation saying, "The weather is too hot." This meant there was too much of a law enforcement presence in the area for an attack to be contemplated.* In the same year, a New York cop, patrolling a Queens subway station after midnight, noticed some men filming trains. When he questioned them, they feigned an inability to speak English. An officer of Middle Eastern background was summoned. He spoke Farsi, so he was able to converse with them in their own language. This flustered them to the point that their English rapidly improved and they admitted they were security guards at the Iranian Embassy. Detectives who investigated the incident suspected that they were intelligence officers, possibly planning a terrorist act. The NYPD reported the men to the U.S. State Department, which ordered them out of the country.

Though rarely discussed publicly, there are police officers equipped with radiation detectors who quietly prowl the streets. The NYPD takes seriously the possibility of a terrorist attempt to detonate a nuclear device or, more likely, a dirty bomb.

Following the bombings in the Madrid subway in 2004 and the London underground in 2005, Commissioner Kelly flooded the New York subways

---

* The caller was a truck driver licensed to carry hazardous materials, whom police suspected was plotting to bring down the bridge.

with cops. The Madrid terrorists had planted explosives and fled. The London ones were suicide bombers who wore backpacks. So the NYPD began spot-checking people carrying bags in the subway. Those who refused to allow the police to search their bags were not allowed on trains. Civil liberties lawyers filed suit, arguing that it was not only a violation of constitutional rights but a waste of time, because a bomber would simply go to another subway station until he was allowed to board a train. Anyone with an understanding of criminal psychology recognized that the police tactic was well conceived. Certain events attract copycats. Someone, hearing about the bombings in Europe, might decide to plant a bomb in the New York subways to highlight his own grievances. However, were he to notice intensive police activity near a target area, he might rethink his options. Trained terrorist teams, observing the police activity, would likely regroup. In the meantime, they could be infiltrated by an informer, their conversations might be intercepted, or their superiors might decide the risk of failure was too great and call the project off. A judge dismissed the suit.

The possibilities for attack are endless. On May 1, 2010, in Times Square, shortly before theater goers began arriving to attend the evening performances, two vendors noticed smoke coming from a Nissan Pathfinder. When police and firefighters examined the vehicle they discovered a cache of explosives powerful enough to kill or injure hundreds of passersby. The device had been set by a U.S. citizen of Pakistani origin. Luckily he had not armed it correctly. Police took him off an airliner bound for Dubai, and under interrogation he talked freely and expressed no regrets other than he had failed in his mission. Apparently he had undertaken it for the Taliban. Brought to trial he was sentenced to life imprisonment. Undoubtedly other would-be terrorists have studied his technical mistakes so that they will not repeat them.

On 9/11 the response of public safety forces to the World Trade Center disaster was disjointed. Some off-duty cops and firefighters, as well as civilian volunteers, assigned themselves to duty at the scene. Their presence only added to the confusion. While most were well meaning, some civilians used the occasion to perpetrate scams or steal valuables. Under Kelly the NYPD responds to possible disasters according to a tightly controlled procedure. If police receive a report of a suspected bomb at some location, they will send a relatively small force to the scene, while other officers screen off the area so that any terrorist observing the target location cannot chart police procedures. Abroad it has been the practice of some groups, such as Hamas, to detonate hidden bombs at sites after rescuers arrive. This not only adds to the casualty list, but it strikes at the security forces themselves. In a major plot it would be a means to weaken security units, making it easier for terrorists to launch a much larger attack at another location. The terrorist strike against Mumbai began with an assault on the local police station. By maintaining strict control over its forces, the NYPD also lessens the possibility that terrorists could use stolen uniforms to infiltrate the police ranks. As in London, the Lower Manhattan financial district is surrounded by a "ring of steel": surveillance cameras that cover the entire area and in some cases can even identify the faces of known terrorists. License plate scanners are able to read the plates of vehicles entering Manhattan. Barriers block vehicle access to sensitive locations.

The NYPD efforts have not been carried out without criticism. In the last week of August 2004, the Republican national convention was held in New York City. For months before, various groups were engaged in attempts to recruit people to come to New York and protest the Bush administration's Iraq policy. Many postings on the Internet spoke of creating disorder and engaging in violence during the time of the convention. In previous years, traveling bands of violent protesters had staged street riots in conjunction with economic summit conferences in various cities. In Seattle in 1999, during a meeting of the World Trade Organization, an estimated fifty thousand to a hundred thousand protesters engaged in acts of violence, destroyed property, set fires, overturned police and emergency vehicles, and looted local stores. For a time they paralyzed the city. In Genoa, Italy, in 2001, two hundred thousand people protested against the G8 summit. Some demonstrators rioted, set fires, and engaged in vandalism. In San Francisco in 2003, antiwar protesters shut down a large portion of the city. During the course of the disturbance, protesters fired bolts from slingshots at the police. That year in Miami, twenty thousand people engaged in protests against a free-trade meeting. Again, there were violent clashes with police and fires set.

Months before the New York convention opened, specific plans appeared on websites urging various groups to engage in "a day of chaos on Tuesday,

August 31." Other sites gave lists of the hotels where various delegations would stay and Broadway shows they would attend, encouraging protesters to harass them. Tactics on how to attack police were openly discussed. Given that an estimated million people were expected in New York, the NYPD was prepared to deal with the various threats.

On August 29, the first day of the convention, between one-half and three-quarters of a million people marched through the streets of New York. Security was massive, and the protesters were kept away from the convention site at Madison Square Garden. About 250 arrests were made, mostly for minor violations. On August 31, the "day of chaos," the protesters were out in force. Again police channeled the demonstrating groups away from the convention center and kept a close eye on individuals and groups suspected of planning acts of terrorism. Twelve hundred people were arrested. Police had the option to issue summonses, but instead they sent prisoners to central booking to be questioned and fingerprinted—a process that would take several days. Many of those arrested were held in a rented facility at Pier 57 along the Hudson River. The place had previously been used as a garage for city buses and was not in condition to receive guests. Some of the protesters called it Guantánamo on the Hudson. Protest leaders and their lawyers complained that the police procedure was meant to prevent the arrestees from any further participation in demonstrations. Cops countered that since arrestees often gave false names, only by questioning and fingerprinting them could a proper legal case be assembled and people wanted on other criminal charges be identified. On the larger issues, both sides have a point. Some protesters hoped to compel the convention to be halted or forced to leave New York. A few wanted blood to flow in the streets. However, some of those caught up in the arrests were simply people who had been peacefully protesting. Over the next eight years there would be continuing litigation over the arrests, with the legal issues yet to be resolved.

It was not only antiwar protesters who criticized the police but conservative business interests. When the NYPD finally got to review the plan for the proposed Freedom Tower, it refused to sign off. The front of the structure was only a few yards back from a busy highway traversed by trucks. Deputy Commissioner Sheehan saw it as an open invitation to truck bombers. Even though the building had been designed so that it would not topple, casualties could have resulted, and the damage that might result from an explosion would require that the facility be closed for repair. In normal times, police department objections could have been pushed aside by the powerful development community backed by politicians. But in a city where nearly three thousand people had died a few years earlier, it was politically impossible to oppose such strong opposition from the NYPD. The plan was scrapped.

Kelly's recruitment of top outside talent for the police department and the NYPD's working relationships with foreign security services recall the World War I period, when the department brought in outsiders to man key positions and received help from Allied intelligence. The way the NYPD has assumed the lead position in security locally is reminiscent of how the department operated under Commissioner Arthur Woods from 1914 to 1917. Other American police departments, such as that in Los Angeles, have adopted some of the features of the New York security model.

———

For the first time since World War II, the United States appears to be in the process of creating a coherent security system. Rather than concocting it overnight, as happened with DHS, a truly effective one is probably going to emerge out of a process of trial and error, and that may be a good thing. In 1959 a Yale social scientist, Charles Lindblom, challenged the popular notion that all problems could be solved by employing a comprehensive, rational, scientific approach to decision making. He mockingly titled it "the science of muddling through." Lindblom argued that in the real world, "branch" or incremental planning provides better solutions than more comprehensive "root" planning. His article appeared two years before President Kennedy's administration, staffed by "the best and brightest," took office. A leading light among them was Secretary of Defense Robert McNamara, a former Harvard Business School professor who had advanced to president of the Ford Motor Company through his ability to utilize scientific management techniques of the operations research variety. When Vice President Lyndon Johnson excitedly described to House Speaker Sam Rayburn the quality of his cabinet colleagues—"[McGeorge] Bundy, who was Dean at Harvard, and McNamara, who headed Ford"—Rayburn observed that he would feel better if one of them had ever run for sheriff. As it turned out,

Bundy, McNamara, and the "whiz kids" who worked for them led America into the Vietnam disaster. That experience demonstrated that it is possible to place too much faith in experts and scientific methods. In contemporary times, the failure of hedge funds, run by "wunderkinds" and operated according to "foolproof" economic risk models, are an example of this.

In the past few years some very talented individuals have begun working in the field of domestic security. Brilliant thinkers are constantly turning out studies proposing innovative ideas. It would be a good idea, though, if all the new talent were required to read David Halberstam's book on Vietnam, *The Best and the Brightest.* In it he described how the "wise men" and their whiz kids failed in Vietnam. Brilliance can lead to hubris, and to paraphrase Speaker Rayburn, it would be more reassuring if some of the current crop of whiz kids had ever walked a beat or investigated a mugging.

In the spirit of Lindblom, I will resist the temptation to present a full-blown plan for making America safe. Instead I will examine a few of the key issues currently on the policy agenda.

At the federal level, a common proposal to improve domestic security is that an MI5 domestic security–type agency be established. If, in the midst of the present crisis, an MI5 were to be created from the ground up, many problems would arise. In the first place, its composition and duties would be determined by political and bureaucratic compromises. In 1980 the U.S. rescue mission to free the embassy hostages in Tehran was organized so that the Army, Navy, Air Force, and Marines all got a piece of the action. The result was a fiasco, which contributed greatly to President Carter being defeated for reelection.

Cops have always looked down on investigators who do not have arrest power or carry firearms. Thus, every conceivable group has sought such authority for its members. MI5 would be no different. An American MI5 would probably end up as a conventional law enforcement agency. On the other hand, if it did not make raids and stage perp walks, Congress and the media would declare it a failure. At worst, it might constitute a secret police force of a type previously unknown to the United States. Better that federal-level security investigations be left to the FBI, whose agents have investigative experience and a grounding in law and are under the overall supervision of Department of Justice attorneys.

Then there is the question of what to do about DHS. If it is not meant to take over the CIA's duty of gathering foreign intelligence or replace the FBI as the principal domestic intelligence agency, is its role simply as a catchall for everything that's left? There have been suggestions that it be divested of some of its tasks and scaled down to performing certain such core missions as safeguarding national transportation networks and protecting the border and entry points to the United States. As protector of the borders, the agency would be the principal cabinet department dealing with immigration issues.

At the federal level, the president and Congress will determine the respective roles of the FBI and DHS, though powerful bureaucrats may have an equally strong input. In his time J. Edgar Hoover was able to position the FBI to play a dominant role in dealing with the key problems of particular eras. In the 1930s the bureau took the lead in the fight against public enemies like the Dillinger gang. In the 1940s Hoover secured for the FBI the top position in domestic security efforts against spies and saboteurs. In the 1950s he was a cold warrior, turning his bureau loose on domestic Communists and their sympathizers. In the twenty-first century, the agency that can convince the public that it is the leading bulwark against terrorists will likely assume preeminence in federal law enforcement.

The United States has never had a European-style ministry of the interior, with authority over the country's police, or maintained a national constabulary as exists in some European countries. However, if an agency like the DHS were to be headed by an ambitious empire builder—perhaps an Attorney General Palmer type with an eye on the White House—it might seek new missions, such as conducting field patrols in U.S. cities.* If America is to go that route, it should not be done by simply inserting a paragraph in an omnibus law. Instead, there should be a vigorous national debate so the public will have a true appreciation of what they are getting into.

At present, there is still not a balance between federal and state roles in domestic security. Local agencies are the first line of defense. Despite the fact that the DHS has the lead role in airline security, all airports have detachments of state or local police on duty. After the plane crashed into the Pentagon on 9/11, headquarters for the world's most powerful military machine,

---

* The current wave of violence by Mexican drug cartels may cause some officials to suggest that DHS be used to supplement state and local police in the Southwest.

the resultant fire was extinguished by the Arlington County, Virginia, Fire Department. It is unrealistic to believe that the NYPD, with more than forty thousand employees, or other large police departments, like Los Angeles or Chicago, are going to take a backseat to a federal agency in the task of protecting the world's most important cities. Partnership between local and federal law enforcement is a better answer than placing security totally in the hands of the national government.

On the other hand, not every American police department can maintain full-fledged counterterrorist units. Not only would an attempt to do so stretch resources to the breaking point, but it also would undoubtedly lead to abuses by half-trained investigators. The logical solution is to create regional squads. But given petty rivalries, this will be difficult. In the New York metropolitan area, the NYPD would be the obvious agency to control all counterterrorist investigations from New Haven to Newark. But New Jersey, Connecticut, and the New York suburbs would never agree to such an arrangement.

In the final analysis, governors and legislatures may create regional task forces, and between the White House and the state capitals, they may reach agreement on federal-state cooperation.

In New York City, starting from a virtual zero base, Commissioner Ray Kelly has made the NYPD a major domestic security agency, recognized as such by U.S. and foreign governments. Despite past difficulties, the FBI headquarters has mandated that its New York personnel work closely with the NYPD. Reports from all law enforcement and security agencies are processed through a fusion center where disparate pieces are assembled into comprehensive reports.

When Kelly leaves his job (and he is already the second-longest serving commissioner in the 110-year history of the office), a new mayor or police commissioner may decide that it is too costly to maintain the present level of effort in counterterrorist operations. This is especially true because city revenues are falling as a result of the depressed economy. The police force now has thirty-four thousand officers, whereas at the beginning of the decade it had more than forty thousand. The degree of professionalism the

NYPD has achieved in counterterrorism is owing to the fact that its specialized officers engage in extensive training and field exercises. If the department head count is drastically reduced, there will probably be attempts to shift counterterrorism duties to the regular patrol complement, which will handle them between responding to street crimes and domestic disturbance calls. This would be akin to the Army using ordinary infantry companies to carry out special-forces operations. The cutbacks may also lead to the withdrawal of NYPD detectives from overseas. If so, the police would be back to total reliance on the FBI for intelligence information. Worse, it is likely to be seen by terrorist organizations as a signal that U.S. defenses are being lowered.

Despite past history, U.S. security forces have not moved to the phase where constitutional and legal rules are set aside in favor of "achieving victory." However, America has not experienced an extensive or prolonged terrorist campaign within its own borders. If it were to sustain the kind of bombings and attacks common in Israel, or the Mexican drug wars overflowed into the United States, it is possible that there could be large-scale crackdowns such as the preventive detention of individuals who, because of their words or their ethnic identity, are deemed security risks. In April 2010 Arizona adopted security laws that many critics see as opening the door to harassment of Mexicans and other person of Hispanic origin. If history is any gauge, calls for severe action will not come exclusively from the right but also from many liberals.

In 2010 when the Department of Justice announced that the KSM (Khalid Shaikh Mohammed) terrorist group would be tried in New York City, many New Yorkers panicked and demanded that the trial he moved away from the city. A reasonable argument could be offered that foreign terrorists captured abroad should not be tried in civilian courts and thereby receive the legal protections afforded U.S. citizens. A less defensible argument was that holding the trial would spark an attack on the city. If the United States cannot conduct government business in its principal city for fear of displeasing someone somewhere, it opens the door for any group to impose its veto in America's domestic affairs.

One lesson from the past is that American leaders should not underestimate the strength of our people and institutions or gauge every enemy to be ten feet tall. In World War I it was believed that German Americans might rise in armed revolt. Anyone who opposed the war was deemed to be the same as a "Hun." In the post–World War I Red Scare or the McCarthyism that followed World War II, officials and private citizens succumbed to the belief that a handful of radicals could overthrow the U.S. government.

In 1990, when New York City recorded 2,245 murders, many national and international publications forecast "the end of the Big Apple." Within a few years, the murder rate had drastically decreased, and New York City was again the in place to live and work.

Even in such spheres as economics, Americans tend to panic easily. In the 1980s it was freely predicted that Japan would emerge as the superpower of the world. Today some believe that China will eventually be in control of the U.S. economy. Since the current recession began in 2008, "wise men and women" have forecast the rapid decline of America's standing in the world. Such predictions were heard during the Depression of the 1930s and post-Vietnam, but they did not come to pass. More astute observations about America have come from foreign enemies such as Captain Rintelen in World War I and Admiral Yamamoto in World War II, both of whom understood the innate power and stability of the United States.

Still, new problems always arise. In the fall of 2011, Wall Street, the historic target of so many protests, was "occupied" by several thousand demonstrators. From their base in an adjacent park, they protested financial practices they believed led to the 2008 economic crisis. The "occupy" movement has stimulated similar action across the country. Locally there have been some confrontations with the police. While it is too early to forecast what will happen, New York City will likely be at the center of events, and on occasion a target of violence. Dealing with its problems will require reasonable responses based on careful analyses. Throughout the twentieth century, despite many mistakes and difficulties, New York City and the country at large were able to overcome the challenges they faced. The twenty-first century need not be any different.

ACKNOWLEDGMENTS

I wish to express my gratitude to the following organizations who were helpful to me in the writing of the book: the NYPD, the FBI, the Library of Congress, the National Security Agency, the National Archives, the John Jay College of Criminal Justice Library, and the Westchester County Library system.

Among individuals I wish to thank are NYPD commissioner Ray Kelly; deputy commissioners Paul Brown, David Cohen, and Mike Farrell; Anthony Bouza; Joe Dunne; John Earl Haynes; Martin Mitchell; and Larry Sullivan.

At Potomac I am grateful for the guidance provided by Elizabeth Demers, my editor; Kathryn Owens, senior production editor; Elizabeth Norris, assistant editor; Laura Briggs, publicity and marketing manager; and Claire Noble, former publicity and marketing manager.

There are also a number of people who are no longer alive who, over the years, have influenced my thoughts on the subject matter of this book. There are so many that to list them would require many pages. I am also not sure that all of them would want to be identified. Indeed, some living persons have preferred not to be cited. In any event, my thanks to all of them.

REFERENCES

Introduction

The great game: Kipling, *Kim*, and Hopkirk, *The Great Game* and *Like Hidden Fire*. Books that describe the workings of the Great Game in the days of the British Empire: Kipling, circa 1880s, Hopkirk, *World War I*.

The war in New York: Hough, *The Web*. The official history of the American Protective League.

Citations

1 Rudyard Kipling, *Kim* (London: Cassell, 1901).

2 Peter Hopkirk, *Like Hidden Fire: The Plot to Bring Down the British Empire* (New York: Kodansha International, 1994), 2.

3 Emerson Hough, *The Web: A Revelation of Patriotism* (Chicago: Reilly & Lee, 1919), 195.

4 David Johnston and William K. Rashbuam, "New York Police Fight with U.S. on Surveillance," *New York Times*, November 19, 2008.

1. Guarding America's Greatest City: Security Policing Before 1914

The Draft Riots, the railroad strike, and other disorders of the 1870s: Bernstein, *Draft Riots* and Cook, *Armies of the Street*, cover the events of July 1863 and other riots of the period. Bruce, *1877*, describes the disorders that occurred in New York and nationally in that tumultuous year.

Goldman, Berkman and Most, the McKinley assassination: Drinnon, *Rebel in Paradise* and Goldman, *Living My Life*. The former is sympathetic to Emma Goldman but is balanced in its analysis of facts. Emma's own account of her life explains why she remains a sympathetic figure while Berkman and Most do not. For Most, see Trautmann, *Voice of Terror*. Rauchway, *Murdering McKinley*, and Tunney, *Throttled*.

Law enforcement and detective agencies: (The New York police) Lardner and Reppetto, *NYPD*, and Riis, *Making of an American*, contain an illuminating picture of Inspector Byrnes. (U.S. Secret Service) Bowen and Neal, *US Secret Service*, is a semiofficial history. Melanson and Stevens, *The Secret Service*, is an independent account. Wilkie and Luther, *American Secret Service Agent*, is the story of turn-of-the-century operative Don Wilkie, son of John Wilkie, chief of the service. (William Burns) Caesar, *Incredible Detective*, and Hunt, *Front Page Detective*, are favorable portraits of the subject. Gage, *The Day Wall Street Exploded*, is critical of him. (The Pinkertons) Horan, *The Pinkertons*, and Lukas, *Big Trouble*. The former is the semiofficial history of the agency, and the other is a highly critical account of it, concentrating on the 1905 Idaho bombing case. (Creation of the FBI) Corson, *Armies of Ignorance*; Powers, *Secrecy and Power*; and Whitehead, *The FBI Story*. (General) Jefferys-Jones, *American Espionage*. Another useful work on U.S. intelligence is Miller, *Spying for America*.

Claude Dansey and the British secret services: Read and Fisher, *Colonel Z*, is the definitive biography of Dansey. Andrew, *Her Majesty's Secret Service*, is a first-rate examination of British intelligence. Deacon, *British Secret Service*, is a popular account. West's MI5 and MI6 cover the ground on those agencies but do not offer much elaboration. Allason's *The Branch* provides a similar treatment for Scotland Yard's security section. This is not surprising since Allason is the real name of Nigel West. None of the three is an authorized history, though they appear to have benefited greatly from informal cooperation. Most of the authorized histories are suitable only as antidotes for insomnia. Andrew's authorized thousand-page history of MI5 is an exception. Conrad, *Secret Agent*, is a master literary figure's rendering of the ethos of British security policing in the early twentieth century.

The Bresci circle and the threats to Rockefeller: Lardner and Reppetto, *NYPD*, and Tunney, *Throttled*, cover the Bresci circle. Gallagher, *All the Right Enemies*, is a biography of Carlo Tresca, who led the anarchists' protests.

Citations

1   Augustine E. Costello, *Our Police Protectors* (New York: C. F. Roper, 1885), 199.

2   *Pollock v. Farmers' Loan & Trust Co.*, 157 U.S. 429 (1895).

3   Eric Rauchway, *Murdering McKinley: The Making of Theodore Roosevelt's America* (New York: Hill and Wang, 2003), 97.

4   "Topic of the Times, Apologies Due to a Detective," *New York Times*, December 4, 1911.

5   Thomas A. Bailey, *A Diplomatic History of the American People* (New York: F. S. Crofts, 1940), 191–201, 209–210.

2. The Manhattan Front: The Undeclared War, 1914–1917

The Wall Street meeting, July 1914: Chernow, *The House of Morgan* and McAdoo, *Crowded Years*. The definitive history of the House of Morgan and its offshoots.

The Mitchell administration and the NYPD: Lewinson, *John Purroy Mitchel*, Lardner and Reppetto, *NYPD*.

The preparedness movement: Hagedorn, *Leonard Wood Volume 2*, Millis, *Road to War*. The Millis book is the definitive work on the preparedness movement. However, it reflects the pacifist and antiwar sentiments dominant among the American elite in the mid-1930s when the book was written.

German sabotage campaign: Gerrard, *My Four Years in Germany*, is an account of U.S. relations with the kaiser's government. Millman, *The Detonators*; Witcover, *Sabotage at Black Tom*. Landau, *The Enemy Within*, covers Black Tom. Landau was one of the principal investigators in the postwar lawsuit against Germany. Tunney, *Throttled*, is useful for its inside account of NYPD operations. Rintelen, *Dark Invader*, and Voska, *Spy and Counterspy*, must be taken with grains of salt. See also *New York Times* obituary, Frank Burke, May 31, 1942, and Frank Polk, February 8, 1943.

British intelligence operations: Andrew, *Her Majesty's Secret Service*, is first rate. Tuchman, *The Zimmerman Telegram*, is a classic. Thomson, *Scotland Yard*, presents the police side of counterintelligence. Brust, *In Plain Clothes*, contains interesting observations by a special branch detective.

Scenes at the Metropolitan Opera: Described in Millis, *Road to War*, pages 441–42, 459.

Citations

1   *Testimony Joint Legislative Committee to Investigate Public Service Commission.* New York State Legislature. Albany, NY: V.S. Lyon, 1916, 99–111.

2   Ron Chernow, *The House of Morgan: An American Banking Dynasty and the Rise of Modern Finance* (New York: Atlantic Monthly Press, 1990), 186.

3   Julian F. Jaffe, *Crusade Against Radicalism: New York During the Red Scare* (Port Washington, NY: Kennikat, 1972), 48–49.

4   Johann von Bernstorff, *The Memoirs of Count Bernstorff* (London: W. Heinemann, 1936), 103.

5   Martin Gilbert, *Churchill: A Life*, vol. 3 (New York: Henry Holt, 1991), 359.

3. The Storm Center of America: New York at War, 1917–1918

Antiwar rally, June 1917: There are a number of *New York Times* stories about draft resistance in New York at the beginning of World War I. Among the most informative are "Anarchists Awed by Police Clubs," June 15, 1917; "Emma Goldman and A. Berkman Behind Bars," June 16, 1917; and "Convict Berkman and Miss Goldman, Both off to Prison," July 10, 1917.

On U.S. counterintelligence: (MID) Bidwell, *History of Military Intelligence*; Cramer, *Newton Baker*; Talbert, *Negative Intelligence*; Van Deman, *Final Memorandum*. (ONI) Dorwart, *Office of Naval Intelligence, 1865–1918*; and Davis, *FDR: The Beckoning of Destiny*. Talbert and Dorwart provide considerable detail. (APL) Hough, *The Web*, and Jensen, *Price of Vigilance*. The former is the official history of the organization, the latter a denunciation of it. See also *New York Times* obituaries, A. Bruce Bielaski, February 20, 1964, and William Flynn, October 15, 1928.

Targets of U.S. security: (Victorica case) Read and Fischer, *Colonel Z*, and Yardley, *American Black Chamber*. (Roger Baldwin) Lamson, *Roger Baldwin*, and *New York Times* obituary, August 27, 1981. (Goldman) Drinnon, *Rebel in Paradise!*. (Big Bill Haywood) *Bill Haywood's Book*. (Slacker Raids) Hough, *The Web*; Jensen, *Price of Vigilance*; and Talbert, *Negative Intelligence*.

New York elections as war referenda: (1917 mayoral contest) Lewinson, *John Purroy Mitchel*. (1918, 14th District) Garrett, *LaGuardia Years*, and Kessner, *Fiorello LaGuardia*.

Citations

1   James W. Gerard, *My Four Years in Germany* (London: Hodder and Stoughton, 1917), 237.

2   See last paragraph on p. 259 on antiwar rally, June 1917.

3   William Allen White, *Woodrow Wilson* (Boston: Houghton Mifflin, 1924), 355–56.

4   Richard G. Powers, *Broken* (New York: Free Press, 2007), 88.

5   Ibid.

6   William A. Corson, *Armies of Ignorance* (New York: Dial, 1977), 590.

7   Hough, *The Web*, 195.

8   Emma Goldman, *Living My Life* (Da Capo, 1970), 477.

9   Ibid., 463–64.

10   Peggy Lamson, *Roger Baldwin* (Boston: Houghton Mifflin, 1976), 90.

4. From Red Scare to Black Chamber: 1919–1930

Red Raids, Palmer, Flynn, and Hoover: Murray, *Red Scare*; Jaffe, *Crusade against Radicalism*; and Powers, *Secrecy and Power*. Surprisingly, despite his condemnation of the government's efforts, Murray's book contains only three brief mentions of J. Edgar Hoover. This suggests that, in 1955, it was not easy for a professor to write negatively about the FBI director. Russell, *A City in Terror*, describes the Boston police strike.

The Wilson administration following the president's collapse: Levin, *Edith and Woodrow*; Medved, *The Shadow Presidents*; and Smith, *When the Cheering Stopped*. The Levin book relates the feud between Mrs. Wilson and Lord Grey.

The Wall Street bombing: Gage, *The Day Wall Street Exploded*. (On the Galleanists) Russell, *Sacco and Vanzetti*, and Watson, *Sacco & Vanzetti*.

Spies and counterspies: Meir, *The Lost Spy*, is an account of a 1920s Soviet operative working in New York City. Yardley, *American Black Chamber*. Kahn, *The Reader of Gentlemen's Mail*, is a biography of Yardley.

The Room: Persico, *Roosevelt's Secret War*, and Chan, "If These Walls Could Talk." Persico tells the story of FDR and The Room. Chan describes the meetings that took place there.

Union Square riot: Whalen, *Mr. New York*, is his autobiography. For critical accounts of Whalen, see LaGuardia bios by Garrett and Kessner.

Citations

1 Roy Talbert Jr., *Negative Intelligence* (Jackson: University of Mississippi Press, 1991), 147–48.

2 "On Pacific List, But Serve Nation," *New York Times*, January 26, 1919.

3 Editorial, "The Bomb Conspirators," *New York Times*, June 4, 1919.

4 Richard Drinnon, *Rebel in Paradise* (Chicago: University of Chicago Press, 1961), 253.

5 Ibid.

6 Beverly Gage, *The Day Wall Street Exploded* (New York: Oxford University Press, 2009), 238.

7 Robert K. Murray, *Red Scare* (Minneapolis: University of Minnesota Press, 1955), 238.

8 Gage, photo section of *The Day Wall Street Exploded*.

9 Ernest Jerome Hopkins, *The Mooney Case* (Cambridge, MA: DaCapo, 1970), VII.

5. Countdown to War: 1931–1940

Incident at Pier 84: Breuer, *Hitler's Underground War*, and Zacharias, *Secret Missions*.

New York in the 1930s: Allen, *Since Yesterday*, describes city life. (On the supposed plan to overthrow the Roosevelt administration) Archer, *The Plot to Seize the White House*. (The Bonus Army) Talbert, *Negative Intelligence*. (Morgan hearings) Chernow, *The House of Morgan*. (NYPD handling of strikes) Garrett, *The LaGuardia Years*, and Kessner, *Fiorello LaGuardia*.

German espionage in the United States: Breuer, *Hitler's Underground War*; Farago, *The Game of the Foxes*; and Kahn, *Hitler's Spies*. (Canaris) Brown, C, and West, *British Secret Intelligence*. An inside account of the operations of German intelligence in the Hitler era is Schellenberg (chief of the Nazi Party Secret Service), *The Labyrinth*. The *New York Times* of that era contains many stories on the arrest of Rumrich and his confederates. Among the most useful are "Spy Hunt Pressed by Agents," February 28, 1938; and "Doctor [Griebel] Watched in Spy Inquiry," March 1, 1938. For a summary of the investigation linking Rumrich, Griebel, Moog, Hoffman, and others, see Russell Owen, "Nation's Spy Hunt Full of Surprises," June 5, 1938. Another recap is written by the *Times* top military expert, Hanson W. Baldwin, "A Spy Thriller in Real-life," June 26, 1938. Turrou's difficulties with the Department of Justice are cited in "Turrou Spy Story Barred in Press," June 23, 1938.

American Nazis and fascists (Coughlin, Kuhn and McWilliams): Carlson, *Undercover*. (The assault on the police in the Bronx) McAllister, *The Kind of Guy I Am*. (Winchell) Mosedale, *Men Who Made Broadway*.

America First: Berg, *Lindbergh*.

World's Fair bombing: Among *New York Times* stories, the most informative include "Police Die in Blast," July 5, 1940; "War Atmosphere Created by Blast," July 5, 1940; and "100 Examined in Bomb Roundup," July 6, 1940.

IRA relationships with Nazis: Carter, *Shamrock and Swastika*.

NYPD domestic security operations: See Ulasewicz, *The President's Private Eye*. A highly critical account of Red Squads in general is contained in Donner, *Protectors of Privilege*.

Citations

1   Zacharias, *Secret Missions* (New York: G. P. Putnam's Sons, 1946), 152–53.

2   Talbert, *Negative Intelligence*, 239.

3   John Roy Carlson, *Undercover* (New York: E. P. Dutton, 1943), 54.

4   Richard G. Powers, *Secrecy and Power* (New York: Free Press, 1987), 236.

5   Thomas Kessner, *Fiorello H. LaGuardia* (New York: McGraw-Hill, 1986), 352.

6. All the President's Men: June 1940–December 1941

On the BSC in New York: Brown, C. (Bio of Sir Stuart Menzies) Cull, *Selling War*; Farago, *The Game of the Foxes*; Hyde, *Room 3603*; Stevenson, *A Man Called Intrepid*; and Read and Fisher, *Colonel Z*. In Chapter 6 I noted scholars' questions about the validity of the *Intrepid* book.

On German networks in New York: Breuer, *Hitler's Underground War*. The arrest of members of the Ludwig ring was extensively covered in the *New York Times*. Among the key stories are "Girl 18 [Lucy Boehmler] Accuses Nazi Spy Suspects," February 4,

1942. For more on the conviction of Ludwig and the lesser figures, see "6 Nazi Spies Guilty in First War Trials," March 7, 1942; "3 Spy Ring Leaders Get 20 Years," March 14, 1942; and "Girl Spy [Boehmler] Gets 5 Years in Prison," March 21, 1942.

U.S. security forces: (The papers of A. Berle) Berle and Berle, *Navigating the Rapids*. (On Hoover and the FBI) Jeffery-Jones, *The FBI*, and Powers, *Secrecy and Power*. (On FDR's personal spies) Persico, *Roosevelt's Secret War*. (On ONI) Dorwart, *Conflict of Duty*. (On MID) Bidwell, *History of the MID*. The anecdote about FDR ordering G-2 not to tell the secretary of war about intercepting messages is on page 336, n. 17. (On Donovan) Brown, *Last Hero*. (On the Popov case) Masterman, *The Double Cross System*. Popov, *Spy/Counterspy*, is Tricycle's own story. West, *MI6 Secret Operations*, questions Masterman's interpretation and Popov's account of the Pearl Harbor questionnaire. On the attack see Wohlstetter, *Pearl Harbor*.

Description of events on December 7, 1941: Goldstein, "Football Sunday, December 7, 1941," *New York* Times, December 7, 1980, and Weintraub, *Journey into War*.

Citations

1   Gene Smith, *Dark Summer* (New York: Collier Edition, 1989), 146.

2   Anthony Cave Brown, *Last Hero* (New York: Times Books, 1982), 159.

3   A. Scott Berg, *Lindbergh* (New York: G. P. Putnam & Son, 1998), 427.

7. Enemies Real and Imagined: 1942–1945

The *Normandie* fire: Jamison, *Jumping Spark*, and Diehl, *Over Here*.

Fascists operating after Pearl Harbor: Breuer, *Hitler's Underground War*, and Carlson, *Undercover*.

On the ONI-Mafia partnership: Campbell, *The Luciano Project*, and Reppetto, *American Mafia*.

The submarine saboteurs (Operation Pastorius): Kahn, *Hitler's Spies*; Lamphere, *The FBI-KGB War*; and Rachlis, *They Came to Kill*. The last is a full account of the case. On the next wave of saboteurss see Gimpel, *Agent 146*.

The murder of Carlo Tresca: Gallagher, *All the Right Enemies*, and Reppetto, *American Mafia*.

Zacharias and U. S. intelligence: Dorwart, *Conflict of Duty*, and Zacharias, *Secret Missions*.

New York during World War II: Goldstein, *Helluva Town*.

Citations

1   "Catastrophe: carelessness," *Time*, February 23, 1942, 17.

2   Joseph E. Persico, *Roosevelt's Secret War* (New York: Random House, 2001), 147.

3   Dorothy Gallagher, *All the Right Enemies* (New York: Pelican Books, 1989), 237. The remark originally comes from Gosch and Hammer, *The Last Testament of Lucky Luciano*, a work that has been discounted by experts on organized crime.

4   Persico, *Roosevelt's Secret War*, 447.

5   Zacharias, *Secret Missions*, 208.

8. The Journey to 9/11: New York Security in the Second Half of the Twentieth Century

America in 1900: Allen, *The Big Change*.

The changing of the guard following World War II: Jeffrey-Jones, *The FBI*; Corson, *Armies of Ignorance*; and Riebling, *The Wedge*.

Counterespionage in New York City: Lamphere, *FBI-KGB War*. (NYPD operations) Ulasewicz, *The President's Private Eye*. (On the Lieutenant Miller case) Thompson, "New York's Communist Cop" supplemented by *New York Times*, "Policeman Missing on Day of His Trial," July 18, 1953; "Red Guilt Proved, Police Trial Holds," July 24, 1953; "Monaghan Ousts Miller as a Red," July 28, 1953. On "Chester" see Haynes and Klehr, *Venona*, 222–225.

Soviet espionage: The various works of Haynes and Klehr have been generally accepted in the scholarly world. See bibliographical listings on the Amerasia case, Venona, the world of American Communism, and the work of the KGB. Andrew and Mitrokhin's *Sword and Shield* is also a valuable account of KGB operations in America. On the lingering doubts about Hiss and Rosenberg, see Jacoby, *Alger Hiss*, and Sam Roberts, "Rosenberg May Have Enlisted 2 Spies," *New York Times*, January 18, 2009. The latter story includes an admission of spying by the last remaining defendant in the Rosenberg case.

The disappearance of Galíndez: Ulasewicz, *The President's Private Eye*, and interview, Anthony Bouza. Representative *New York Times* stories on the affair are "Galíndez Search by the FBI is Urged," March 21, 1956; "FBI Denounced in the Galíndez Case," April 26, 1956; and "Galíndez Reported Murdered on a Ship," May 30, 1956 (a claim that investigators later labeled "a red herring.")

1960's disturbances: (San Francisco Riot of 1960 and Chicago Convention of 1968) Author present at both. (U.S. security operations in the '60s) Theoharis, *The FBI and American Democracy*, is a critical account. (On New York cop killings) Daley, *Target Blue*. (Bombings in New York) Esposito and Gerstein, *Bomb Squad*.

Citations

1   David McCullough, *Truman* (New York: Simon & Schuster, 1992), 388.

2   Curt Gentry, *J. Edgar Hoover: The Man and the Secrets* (New York: Norton, 1991), 235.

3   C. P. Trussell, "FBI Chief Says Reds Incite Youth," *New York Times*, July 18, 1960.

9. 9/11 and Beyond: The Twenty-First Century

The 9/11 attack: (John O'Neill) Weiss, *The Man Who Warned America*, and Wright, *The Looming Tower*. (FBI-CIA rivalries) Miller et al., *The Cell: Inside 9/11*. See also *The 9/11 Commission Report*. General studies of counterintelligence are Riebling, *The Wedge*, and Clark, *Against All Enemies*.

Commissioner Kelly's counterterrorist program: Inside accounts include Dickey, *Securing the City*, and Sheehan, *Crush the Cell*.

Policy framework: Lindblom, "The Science of Muddling Through."

Citations

1   Lawrence Wright, *The Looming Tower* (New York: Knopf, 2006), 274.

2   David Johnston and James Risen, "FBI is Investigating a Senior Counterterrorist Agent," *New York Times*, August 19, 2001.

3   Mark Mazzetti, "Nominee Promises Action as U.S. Intelligence Chief," *New York Times*, July 21, 2010.

4   Statement made by intelligence official to author in early 2011.

BIBLIOGRAPHY

Books

Allason, Rupert. *The Branch: A History of the Metropolitan Police Special Branch, 1883–1983*. London: Secker and Warburg, 1983.

Allen, Frederick Lewis. *Since Yesterday: The Nineteen Thirties in America*. New York: Harper, 1940.

———. *The Big Change: America Transforms Itself, 1900–1950*. New York: Harper, 1952.

Andrew, Christopher. *Her Majesty's Secret Service: The Making of the British Intelligence Community*. New York: Viking, 1986.

———. *For the President's Eyes Only: Secret Intelligence and the American Presidency from Washington to Bush*. New York: HarperCollins, 1995.

———. *Defend the Realm: The Authorized History of MI5*. New York: Vintage Books, 2010.

Andrew, Christopher, and Vasili Mitrokhin. *The Sword and the Shield: The Mitrokhin Archive and The Secret History of the KGB*. New York: Basic Books, 1999.

Archer, Jules. *The Plot to Seize the White House*. New York: Hawthorn Books, 1973.

Bailey, Thomas A. *A Diplomatic History of the American People*. 10th ed. Englewood Cliffs, NJ: Prentice-Hall, 1980.

Berg, A. Scott. *Lindbergh*. New York: G. P. Putnam & Son, 1998.

Berle, Beatrice Bishop and Travis B. Jacobs, eds. *Navigating the Rapids, 1918–71: From the Papers of Adolph A. Berle*. New York: Harcourt Brace Jovanovich, 1973.

Bernstein, Iver. *The New York City Draft Riots: Their Significance for American Security and Politics in the Age of the Civil War*. New York: Oxford University Press, 1990.

Bernstorff, Johann. *The Memoirs of Count Bernstorff*. New York: Random House, 1936.

Bidwell, Bruce. *History of the Military Intelligence Division of the Department of the Army General Staff, 1775–1941*. Frederick, MD: University Publications of America, 1986.

Bouza, Anthony V. *Police Intelligence: The Operations of an Investigative Unit*. New York: AMS, 1976.

Bowen, Walter S., and Harry Edward Neal. *The United States Secret Service*. Philadelphia: Chilton, 1960.

Breuer, William. *Hitler's Undercover War: The Nazi Espionage Invasion of the U.S.A.* New York: St. Martin's, 1989.

Brown, Anthony Cave. *The Last Hero: Wild Bill Donovan*. New York: Times Books, 1982.

———. *C: The Secret Life of Sir Stewart Menzies, Spymaster to Winston Churchill*. New York: Macmillan, 1987.

Bruce, Robert J. *1877: Year of Violence*. Chicago: Quadrangle Edition, 1970.

Brust, Harold. *In Plain Clothes: Further Memoirs of a Political Police Officer*. London: Stanley Paul, 1937.

Caesar, Gene. *Incredible Detective: The Biography of William J. Burns*. Englewood Cliffs, NJ: Prentice-Hall, 1968.

Campbell, Rodney. *The Luciano Project: The Secret Wartime Collaboration of the Mafia and the U.S. Navy*. New York: McGraw-Hill, 1977.

Carlson, John Roy [Arthur Derounian]. *Under Cover: My Four Years in the Nazi Underworld of America—The Amazing Revelation of How Axis Agents and Our Enemies Within Are Now Plotting to Destroy the United States*. New York: E. P. Dutton, 1943.

Carter, Carole. *The Shamrock and The Swastika: Counter Espionage in Ireland in WWII*. Palo Alto, CA: Pacific Books, 1977.

Chernow, Ron. *The House of Morgan: An American Banking Dynasty and the Rise of Modern Finance*. New York: Simon & Schuster, 1990.

Clarke, Richard A. *Against All Enemies: Inside America's War on Terror*. New York: Free Press, 2004.

Conrad, Joseph. *The Secret Agent: A Simple Tale*. New York: Modern Library, 2004. First published 1907 by Harper & Brothers.

Cook, Adrian. *The Armies of the Streets: The New York City Draft Riots of 1863*. Lexington: University Press of Kentucky, 1974.

Corson, William A. *The Armies of Ignorance: The Rise of the American Intelligence Empire*. New York: Dial, 1977.

Costello, Augustine E. *Our Police Protectors: A History of the New York Police*. Montclair, NJ: Patterson Smith, 1972. First published 1885 by C. F. Roper.

Cramer, C. H. *Newton D. Baker: A Biography*. Cleveland, OH: World Publishing Company, 1961.

Cull, Nicholas John. *Selling War: The British Propaganda Campaign against American "Neutrality" in World War II*. New York: Oxford University Press, 1995.

Daley, Robert. *Target Blue*. New York: Delacorte, 1973.

Davis, Kenneth S. *FDR: The Beckoning of Destiny, 1882–1928*. New York: G. P. Putnam's Sons, 1971.

Deacon, Richard. *A History of the British Secret Service*. London: Granada Publishing, 1980.

Dickey, Christopher. *Securing the City: Inside America's Best Counterterror Force—The NYPD*. New York: Simon & Schuster, 2009.

Diehl, Lorraine. *Over Here: New York City During World War II*. New York: Smithsonian, 2010.

Donner, Frank J. *Protectors of Privilege: Red Squads and Police Repression in Urban America*. Berkeley: University of California Press, 1990.

Dorwart, Jeffery M. *The Office of Naval Intelligence: The Birth of America's First Intelligence Agency, 1865–1918*. Annapolis, MD: Naval Institute Press, 1972.

———. *Conflict of Duty: The U.S. Navy's Intelligence Dilemma, 1919–45*. Annapolis, MD: Naval Institute Press, 1983.

Drinnon, Richard. *Rebel in Paradise: A Biography of Emma Goldman*. Chicago: University of Chicago Press, 1961.

Esposito, Richard and Ted Gerstein. *Bomb Squad: A Year Inside the Nation's Most Exclusive Police Unit*. New York: Hyperion, 2007.

Farago, Ladislas. *The Game of the Foxes*. New York: McKay, 1971.

Gage, Beverly. *The Day Wall Street Exploded: A Story of America in Its First Age of Terror*. New York: Oxford University Press, 2009.

Gallagher, Dorothy. *All the Right Enemies: The Life and Murder of Carlo Tresca*. New York: Pelican Books, 1989.

Garrett, Charles. *The LaGuardia Years: Machine and Reform Politics in New York City.* New Brunswick, NJ: Rutgers University Press, 1961.

Gentry, Curt. *J. Edgar Hoover: The Man and the Secrets.* New York: Norton, 1991.

Gerard, James W. *My Four Years in Germany.* New York: George H. Doran, 1917.

Gilbert, Martin. *Churchill: A Life.* Vol. III. New York: Henry Holt, 1991.

Gimpel, Erich. *Agent 146: The True Story of a Nazi Spy in America.* New York: St. Martin's, 1957.

Giuliani, Rudolph. *Leadership.* New York: Hyperion, 2002.

Goldman, Emma. *Living My Life.* New York: Da Capo, 1970. First published 1931 by A. A. Knopf.

Goldstein, Richard. *Helluva Town: The Story of New York City During World War II.* New York: Free Press, 2010.

Hagedorn, Herman. *Leonard Wood: A Biography.* Vol. 2. New York: Harper, 1931.

Haynes, John Earl, and Harvey Klehr. *Venona: Decoding Soviet Espionage Operations in America.* New Haven, CT: Yale University Press, 1999.

Haynes, John Earl, Harvey Klehr, and Alexander Vassiliev. *Spies: The Rise and Fall of the KGB in America.* New Haven, CT: Yale University Press, 2009.

Haywood, William D. *Bill Haywood's Book: The Autobiography of William D. Haywood.* New York: International Publishers, 1929.

Hopkins, Ernest Jerome. *What Happened in the Mooney Case?* Cambridge, MA: DaCapo, 1970. First published 1932 by Brewer, Warren & Putnam.

Hopkirk, Peter. *The Great Game: On Secret Service in High Asia.* New York: Kodansha, America, Inc., 1990.

Horan, James D. *The Pinkertons: the Detective Dynasty That Made History.* New York: Crown, 1967.

Hough, Emerson. *The Web.* New York: Arno, 1969 (original, 1919).

Hunt, William R. *Front Page Detective: William J. Burns and The Detective Profession, 1880–1930.* Bowling Green, OH: Bowling Green State University Popular Press, 1990.

Hyde, H. Montgomery. *Room 3603: The Story of the British Intelligence Center in NewYork During World War II.* New York: Fararr, Strauss, 1964.

Jacoby, Susan. *Alger Hiss and the Battle for History.* New Haven, CT: Yale University Press, 2009.

Jaffe, Julian F. *Crusade Against Radicalism: New York during the Red Scare, 1914–24.* Port Washington, NY: Kennecott, 1972.

Jeffreys-Jones, Rhodri. *American Espionage: From Secret Service to CIA.* New York: Free Press, 1977.

———. *The FBI: A History.* New Haven, CT: Yale University Press, 2007.

Jensen, Joan M. *The Price of Vigilance.* New York: Rand McNally, 1968.

Kahn, David. *Hitler's Spies: German Intelligence in World War II.* New York: Macmillan, 1978.

———. *Like Hidden Fire: The Plot to Bring Down the British Empire.* New York: Kodansha, America, Inc., 1994.

———. *The Reader of Gentlemen's Mail: Herbert O. Yardley and the Birth of American Code Breaking.* New Haven, CT: Yale University Press, 2004.

Kerik, Bernard B. *The Lost Son: A Life in Pursuit of Justice.* New York: ReganBooks, 2001.

Kessner, Thomas. *Fiorello H. LaGuardia: The Making of Modern New York.* New York: McGraw-Hill, 1986.

Kipling, Rudyard. *Kim.* New York: Doubleday, Page, 1901.

Klehr, Harvey. *The Amerasia Spy Case: Prelude to McCarthyism.* Chapel Hill: University of North Carolina Press, 1986.

Klehr, Harvey, and John Earl Haynes. *The Secret World of American Communism.* Translated by F. I. Firsov. New Haven, CT: Yale University Press, 1995.

Lamphere, Robert J. and Tom Schactman. *The FBI-KGB War: A Special Agent's Story.* New York: Random House, 1986.

Lamson, Peggy. *Roger Baldwin: Founder of the American Civil Liberties Union.* Boston: Houghton Mifflin, 1976.

Landau, Henry. *The Enemy Within: The Inside Story of German Sabotage in America.* New York: G. P. Putnam's Sons, 1937.

Lardner, James and Thomas Reppetto. *NYPD: A City and Its Police.* New York: Henry Holt, 2000.

Levin, Phyllis Lee. *Edith and Woodrow: The Wilson White House.* New York: Scribner, 2001.

Lewinson, Edwin R. *John Purroy Mitchel: The Boy Mayor of New York.* New York: Astra Books, 1965.

Lukas, Anthony. *Big Trouble: A Murder in a Small Western Town Sets Off a Struggle For the Soul of America*. New York: Simon & Schuster, 1997.

Masterman, J. C. *The Doublecross System in the War of 1939–45*. New Haven, CT: Yale University Press, 1972.

McAdoo, William Gibbs. *Crowded Years*. Port Washington, NY: Kennikat, 1931.

McAllister, Robert. *The Kind of Guy I Am*. New York: McGraw-Hill, 1957.

McCullough, David. *Truman*. New York: Simon & Schuster, 1992.

Medved, Michael. *The Shadow Presidents: The Secret History of the Chief Executives and Their Top Aides*. New York: Times Books, 1977.

Meir, Andrew. *The Lost Spy: An American in Stalin's Secret Service*. New York: Norton, 2008.

Melanson, Phillip, and Peter F. Stevens. *The Secret Service: The Hidden History of an Enigmatic Agency*. New York: Carroll and Graf, 2002.

Miller, John, and Michael Stone with Chris Mitchell. *The Cell: Inside the 9/11 Plot and Why the FBI and CIA Failed to Stop It*. New York: Hyperion, 2002.

Miller, Nathan. *Spying for America: The Hidden History of U.S. Intelligence*. New York: Dell Publishing, 1989.

Millis, Walter. *Road to War: America 1914–1917*. Boston: Houghton Mifflin, 1935.

Millman, Chad. *The Detonators: The Secret Plot to Destroy America and an Epic Hunt for Justice*. New York: Little, Brown, 2000.

Mosedale, John. *The Men Who Invented Broadway: Damon Runyon, Walter Winchell & Their World*. New York: Richard Marek, 1981.

Murray, Robert K. *Red Scare: A Study in National Hysteria, 1919–20*. Minneapolis: University of Minnesota Press, 1955.

National Commission on Terrorists Attacks upon the United States. *The 9/11 Commission Report: Final Report of the National Commission on Terrorist Attacks upon the United States*. New York: Norton, 2004.

Persico, Joseph E. *Roosevelt's Secret War: FDR and World War II Espionage*. New York: Random House, 2001.

Popov, Dusko. *Spy/Counterspy: The Autobiography of Dusko Popov*. New York: Grosset & Dunlap, 1974.

Posner, Richard A. *Countering Terrorism: Blurred Focus, Halting Steps*. Lanham, MD: Rowman & Littlefield, 2007.

Powers, Richard G. *Secrecy and Power: The Life of J. Edgar Hoover.* New York: Free Press, 1987.

———. *Broken: The Troubled Past and Uncertain Future of the FBI.* New York: Free Press, 2007.

Rachlis, Eugene. *They Came to Kill: The Story of 8 Nazi Saboteurs in America.* New York: Random House, 1961.

Rauchway, Eric. *Murdering McKinley: The Making of Theodore Roosevelt's America.* New York: Hill & Wang, 2003.

Read, Anthony and David Fisher. *Colonel Z: The Secret Life of a Master of Spies.* New York: Viking Penguin, 1985.

Reppetto, Thomas. *American Mafia: A History of Its Rise to Power.* New York: Henry Holt, 2004.

Riebling, Mark. *Wedge: The Secret War Between the FBI and CIA.* New York: Knopf, 1994.

Riis, Jacob. *The Making of an American.* New York: Macmillian, 1901.

Rintelin, Franz von. *The Dark Invader: Wartime Reminiscences of a German Naval Intelligence Officer.* New York: Macmillan, 1933.

Roth, Andrew. *Infamous Manhattan: A Colorful Walking Tour of New York's More Notorious Crime Sites.* New York: Carol Publishing Group, 1996.

Russell, Francis. *A City in Terror.* New York: Viking, 1975.

———. *Sacco and Vanzetti: The Case Resolved.* New York: Harper & Row, 1986.

Schellenberg, Walter. *The Labyrinth.* New York: Harper, 1956.

Sheehan, Michael A. *Crush the Cell: How to Defeat Terrorism without Terrorizing Ourselves.* New York: Crown Publishers, 2008.

Smith, Gene. *When the Cheering Stopped: The Last Years of Woodrow Wilson.* New York: Morrow, 1964.

———. *The Dark Summer: An Intimate History of the Events that Led to World War II.* New York: Collier Edition, 1989.

Stevenson, William. *A Man Called Intrepid: The Secret War.* New York: Harcourt Brace Jovanovich, 1976.

Talbert, Roy Jr. *Negative Intelligence: The Army and the American Left, 1917–1941.* Jackson: University of Mississippi Press, 1991.

Theoharis, Athan G. *The FBI and American Democracy: A Brief Critical History.* Lawrence: University of Kansas Press, 2004.

———. *The Quest for Absolute Security: The Failed Relations among U.S. Intelligence Agencies*. Chicago: Ivan R. Dee, 2003.

Thomson, Sir Basil. *The Story of Scotland Yard*. New York: Doubleday Doran, 1936.

———. *Queer People*. London: Hodder and Stoughton, 1922.

Trautmann, Frederic. *The Voice of Terror: A Biography of Johann Most*. Westport, CT: Greenwood, 1980.

Tuchman, Barbara. *The Zimmermann Telegram*. New York: Viking, 1958.

Tunney, Thomas J. *Throttled!: The Detection of German and Anarchist Bomb Plotters . . . as told to Paul Merrick Hollister*. Boston: Small, Maynard, 1919.

Turrou, Leon G. *Nazi Spies in America*. New York: Random House, 1939.

———. *Where My Shadow Falls: Two Decades of Crime Detection*. Garden City, NY: Doubleday, 1949.

Ulasewicz, Tony, with Stuart A. McKeever. *The President's Private Eye: The Journey of Detective Tony U from NYPD to the Nixon White House*. Westport, CT: MACSAM, 1990.

Van Deman, Ralph H. *Final Memoranda 1865–1952*. Edited by Ralph E. Weber. Wilmington, DE: Scholarly Resources, 1988.

Voska, Emanuel V., and Will Irwin. *Spy and Counterspy*. New York: Doubleday Doran, 1940.

Watson, Bruce. *Sacco & Vanzetti: The Men, the Murders and the Judgment of Mankind*. New York: Penguin, 2007.

Weintraub, Stanley. *Long Day's Journey into War: December 7, 1941*. New York: Truman Talley Books, 1991.

Weiss, Murray. *The Man Who Warned America: The Life and Death of John O'Neill*. New York: Regan Books, 2003.

West, Nigel. *MI5: British Security Service Operations, 1909–1945*. London: Bodley Head, 1981.

———. *MI6: British Secret Intelligence Operations, 1909–1945*. New York: Random House, 1985.

———. *A Thread of Deceit: Espionage Myths of World War II*. New York: Random House, 1985.

Whalen, Grover. *Mr. New York: The Autobiography of Grover Whalen*. New York: G. P. Putnam's Sons, 1955.

White, William Allen. *Woodrow Wilson*. Boston: Houghton Mifflin, 1924.

Whitehead, Don. *The FBI Story*. New York: Random House, 1956.

Wilkie, Don, with Mark Lee Luther. *American Secret Service Agent*. New York: Frederick A. Stokes, 1934.

Witcover, Jules. *Sabotage at Black Tom: Imperial Germany's Secret War on America*. Chapel Hill, NC: Algonquin Books, 1989.

Wohlstetter, Roberta. *Pearl Harbor: Warning and Decision*. Palo Alto, CA: Stanford University Press, 1962.

Wright, Lawrence. *The Looming Tower: Al-Qaeda and the Road to 9/11*. New York: Knopf, 2006.

Yardley, Herbert. *The American Black Chamber*. Indianapolis, IN: Bobbs-Merrill, 1931.

Zacharias, Ellis M. *Secret Missions: The Story of an Intelligence Officer*. New York: G. P. Putnam's Sons, 1946.

Articles

Chan, Sewell. "If These Walls Could Talk, What They Would Say Might Be Classified." *New York Times*, July 11, 2006, B5.

Editorial. "The Bomb Conspirators." *New York Times*, June 4, 1919.

Goldstein, Richard. "Football, December 7, 1941. Suddenly the Games Did Not Matter." *New York Times*, December 7, 1980, Sunday Sports Section, p. 6.

Jamieson, Wendell. "Jumping Spark, Normandie 1942" in *Big Town Big Time*. Edited by Jay Maeder. *New York Daily News*, 1999.

Johnston, David and James Risen. "FBI is Investigating a Senior Counter Terrorist Agent." *New York Times*, August 19, 2001.

Lindblom, Charles E. "The Science of Muddling Through." *Public Administration Review* 19 (1959): 79–88.

Manchester, Harland. "The Black Tom Case." *Harper's*, December 1939, 60–69.

Mazzetti, Mark. "Nominee Promises Action as U.S. Intelligence Chief." *New York Times*, July 21, 2010.

Thompson, Craig. "Topics of the Times, Apologies Due to a Detective." *New York Times*, December 4, 1911.

——. "On Pacific List, But Serve Nation." *New York Times*, January 26, 1919.

——. "Catastrophe: carelessness." *Time*, February 23, 1942, 17.

———. "New York's Communist Cop." *Saturday Evening Post*, March 20, 1954.

Trussell, C. P. "FBI Chief Says Reds Incite Youth." *New York Times*, July 18, 1960.

INDEX

ABOUT THE AUTHOR

Thomas A. Reppetto, a former commander of detectives in the Chicago Police Department, received his doctorate from Harvard and was professor, dean, and vice president at City University of New York's John Jay College of Criminal Justice. From 1979 to 2005 he was the president of the Citizens Crime Commission of New York City, a watchdog and research organization on crime and criminal justice. In 1986 he was named New York State Governor's Law Enforcement Executive of the Year. Reppetto is the author of *NYPD: A City and Its Police* (2000), *American Mafia: A History of Its Rise to Power* (2004), *Bringing Down the Mob: The War Against the American Mafia* (2006), and *American Police: The Blue Parade, 1845–1945* (2010).